Mike Meyers' CompTIA A+® Guide to 802: Managing and Troubleshooting PCs Lab Manual

Fourth Edition

(Exam 220-802)

Mike Meyers
Scott Strubberg
Aaron Verber

D1380681

New York   Chicago   San Francisco
Lisbon   London   Madrid   Mexico City
Milan   New Delhi   San Juan
Seoul   Singapore   Sydney   Toronto

McGraw-Hill books are available at special quantity discounts to use as premiums and sales promotions, or for use in corporate training programs. To contact a representative, please e-mail us at bulksales@mcgraw-hill.com.

Mike Meyers' CompTIA A+® Guide to 802: Managing and Troubleshooting PCs Lab Manual, Fourth Edition (Exam 220-802)

Copyright © 2013 by The McGraw-Hill Companies. All rights reserved. Printed in the United States of America. Except as permitted under the Copyright Act of 1976, no part of this publication may be reproduced or distributed in any form or by any means, or stored in a database or retrieval system, without the prior written permission of publisher, with the exception that the program listings may be entered, stored, and executed in a computer system, but they may not be reproduced for publication.

All trademarks or copyrights mentioned herein are the possession of their respective owners and McGraw-Hill makes no claim of ownership by the mention of products that contain these marks.

1234567890   QDB QDB   109876543

ISBN   978-0-07-179515-9
MHID   0-07-179515-4

Sponsoring Editor
Timothy Green

Editorial Supervisor
Janet Walden

Project Manager
Yashmita Hota,
Cenveo® Publisher Services

Acquisitions Coordinator
Stephanie Evans

Technical Editor
Christopher A. Crayton

Copy Editors
William McManus and
Emily Rader

Proofreaders
Emily Rader and Susie Elkind

Indexer
Jack Lewis

Production Supervisor
George Anderson

Composition
Cenveo® Publisher Services

Illustration
Cenveo® Publisher Services

Art Director, Cover
Jeff Weeks

To students young and old who keep the faith, that
with hard work and diligence you will succeed.

About the Authors

Mike Meyers, lovingly called the "AlphaGeek" by those who know him, is the industry's leading authority on CompTIA A+ certification. He is the president and cofounder of Total Seminars, LLC, a provider of PC and network repair seminars, books, videos, and courseware for thousands of organizations throughout the world. Mike has been involved in the computer and network repair industry since 1977 as a technician, instructor, author, consultant, and speaker. Author of numerous popular PC books and videos, Mike is also the series editor for the highly successful *Mike Meyers' Certification Passport* series, the *Mike Meyers' Computer Skills* series, and the *Mike Meyers' Guide To* series, all published by McGraw-Hill.

Scott Strubberg is a master teacher in computer maintenance and networking. He began his career in IT as a consultant and technician, earning the CompTIA A+, CompTIA Network+, and CompTIA Security+ certifications along the way. Scott taught in the public school system for over half a decade and, after joining Total Seminars, has led computer training courses all over the United States. Scott has worked as a mentor to countless teachers and takes great pleasure inventing labs that make learning computer and networking subjects entertaining as well as productive.

Aaron Verber graduated from the University of Wisconsin, Eau Claire, with a focus on the spoken and sung word, and turned a passion for computers and a love of English into a career in computer training. Aaron has edited numerous books on computer maintenance, troubleshooting, and networking, including the best-selling *All-in-One CompTIA A+ Exam Guide*, by Michael Meyers. Aaron puts his CompTIA A+ certification to good use crafting informative and creative labs suitable for all learners.

About the Technical Editor

Christopher A. Crayton (MCSE, MCP+I, CompTIA A+, CompTIA Network+) is an author, technical editor, technical consultant, security consultant, and trainer. Formerly a computer and networking instructor at Keiser College (2001 Teacher of the Year), Chris has also worked as network administrator for Protocol and at Eastman Kodak Headquarters as a computer and network specialist. Chris has authored several print and online books on topics ranging from CompTIA A+ and CompTIA Security+ to Microsoft Windows Vista. Chris has provided technical edits and reviews for many publishers, including McGraw-Hill, Pearson Education, Charles River Media, Cengage Learning, Wiley, O'Reilly, Syngress, and Apress.

Contents at a Glance

Contents

Acknowledgments

The crew at Total Seminars contributed mightily to this edition. Our Editor in Chief, Scott Jernigan, helped manage the flow of the textbook and provided direction for the accompanying lab manual. Michael Smyer and Ford Pierson provided stellar art, editing, and help with labs. Doug Jones and Dave Rush, fellow instructors at Total Seminars, added great feedback and support on the many labs in this book.

Our acquisitions editor, Tim Green, and his trusty assistant, Stephanie Evans, did a superb job managing priorities and adding tons of encouragement and praise as the book unfolded. Thanks!

Chris Crayton, our technical editor, did a great job on this edition. Thank you for helping make this book happen.

On the McGraw-Hill side, the crew once again demonstrated why McGraw-Hill is the best in show as a publisher. With excellent work and even better attitude, this book went together smoothly.

Additional Resources for Teachers

This lab manual supplements the *Mike Meyers' CompTIA A+ Guide to 802: Managing and Troubleshooting PCs, Fourth Edition (Exam 220-802)* textbook, which includes an instructor Web page available online at:

www.mhprofessional.com/certification802

McGraw-Hill Professional's Web site hosts the instructor support materials for this textbook, providing resources for teachers in a format that follows the organization of the textbook and lab manual.

This site includes the following:

- Answer keys to the Mike Meyers' 802 Lab Manual activities

- Answer keys to the end-of-chapter activities in the 802 textbook

- Access to test bank files and software that allows you to generate a wide array of paper- or network-based tests and that features automatic grading. The test bank includes:

  - Hundreds of practice questions and a wide variety of question types categorized by exam objective, enabling you to customize each test to maximize student progress

  - Blackboard cartridges and other formats may also be available upon request; contact your sales representative

- Engaging PowerPoint slides on the lecture topics that include full-color artwork from the book

- The Instructor's Manual, which contains learning objectives, classroom preparation notes, instructor tips, and a lecture outline for each chapter

Please contact your McGraw-Hill sales representative for details.

Chapter 1

The Path of the PC Tech

Lab Exercises

Well, now you've really done it. The fact that you hold this lab manual in your hands says one thing loud and clear—you're deadly serious about getting that CompTIA A+ certification! Good. Even though the CompTIA A+ 220-802 exam is considered entry level, you need to take it seriously if you want to pass.

Because you're serious, I'm going to let you in on a secret: The key to passing this is preparation. When I say "preparation," I'm not talking about studying, although studying is important! I'm talking about *preparing to study*. You need to know exactly how to study for this exam, and you need to have the right tools to get that studying done. Sure, you have a textbook and a lab manual, but you're not ready to hit the books just yet.

In this chapter, you'll learn how to start studying for the CompTIA A+ 220-802 exam. First, you'll organize what you need to study. Second, you'll explore how the CompTIA A+ certification helps move you toward more advanced certifications. Finally, you'll get some ideas on how to gather equipment so that you can reinforce what you read with real hardware and software. So stay serious, roll up your sleeves, and start preparing to study for the CompTIA A+ 802 exam!

 60 MINUTES

Lab Exercise 1.01: Preparing to Study

Back in the 1980s, there was a popular TV show called *The A-Team*, starring George Peppard and Mr. T. It wasn't the greatest TV show, but I always remember one repeated line: "I love it when a plan comes together!" I want you to feel like that while you prepare for your CompTIA A+ certification. In fact, just for fun, let's call ourselves the "A+ Team" as we get ready to knock those exams right into next week's episode!

Learning Objectives

This lab helps you lay out a logical path for your studies. To do this, you need to deal with three issues: determining your weak points, checking your study habits, and scheduling the exam.

At the end of this lab, you'll be able to

- Identify the CompTIA A+ topics you need to learn
- Develop a good study plan
- Schedule the CompTIA A+ exams

Lab Materials and Setup

The materials you need for this lab are

- A PC with Internet access
- A phone

Getting Down to Business

Total Seminars has been teaching CompTIA A+ certification for years. We've developed a handy template that will show you what you need to study and how much time you need to devote to preparing for the CompTIA A+ 802 exam. These tables are shown in the *Mike Meyers' CompTIA A+ Guide to 802: Managing and Troubleshooting PCs* textbook, but with extra steps added to help you determine the topics you need to study.

Step 1   For each skill listed in the table that follows, circle the number that corresponds to the amount of experience you have: None, Once or Twice, Every Now and Then, or Quite a Bit. You'll use that number to calculate the total number of hours you need to study for the exam.

Tech Task	Amount of Experience			
	None	**Once or Twice**	**Every Now and Then**	**Quite a Bit**
Installing and configuring hard drives	12	10	8	2
Repairing printers	6	5	4	3
Repairing boot problems	8	7	7	5
Repairing portable computers	8	6	4	2
Configuring mobile devices	4	3	2	1
Using the command line	8	8	6	4
Installing and optimizing Windows	10	8	6	4
Using Windows XP	6	6	4	2
Using Windows Vista	8	6	4	2

(continued)

Tech Task	Amount of Experience			
	None	Once or Twice	Every Now and Then	Quite a Bit
Using Windows 7	8	6	4	2
Configuring NTFS, Users, and Groups	6	4	3	2
Configuring a wireless network	6	5	3	2
Configuring a software firewall	6	4	2	1
Removing malware	4	3	2	0
Using OS diagnostic tools	8	8	6	4
Using a volt-ohm meter	4	3	2	1

Great! You now have a good feel for the topics you need to study. Now you need to determine the total study time. First, add up the numbers you've circled. Then add the result to the number from the following table that corresponds to your experience. The grand total is the number of hours you should study to be ready for the exam.

Months of Direct, Professional Experience...	Hours to Add to Your Study Time...
0	50
Up to 6	30
6 to 12	10
Over 12	0

A total neophyte usually needs around 120 hours of study time. An experienced tech shouldn't need more than 30 hours.

You'll need to spend _____ hours studying for the CompTIA A+ certification exam.

Step 2   Go to the Computing Technology Industry Association (CompTIA) Web site and download a copy of the exam objectives for the CompTIA A+ 220-802 exam. As of this writing, you can find them here:

http://certification.comptia.org/Training/testingcenters/examobjectives.aspx

You have to fill out a short form (requiring your name, e-mail address, and country of residence) before you can view the objectives. Bear in mind, however, that CompTIA changes its Web site more often than TV networks invent new reality shows, so be prepared to poke around if necessary! Compare what you circled in the tables to the CompTIA A+ exam objectives. Note that any single tech task in the table covers more than one exam objective on the CompTIA A+ 220-802 exam. In the table that follows, list the top five exam objectives that you think will challenge you the most as you begin your journey toward CompTIA A+ certification.

Exam	Objective
Example: 220-802	*1.2 Given a scenario, install and configure the operating system using the most appropriate method.*

Step 3   If you are taking this course at your high school, career center, or community college, ask your instructor about the most effective ways to learn and study. If you're studying on your own, think about your favorite teachers from the past and list which methods they used that helped you best learn the material.

1. _____

2. _____

3. _____

Step 4   Now that you know which topics are most important to you and how much time you need to devote to studying them, you need to develop your study plan. Take the amount of time you've set aside and determine how many days you have to prepare. Consider work, holidays, weekends, and anything else that will affect your study time.

Ask your instructor when he or she plans to have you take the certification exams. Every school handles the exam differently. It's important that you know how getting certified at your school works so that you'll know what to expect down the road.

If you aren't taking a course, you need to pick a day to take the exam. Keep in mind how much time you'll need to study, but don't put it off so long that you get lazy. Challenge yourself to take the exam as soon as you feel comfortable.

Enter the number of days you have to prepare for the CompTIA A+ 220-802 exam: _____. You now have your deadline—the day you'll say, "I'm ready to take the exam!"

Step 5   You should also investigate how much it will cost you to take the exam. Several vendors sell vouchers that enable you to take the exam at a discounted price. This step introduces you to a few vendors and their pricing options.

    a.   Visit the following link to begin searching for pricing information:

        www.vue.com/vouchers/pricelist/comptia.asp

    b.   In the Pricing section, click the Pricing Spreadsheet link to download a file containing Pearson VUE's voucher pricing information. Open the downloaded file using Microsoft Excel and record the current cost for a single CompTIA A+ exam voucher for your region.

        Price: _____

    c.   On the same Web site, click the Academic/E2C Member Pricing Spreadsheet link to download another file. Open the file, and then find and record the cost for a single CompTIA A+ exam.

        Price: _____

    d.   Now visit this Web site:

        www.totalsem.com/vouchers/index.php

    e.   At the Total Seminars Web site, listed under Step 1, click the CompTIA A+ certification logo. Find and record the price for a CompTIA A+ Exam Voucher.

        Price: _____

Some vouchers require you to be a member of an academic or technology organization. Check to see which voucher applies to you. You may be eligible for one, two, or even all three pricing options!

Step 6   Go online and schedule your exam with Pearson VUE (www.vue.com). You'll almost certainly need to make a phone call to do this. Make sure you have both a method of payment (credit cards are preferred) and some form of identification when you call. In the United States you need your Social Security number to schedule CompTIA exams. It's very important that you schedule your exam *now*—setting a test date early in the process will help motivate you to study, and keep you from procrastinating!

✔ **Cross-Reference**

For details about taking the CompTIA A+ 220-802 exam, go to the CompTIA Web site (www.comptia.org).

 60 MINUTES

Lab Exercise 1.02: Considering Other Certifications

CompTIA A+ certification may be your first certification, but it certainly should not be your last! The information technology (IT) industry considers obtaining certifications an ongoing process, one that continues as long as you're working in the IT field. You need to appreciate how the CompTIA A+ certification leads into other certifications.

Learning Objectives

This lab helps you learn about the various IT certifications that are available, and how they fit with both your skills and aptitude.

At the end of this lab, you'll be able to

- Understand some of the more common certifications that follow the CompTIA A+ certification
- Plan in what order you might attain those certifications

Lab Materials and Setup

The materials you need for this lab are

- A PC with Internet access

Getting Down to Business

It's time to jump onto the Internet and do a little research! You'll tour some of the more popular IT certifications and see how CompTIA A+ helps you gain these more advanced certifications.

✔ **Cross-Reference**

To review the domains of each CompTIA A+ exam, refer to "The Basic Exam Structure" in Chapter 1 of *Mike Meyers' CompTIA A+ Guide to 802: Managing and Troubleshooting PCs.*

Step 1   Fire up a Web browser and go to this Web address:

http://certification.comptia.org/ExploreCareers/careerpaths.aspx

CompTIA offers many other certifications related to the IT field. Research their certification offerings by clicking the Launch IT Certification Roadmap button. From here, list three careers that most interest you.

1. _____

2. _____

3. _____

Of the three career paths you listed, choose the one that appeals to you the most. You can always change your mind later if you don't like it! List three CompTIA certifications you'll need to become an expert in that field.

1. _____

2. _____

3. _____

List three certifications that CompTIA recommends you take that are *not* CompTIA certifications.

1. _____

2. _____

3. _____

Step 2   CompTIA strongly recommends pursuing CompTIA A+ certification as the starting point to your career in information technology. Why do you think they do that?

_____

_____

_____

Step 3   Now that you've seen some common certifications and career paths that follow the CompTIA A+ certification, write a short paragraph explaining why you chose the career path and certifications that you did.

_____

_____

_____

_____

_____

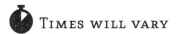 Times will vary

Lab Exercise 1.03: Gathering Equipment

Although it's theoretically possible to obtain CompTIA A+ certification by doing nothing but reading books, you'll be far better prepared for the real world if you can practice with real equipment. You also need some tools so you can take things apart and put them back together. Finally, you need some operating system software, in particular Windows XP, Windows Vista, and Windows 7. If you're taking a course, all of this equipment should be provided to you. If you are not taking a course, you could find yourself spending some serious cash trying to buy everything you need!

Learning Objectives

In this lab, you'll discover some rather interesting ways to get inexpensive or free hardware and software. None of these ideas will work every time, but with a little patience, you'll be amazed how much you can get for very little!

At the end of this lab, you'll be able to

- Acquire inexpensive or free hardware and software

- Acquire a standard PC technician toolkit

Lab Materials and Setup

The materials you need for this lab are

- A phone

- Transportation

- A PC with Internet access

Getting Down to Business

Most of the objectives on the CompTIA A+ 220-802 exam don't require state-of-the-art hardware. If you're willing to use systems that are a few years old, you can get plenty of good hands-on practice with the techniques you need to know to pass the CompTIA A+ 802 exam.

Step 1   Go on a scavenger hunt. Get a list of the smaller "mom and pop" PC repair companies and small PC parts suppliers in your town. Drive to these companies (don't call them) and ask them, "What do you guys do with your broken or obsolete parts?" The vast majority of these stores simply throw the parts away! Ask when they toss stuff and if you can have what they throw away. Most of these companies pay to get rid of equipment and will be glad to give it to you. Oh, and you can forget the big chain stores—they almost never let folks have equipment.

Step 2 Shop the sale bins at the local computer parts stores. You'll always find one or two pieces of equipment at outrageously low prices. Granted, you may end up using a bright pink Barbie keyboard, but if it only costs $3, who cares? Don't forget about rebates—you can often get parts for free after rebate! Really!

Step 3 Tell everyone you know that you're looking for PC hardware. Almost every organization will have occasional in-house sales where they sell older (but still good) PCs, printers, and so on, to employees. If you can get in on some of these sales, you'll have some amazing deals come your way!

✔ **Hint**

You'll often find that older machines still have the Windows 98 or Windows 2000 operating system software installed. If you come across one of these systems, see if you can work with the seller or donor to get the licensed disc. Working with an older operating system (even DOS) will introduce you to the installation and configuration process. Having an operating system installed will also enable you to verify that the hardware is working.

Step 4 Take one weekend to check out local garage sales. People often sell older PCs at a tiny fraction of their original cost. If you're not afraid to barter a bit, you'll get incredible deals—just watch out for equipment that's simply too old to be worthwhile.

✔ **Hint**

I avoid PC flea markets. The problem is that these folks know the value of their computer equipment, so it's often hard to find excellent deals.

Step 5 Locate the local PC user groups in your town—almost every town has at least one. Explain your situation to them; you'll usually find someone who's willing to give you a part or two, and you may also find others who are studying for the CompTIA A+ exams. You may even be able to start or join a study group!

Step 6 Check out the Craigslist page for your area (www.craigslist.org) and look in the For Sale/Computer category. Craigslist is like a big online garage sale, and you can almost always find someone trying to get rid of old PC equipment for next to nothing. Failing that, you can check out their forums, or even place an ad yourself saying that you're looking for old PC parts.

Step 7 Speaking of study groups, try teaming up with as many fellow students as you can to pool cash for parts and to work as a study group. If you're in a course, this is easy—your fellow students are your study group! Have everyone go equipment hunting, using the different methods described to get equipment, and pool the items you find for everyone to use. You might even hold a drawing after you all get certified to choose who gets to keep the equipment.

Step 8   After searching your area—online and off—for the best deals on tools and equipment, record what you think are the three best deals you found. If you can, find out what the full price is for each product so you can see how much money you saved.

1. _____

2. _____

3. _____

Chapter 2
Visible Windows

Lab Exercises

Every good PC technician should know the Windows environment inside and out. This is vital to any troubleshooting scenario, and it won't happen automatically—it takes some practice and discovery on the technician's part. You need to be fluent in navigating the PC from a user's perspective. If there's anything magical about Windows, it's that there's almost always more than one way to get a desired result, and your preferred way might not be the same as your client's. As a good customer-oriented tech, you need to be flexible in your thinking, and this comes only through practice and more practice. As you study and work through these labs, always look for more than one way to access the files or programs you need. Many of the shortcuts and hot keys you'll discover can be invaluable aids for a busy tech!

✔ **Hint**

Windows enables right-click menus for most of its buttons, icons, and other screen elements. Be sure to right-click everything you see in Windows to explore the many context menus and options.

In the field, the PC tech is perceived as the Master of All Things Technical. This might not be a fair assessment—for example, why should a PC hardware technician need to know how to open and close the user's programs?—but that's the way it is. You need to be comfortable and confident with the Windows interface, or you'll lose all credibility as a PC technician. If you show up to service a PC and have trouble moving or resizing a window or locating the information you seek, it won't instill a lot of confidence in your client. There's nothing more embarrassing to a tech than having to ask the user how to find or use a Windows feature!

The creators of the CompTIA A+ 220-802 exam understand this, so they test you on Windows user-level information, such as using power saving settings, changing the appearance of the interface, manipulating files and folders, locating information stored on drives, and using Windows' built-in OS tools. You must also know how to navigate to the basic Windows features—the CompTIA A+ 802 exam is big on identifying paths to features. Although you may already know much of the information about to be covered, the labs in this chapter will help you review and catch any bits and pieces you missed along the way.

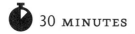 30 MINUTES

Lab Exercise 2.01: The Windows XP Interface

Microsoft Windows XP debuted back in August 24, 2001, succeeding the more business-minded Windows 2000 and the more consumer-driven Windows Me. Windows XP features a slick new interface aimed at both professionals and consumers. Microsoft created four editions of the operating system: Windows XP Home Edition, Windows XP Professional Edition, Windows XP Media Center Edition, and Windows XP 64-bit Edition. Windows XP is Microsoft's longest reigning and supported operating system. People around the world still use it 10 years after it was released.

You can think of Windows XP Home Edition as an abridged version of Windows XP Professional. Media Center Edition is based on the Home Edition, plus some added functionality to simplify access to music, videos, and photos. The major advantages of XP Professional include remote access, tighter security, and the ability to network in domains. If possible, try going through this lab exercise with different editions of Windows XP so that you can see what changes and what stays the same.

Learning Objectives

The main objective of this exercise is to familiarize you with the interface of Windows XP.

At the end of this lab, you'll be able to

- Manipulate and use the taskbar, Quick Launch toolbar, notification area, Start menu, and Recycle Bin

Lab Materials and Setup

The materials you need for this lab are

- A fully functioning PC with Windows XP installed

Getting Down to Business

This lab exercise takes you on a tour of the Windows XP interface. You'll see in detail how the Start menu, taskbar, Quick Launch toolbar, notification area, and Recycle Bin work.

Step 1 Let's begin with the Start menu and the Start button, both located in the lower-left corner of the desktop. The Start menu provides you with easy access to the applications and tools on your computer.

a. Click on the Start button to open the Start menu. Record five of the clickable items in this menu.

_____

b. How many columns does this menu have?

_____

c.   Close the Start menu by clicking on an unused part of the desktop. Then right-click on the Start button to open the context menu. (Remember that you can right-click on just about anything in Windows to find additional options.) Select Properties to open the Taskbar and Start Menu Properties dialog box. The Start Menu tab should be selected already. You should see two options. List them below.

_____ and _____

d.   Click the Customize button to open the Customize Start Menu dialog box (see Figure 2-1). From here, you can control what appears on the Start menu. How many programs are shown by default in the Start menu?

_____

e.   Click OK or Cancel to close the Customize Start Menu dialog box. Click the Classic Start menu radio button, and then click Apply. Close the Taskbar and Start Menu Properties dialog box by clicking OK. Click the Start button and notice the changes that were made. Just like you did for Step 1a, record five of the clickable items in this menu.

_____

f.   Write down how many columns wide this menu system is:

_____

g.   When you are finished recording the information, restore the Start menu to the classic style using the radio buttons.

Figure 2-1 Customize Start Menu dialog box in Windows XP

Step 2   The taskbar displays the applications you are running, such as Microsoft Word, Firefox, or League of Legends. Like the Start menu, the taskbar can be customized to your satisfaction.

a.   Right-click on the taskbar and select Properties. A familiar dialog box should appear. It's the Taskbar and Start Menu Properties dialog box! This time, the Taskbar tab should be selected, displaying the appearance settings for your taskbar. Record the names of the options and their default settings for the Taskbar appearance section:

Option	Default Setting

b.   Uncheck the *Lock the taskbar* checkbox and click Apply. Now click and drag your taskbar to a different corner of the screen (see Figure 2-2). Record what happens when you release the left mouse button.

_____

FIGURE 2-2 Moving the taskbar

c.   The *Group similar taskbar buttons* option does exactly what it sounds like—condenses a lot of taskbar buttons into a single button—but let's find out just how many buttons it takes to make that happen. Close all other applications, and then open Internet Explorer multiple times until the taskbar groups multiple taskbar icons together. How many instances of Internet Explorer did you need to open to group the buttons?

_____

d.   Uncheck the Show Quick Launch checkbox. The Quick Launch toolbar next to the Start button enables you to launch applications with a single click. Record which icons disappear.

_____

→   **Note**

You can add icons to the Quick Launch toolbar by dragging and dropping an icon from your desktop or Windows Explorer into that area.

e.   Using the chart you created earlier, reset the taskbar to its default settings.

Step 3   The lower-right corner of the desktop houses the notification area (see Figure 2-3). Some techs still call it the "systray" or "system tray," but these were never official names. The notification area usually displays icons for applications running in the background. Clicking the left arrow button next to the notification area will expand the area and reveal more icons.

a.   Record a few of the icons from your notification area.

_____

b.   Right-click on the taskbar and click Properties to open the Taskbar and Start Menu Properties dialog box with the Taskbar tab selected. In the Notification area section, click the Customize button. From the Customize Notifications dialog box, you can choose to show or not show the clock, hide inactive icons, and more.

c.   Choose an item you like and click the drop-down box. List the three options you can choose from.

_____, _____, _____

Figure 2-3 The Windows XP notification area

Step 4   When you delete files on your computer, their remains go to the Recycle Bin—unless you want to change how the Recycle Bin operates. Let's try customizing the Recycle Bin:

a.   Right-click the Recycle Bin, select Properties, and investigate each tab. Record the maximum size for Recycle Bin storage on a Windows XP system.

       _____

b.   Does Windows give you the option to delete a file without using the Recycle Bin?

       _____

c.   Try changing the available options. Test your changes by deleting files you don't need. To create a new file, right-click on your desktop and select New. From there, choose any file type you want and name the file. Now delete it.

→ **Note**

While using the default settings, you can permanently delete a file or folder in Windows by selecting the file and pressing SHIFT-DELETE. Be careful! Files deleted in this manner aren't recoverable without a third-party program.

 30 MINUTES

Lab Exercise 2.02: The Windows Vista Interface

On January 30, 2007, Microsoft released Windows Vista. Windows Vista included many improvements to security and big changes to the graphical user interface (GUI). Microsoft created six editions of Vista: Vista Starter, for developing nations; Vista Home Basic and Home Premium, for consumers; and Vista Business, Enterprise, and Ultimate, for businesses and power users. You can get each edition in both 32-bit and 64-bit varieties (except for the Vista Starter edition). Pay close attention to which versions of Vista support which features. This will help you pass your CompTIA A+ 220-802 exam and be a more knowledgeable technician.

Learning Objectives

The main objective of this exercise is to familiarize you with the interface of Windows Vista.

At the end of this lab, you'll be able to

- Manipulate and use the Start menu, taskbar, Quick Launch toolbar, notification area, Sidebar, and Recycle Bin

Lab Materials and Setup

The materials you need for this lab are

- A fully functioning PC with Windows Vista installed

Getting Down to Business

In this lab exercise, you'll take a tour of the Windows Vista interface. You'll see in detail how the Start menu, taskbar, Quick Launch toolbar, notification area, and Recycle Bin work. You'll also look at how the Sidebar works.

Step 1   Modern versions of Windows revolve around the Start button, and Vista is no different. Windows Vista, however, no longer labels the button "Start." The Start button is now just the Windows logo icon. Don't worry, though—it's still the Start button and still opens the Start menu.

a.   Click on the Start button to open the Start menu. Record five of the clickable items in this menu.

_____

b.   How many columns does this menu have?

_____

c.   Windows Vista removed the Run command found in previous versions of the Windows Start menu. What replaced it in Windows Vista?

_____

d.   You can still restore the Run command to the Start menu in Windows Vista. Right-click on the Start menu and select Properties to open the Taskbar and Start Menu Properties dialog box (remember this?). The Start menu radio button should be selected by default. Click the Customize button to open the Customize Start Menu dialog box (see Figure 2-4). You can use this dialog box to change the appearance of the Start menu. Look at the options for Computer.

e.   What are the three options available for customizing Computer?

_____

_____

_____

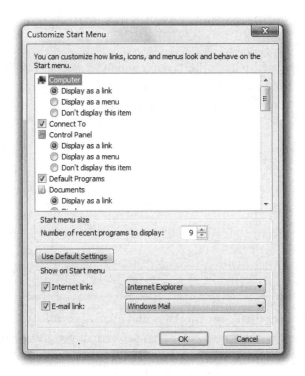

FIGURE 2-4 Customize Start Menu dialog box in Windows Vista

f.   Scroll down the list. Find and check the box for the Run command and click OK. Click OK in the Taskbar and Start Menu Properties dialog box. Click the Start button. You should see the Run command in the Start menu.

g.   You can also revert the entire Start menu to a more classic style. Right-click on the Start button and select Properties. Change to Classic Start menu and click OK. Record the changes to the desktop and the Start menu.

_____

h.   After finishing, return the settings to their original configuration.

Step 2   The Windows Vista taskbar remains similar to the Windows XP taskbar, but with a new glossy finish and a few new features.

    a.   Right-click on the taskbar and select Properties to open the Taskbar and Start Menu Properties dialog box. The Taskbar tab should be selected by default. From here you can adjust the appearance settings for your taskbar. Record the names of the options and their default settings for the Taskbar appearance section.

Option	Default Setting

    b.   Try changing some settings. Uncheck the *Lock the taskbar* checkbox and click Apply. Now click and drag your taskbar to a different corner of the screen. What happens when you release the left mouse button?

    _____

    c.   Open an application—a Web browser will do. The application should appear on the taskbar. Hover your cursor over the application icon in the taskbar. What happens?

    _____

    d.   Uncheck the Show Quick Launch checkbox. Remember from Windows XP that the Quick Launch toolbar next to the Start button enables you to launch applications with a single click. Record what icons disappear.

    _____

➜ **Note**

You can add icons to the Quick Launch toolbar by dragging and dropping an icon from the desktop or Windows Explorer into that area.

    e.   Using the chart you created earlier, reset the taskbar to its default settings once you are finished.

FIGURE 2-5 The Windows Vista notification area

Step 3 The notification area doesn't change much from Windows XP to Windows Vista, though Microsoft did add some new customization options (see Figure 2-5).

a. Right-click on the taskbar and select Properties to open the Taskbar and Start Menu Properties dialog box. Then click the Notification Area tab. List the four system icons you have available to choose from.

_____, _____, _____, _____

b. One of the options, Power, is grayed out when using a desktop PC. Why do you think that is?

_____

Step 4 The Recycle Bin still handles all of your deleted files in Windows Vista, just like it did in Windows XP.

a. Right-click on the Recycle Bin and select Properties to view the options you have available. Record the default custom size for Recycle Bin storage on your Windows Vista system.

_____

→ **Note**

If you are in a classroom environment with other students doing this lab, check with them and see if their Recycle Bin size is the same as yours. Depending on the size of the hard drives, you may see different results.

b. Windows usually asks for confirmation when you choose to delete a file. Is there a way you can turn off that feature in this area? What would be a benefit to a feature like that?

_____

_____

c. What is the maximum size of the Recycle Bin on your computer?

_____

d. When finished, return the Recycle Bin to its default settings.

Step 5   One of Windows Vista's new features is the Windows Sidebar. The Sidebar sits on one side of your desktop and holds little programs called Gadgets. There are thousands of Gadgets on Microsoft's Web site that provide such things as weather reports, puzzles, or your *World of Warcraft* stats. You may notice a large analog clock in the upper-right corner of your screen—that's a Gadget. Hovering your cursor over the clock or Sidebar area will highlight it.

Right-click on an empty portion of the Sidebar and click Properties. In the Windows Sidebar Properties dialog box, you can select whether the Sidebar appears on the right side or left side of your screen, as well as which monitor it appears on (if you are using multiple monitors). Click the *View list of running gadgets* button.

a.   Record the list of running Gadgets.

_____

_____

b.   Return to your desktop. Right-click on the Sidebar and click Add Gadgets. Add as many Gadgets as you like. How many Gadgets can fit on your screen at once?

_____

 30 MINUTES

Lab Exercise 2.03: The Windows 7 Interface

As of the first half of 2012, Windows 7 is Microsoft's current flagship operating system. It debuted on October 22, 2009 as a replacement to Windows Vista. Windows 7 comes in several editions for consumers and businesses. For consumers, these include Starter, Home Basic, and Home Premium. Out of those three choices, the only one that you can buy in the store is Home Premium. The Starter edition is sold exclusively on portable devices like netbooks, while Home Basic is only available in "emerging markets." For the business and power users, Microsoft created Professional, Enterprise, and Ultimate. Windows 7 comes in 32-bit and 64-bit flavors.

Learning Objectives

The main objective of this exercise is to familiarize you with the interface of Windows 7.

At the end of this lab, you'll be able to

- Manipulate and use the Start menu, taskbar, Quick Launch toolbar, notification area, and Gadgets

Lab Materials and Setup

The materials you need for this lab are

- A fully functioning PC with Windows 7 installed

Getting Down to Business

In this lab exercise, you will take a tour of the Windows 7 interface. You'll see in detail how the Start menu, taskbar, Quick Launch toolbar, and notification area work—you should be pretty familiar with these by now. You'll also see how Gadgets have changed from Windows Vista to Windows 7.

Step 1   Let's begin once again with the Start menu. Windows 7 only uses the Windows logo icon to label the Start button, though if you hover your mouse cursor over the logo, a tooltip labeled "Start" appears.

   a.   Click on the Start button to open the Start menu. Record five of the clickable items in this menu.

   _____

   b.   Write down how many columns wide this menu system is:

   _____

   c.   You can get help about your Microsoft operating system by opening the Start menu and clicking Help and Support. If you're like me, you probably use Google to search for PC troubleshooting solutions, so you may we want to remove this button from the Start menu. Right-click on the Start button and select Properties. This opens the Taskbar and Start Menu Properties dialog box. From here, you can change how your power button works and change the Start menu's privacy settings.

   d.   Record the different ways you can customize the power button.

   _____   _____   _____

   _____   _____   _____

   e.   Click the Customize button to open the Customize Start Menu dialog box (see Figure 2-6). List four Start menu options that can be displayed as a link, as a menu, or not at all.

   _____

   _____

   _____

   _____

   f.   Scroll down the list and uncheck the Help checkbox, and then click OK. Click OK in the Taskbar and Start Menu Properties dialog box. View the changes to your Start menu.

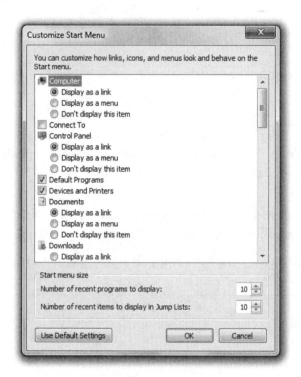

FIGURE 2-6 Customize Start Menu dialog box in Windows 7

Step 2 The Windows 7 taskbar includes a new feature called *pinning*. Pinning enables you to attach any application to the taskbar for later use (see Figure 2-7). I like to think of pinning as what would happen if the taskbar and the Quick Launch toolbar had a baby.

    a. Select any item that is currently on your desktop or in your Start menu. Click and drag the icon onto your taskbar and let go. To truly enjoy this lab, pin at least five icons to the taskbar.

→ **Note**

Don't worry if you make a mistake and accidently pin something to the taskbar that you didn't want pinned to the taskbar. Right-click on the pinned icon and select *Unpin this program from taskbar* to remove it.

    b. Right-click on the taskbar and select Properties, as usual. You'll see the same Taskbar and Start Menu Properties dialog box you saw in Windows XP and Windows Vista.

FIGURE 2-7 Pinning objects to the taskbar

Figure 2-8 Opening multiple instances of Internet Explorer

c. List the four choices for the location of the taskbar on the screen.

_____

d. Leave the Taskbar and Start Menu Properties dialog box open. Open multiple instances of a program. Try using Internet Explorer. To open multiple instances of the same program, right-click on the program's icon in the taskbar. This opens a new type of menu called a Jump List. Click the title of the application, as shown in Figure 2-8. Repeat this about three or four times. Now, move your mouse cursor over the program's taskbar icon (Internet Explorer or whatever program you chose). It should look something like Figure 2-9.

Figure 2-9 Viewing taskbar thumbnails

e.   Return to the Taskbar and Start Menu Properties dialog box. In the *Taskbar buttons* drop-down menu, select *Never combine*. Click Apply. Record the results of selecting and applying this option.

_____

f.   Continue to manipulate and change the settings in this area to get accustomed to how you can affect the taskbar settings. When finished, return the taskbar to the default settings by undoing the changes you made.

Step 3   The Windows 7 notification area remains largely unchanged from previous versions of Windows (see Figure 2-10). There are, however, a few new customization options to learn about.

a.   Right-click on the taskbar and select Properties to open the Taskbar and Start Menu Properties dialog box. Click the Customize button. Record the different Behavior options available in the drop-down menus.

_____

_____

_____

b.   Click the link that says *Turn system icons on or off*. List the five system icons you have available to choose from.

_____, _____, _____, _____, _____

c.   Change some of these settings to manipulate how your notification area looks and acts on your Windows 7 computer. When you are done, click the link *Restore default icon behaviors*. Close the Taskbar and Start Menu Properties dialog box.

d.   Open each of the applications you pinned to your taskbar. Holy cow! That's a lot of applications loaded! You won't be able to see much of your desktop with all of those applications loaded.

e.   Move your cursor to the bottom-right corner of the screen. There is a small rectangular shape to the right of the clock. This is the Show desktop button.

f.   Hover your cursor over this area and record what happens.

_____

FIGURE 2-10 The Windows 7 notification area

g. Right-click the taskbar and select Properties to reopen the Taskbar and Start Menu Properties dialog box. Using your knowledge from the previous steps in this lab exercise, which feature in Windows 7 allowed you to view the desktop?

_____

h. Click Cancel when you are ready to return to the Windows desktop. Return your taskbar to normal by unpinning applications from it.

Step 4 Windows 7 includes an altered version of Windows Vista's Gadgets and Sidebar. While Vista's Gadgets were forced to live a life of servitude on a small strip of screen known as the Sidebar, Windows 7 Gadgets are free to roam the entire desktop. The Sidebar is no more. By default, Windows 7 won't display any Gadgets on your desktop. You have to choose to add them.

a. To add a Gadget, simply right-click anywhere on your desktop and select Gadgets.

b. List three examples of the default Gadgets.

_____

c. Click and drag a few Gadgets to your desktop to get a feel for how they work in Windows 7. Right-click on one of the Gadgets on your desktop. Set the opacity to 20%. Record what happens to the Gadget after you change the opacity.

_____

→ **Note**

If you're an advanced user, open the Windows Task Manager and click on the Processes tab. Look for sidebar.exe. It seems as though the application that runs your Gadgets is still known as sidebar.exe even in Windows 7. Don't worry, though: from a CompTIA A+ certification standpoint, the Sidebar existed only in Windows Vista.

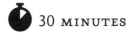 30 MINUTES

Lab Exercise 2.04: Discovering Aero in Windows 7

When Microsoft released Windows Vista, they updated the desktop interface with a new feature called Windows Aero. Aero is the default theme in Windows Vista and Windows 7. To take advantage of this enhanced desktop, you need to have a compatible Windows operating system and a DirectX 9 compatible graphics card with a minimum of 128 MB of video memory, among other requirements.

Learning Objectives

The main objective of this exercise is to familiarize you with the features of Windows Aero and tools to troubleshoot it.

At the end of this lab, you'll be able to

- Understand and explain the different features provided by Windows Aero

- Troubleshoot a PC with problems related to Windows Aero

Lab Materials and Setup

The materials you need for this lab are

- A fully functioning PC with Windows 7 Home Premium, Professional, Enterprise, or Ultimate installed

- Optional: A fully functioning PC with Windows Vista Home Premium, Business, Enterprise, or Ultimate installed

Getting Down to Business

In this lab exercise, we will be exploring the features of Window Aero from the perspective of Windows 7. Aero takes advantage of modern graphics card technologies to create a more appealing user interface. In Lab Exercise 2.03, you explored the Windows 7 interface and found Aero Peek and Jump Lists. These features are a part of Windows Aero, along with a host of others like Shake, Snap, Flip3D, and Transparency (sometimes called Glass). This lab also looks at how to troubleshoot Aero-related problems. In order to use Windows Aero, you need to have Windows 7 Home Premium, Professional, Enterprise, or Ultimate. Windows 7 Starter and Home Basic do not include Aero.

→ **Note**

This lab was designed using Windows 7. Many of the steps will also work for Windows Vista, but there are minor changes between the two. You might try following the steps with both Windows 7 and Windows Vista to see where Microsoft changed things.

Step 1

a. Before you can see the features of Windows Aero, you must select an Aero theme. Right-click on your desktop and select Personalize to open the Personalization applet.

b. You should see at least three different categories of themes by default. List them here.

_____

_____

_____

c.   Choose a theme from the Aero Themes category. Next, click on the Window Color link at the bottom of the applet. This opens the Window Color and Appearance window. From here you can change the colors and intensity of your window borders. Find a color that suits you and select it.

d.   Uncheck the Enable transparency checkbox. Record what happens to your taskbar and window panes as a result.

_____

e.   Check the box again to reenable transparency. Save your changes and exit to your desktop.

Step 2   To make Aero Shake work, we need to create a little chaos and open some applications. Open as many applications as you would like, but at least three. Your desktop should look something like mine, shown in Figure 2-11.

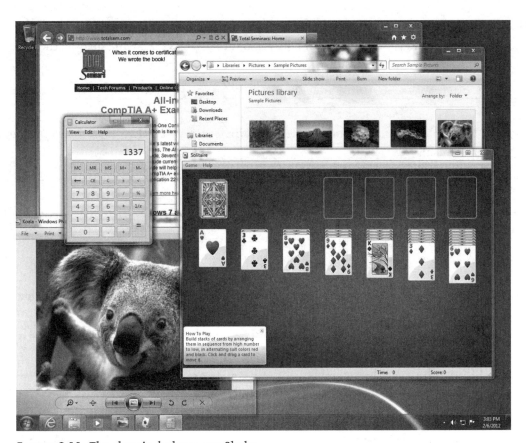

FIGURE 2-11   The chaotic desktop, pre-Shake

Once you have three or more applications open, go to whichever application is active (or in the foreground) and then click and hold on the top of the foreground window. Now, while holding down the mouse button, quickly shake your mouse side to side.

Record what happens.

_____

Step 3 To see Snap in action, open any application. Click and hold the top of the window pane and then drag it to the far-right side of your screen until you can't make your mouse go any further. Release the mouse button and record what happens.

_____

Try snapping the application to the left side of the screen. When might a feature like this be useful?

_____

Step 4 Finally, let's take a look at task switching and Flip3D. Open a few more applications. At least three will do nicely. On your keyboard, press and hold ALT and then press TAB. While holding the ALT key, continue to tap the TAB key. Record the results.

_____

That shortcut key combination has been with us since Windows 3.0. It's older than some of you who are reading this lab manual!

Now, while holding the WINDOWS key, press the TAB key. Record the results.

_____

→ Note

Did you know that Aero is a backronym (an acronym created after the word itself)? It stands for Authentic, Energetic, Reflective, and Open.

Step 5 Troubleshooting Windows Aero is actually a fairly simple process. Aero will either work or it won't. The following steps showcase the Aero troubleshooting tool.

a. Right-click on the desktop and select Screen Resolution. Click on the _Advanced settings_ link to open the Properties dialog box of your graphics card. Click the Monitor tab. In the Colors drop-down list, switch to High Color (16-bit) and record the results.

_____

We have officially made a settings change with how Windows 7 displays colors onscreen, and Aero has a major issue with that, as the following steps reveal.

b.   Click OK in the dialog box and the applet you opened to return to the desktop.

→ Note

While Aero is having problems, try some of the features showcased earlier such as Snap, Shake, and Flip3D. Which features still work and which ones don't?

c.   With your graphics card set to 16-bit color depth, right-click on the desktop and click Personalize. At the bottom of the Personalization window is a troubleshooting tool. Record the title of the link to the troubleshooting tool.

_____

d.   Click the link to open the Aero troubleshooting tool, shown in Figure 2-12.

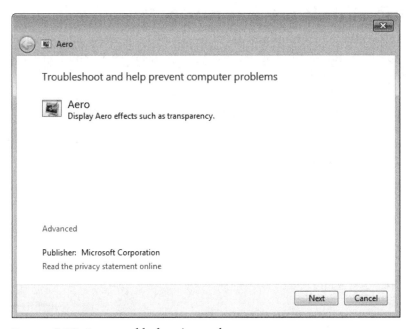

FIGURE 2-12 Aero troubleshooting tool

e. At the bottom of the Aero troubleshooting tool's window is the Advanced link. Click on the link and uncheck the *Apply repairs automatically* checkbox. Click Next to run the troubleshooting tool. Once the tool has been run, a results screen will be presented. List the problems that the Aero troubleshooting tool wants to fix.

_____

f. Click Next to apply the fixes. Your screen will flash a couple of times as it fixes itself. You will then see a summary window. Notice the results of the troubleshooting tool. Click Close.

→ Note

You can also access the Aero troubleshooting tool by clicking the Start button and typing **Aero** into the Start search box. Select *Find and fix problems with transparency and other visual effects.*

 30 MINUTES

Lab Exercise 2.05: Windows Explorer

Windows Explorer enables you to see all the programs and data files on a given storage device. Explorer works with hard drives and removable media such as optical media, USB flash drives, and floppy disks. Both users and techs use this program more than any other when they need to locate and manipulate files and folders.

Learning Objectives

In this lab, you'll explore the Windows file structure.

At the end of this lab, you'll be able to

- Use Windows Explorer
- Understand and use the contents of the Windows and Program Files folders

Lab Materials and Setup

The materials you need for this lab are

- A working computer running Windows XP, Windows Vista, or Windows 7

✔ Hint

You can perform these steps on any Windows system, but some of them may involve functionality that's available only in Windows XP.

Getting Down to Business

When you open a folder icon to view what's inside, you're seeing Windows Explorer in action. It enables you to see and manipulate files, folders, and their organizational structures quickly and easily without memorizing a bunch of commands. Becoming familiar with its ins and outs is vital to becoming an effective PC technician.

Step 1   Begin by looking at the internal directory structure of Windows. Start Windows Explorer by selecting Start | All Programs | Accessories | Windows Explorer. The first place to go exploring in the Windows directory structure is the root directory:

    a.   Locate the My Computer/Computer icon in the left pane of Windows Explorer and click the plus sign (+) or arrow.

    b.   Locate the C: drive icon, and click it once to highlight it. You should not need to click the plus sign or arrow, as clicking the drive's icon automatically expands its contents. The right pane now displays the contents of the root directory of your C: drive (see Figure 2-13).

    c.   List a few examples of folders stored on your C: drive.

_____

You can choose from several different views, or ways of displaying folder contents.

    d.   At the top of the Explorer window, click the icon called Views. (In Windows 7, the icon isn't labeled, but it looks like a set of icons.) You can also access the different views by clicking on the View drop-down menu (located on the left side of the toolbar in Windows XP, and on the right side of the toolbar in Windows Vista and Windows 7).

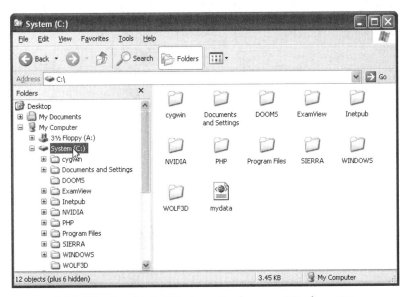

FIGURE 2-13 Viewing C:\ in Windows Explorer on Windows XP

e. List the different views available in your operating system.

_____

_____

When you open the menu, the current view is marked with a large dot or slider icon. You can switch views as often as you like, simply by selecting another view from the list.

f. Find the folders named Windows and Program Files. If you have a 64-bit operating system, you will see Program Files and Program Files (x86). These folders contain the majority of your operating system and program files.

g. Click the Windows folder icon. Look at Figure 2-14 for a sample of what you should see at this point if you're running Windows XP.

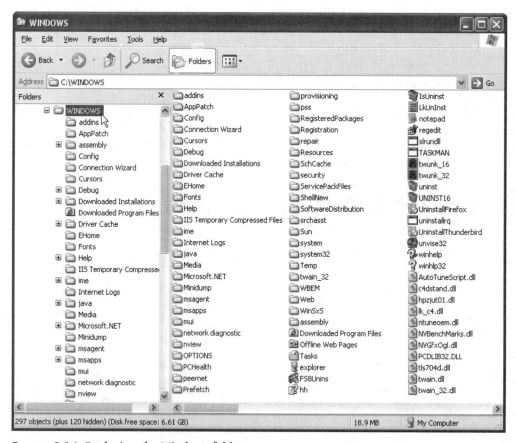

Figure 2-14 Exploring the Windows folder

✖ Warning

Some system administrators may have changed the names of these folders, but in general this is not the best practice. If you need to contact Microsoft for assistance, they always start by directing you to the default folder names, so changing them can increase your troubleshooting time.

Step 2 In the next few substeps, you'll configure your folder options to provide the maximum information about your files and folders. Techs usually find that the more information they have about a component, the easier it is to troubleshoot or configure. Take a moment and explore the different folders and files in the Windows folder. A typical Windows folder has tens of thousands of files and folders (see Figure 2-15). To view the number of files and folders in your Windows folder, right-click the Windows folder icon and select Properties from the drop-down menu.

a.   List the number of files and folders in the Windows folder on your computer.

_____

b.   Return to the root of your C: drive by navigating to it in the left pane or clicking the Back button at the top of Windows Explorer.

c.   Like you did with the Windows folder above, record the total number of files and folders in the root of the C: drive.

_____

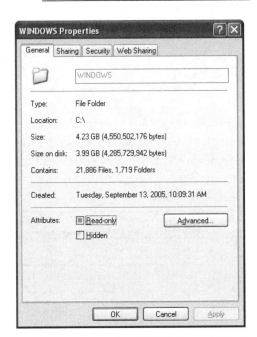

FIGURE 2-15 Viewing the Windows folder's properties

d.   Maximize your Explorer window (if it isn't already) by clicking the small box button next to the × button in the upper-right corner of the window. Then change the view mode to Details.

e.   Notice the column headings across the right pane. List the default column headings.

_____

f.   Click each of the headings to sort by that value. Click any heading again to sort in reverse order. You can also right-click on any column heading to see additional values for sorting.

g.   In Windows XP, select Tools | Folder Options. In Windows Vista/7, select Organize | Folder and search options. Click the View tab of the Folder Options dialog box.

h.   In the Advanced settings area, click the radio button *Show hidden files, folders, and drives*, in Windows 7. This displays all files and folders, even those for which the Hidden attribute has been set.

i.   Remove the checkmark next to *Hide extensions for known file types*. This directs Windows Explorer to display the filename extensions in all views. This is useful for a tech, and these days it also helps users with such things as identifying e-mail viruses hiding as (for instance) FILE.MP3.SCR.

j.   Remove the checkmark next to *Hide protected operating system files (Recommended)*. This will enable you to examine critical system files when you're troubleshooting problems.

k.   Click Apply to commit these changes to the folder view. Before you close the Folder Options dialog box, click Apply to All Folders (Apply to Folders in Windows 7) in the Folder views section. This will apply the Details view to every folder on the system, and enable you to see file extensions, hidden files, and system files in all folders as well.

l.   List the examples of new files or folders that are present on the root of the C: drive after making the preceding changes.

_____

m.   Click on the Windows folder in the left pane. Different files use different extensions. Sort the folders and files by Type (click the Type column heading), and see if you can locate the files with the following extensions. Give a brief description of each extension by searching them on the Internet.

- .INI   _____
- .BMP   _____
- .EXE   _____
- .TXT   _____

n.   Sort the list by Name, and locate these files:

  •   **Explorer.exe**   This is the Windows Explorer application you're using for these exercises.

  •   **Desktop.ini**   This contains the configuration data for your desktop.

✖   **Warning**

Do not alter these files in *any* way! You won't like the results.

Step 3   When working with Windows, it's important to know the key system files that are involved with your operating system and to know how to find them. In Windows XP, use the *Search for files and folders* tool to locate and record the absolute path of any file on your system. If you are using Windows Vista or Windows 7, open the Start menu and type your search terms into the Search bar. Microsoft's more recent operating systems have much more advanced search options. If Windows doesn't find the file you are looking for, click *See more results* and you will be presented with additional search options.

  a.   In Windows XP, you'll first need to click Start | Search | For Files or Folders, then click *All files and folders*, and finally click *More advanced options*. Select the following checkboxes (see Figure 2-16):

  •   Search system folders

  •   Search hidden files and folders

  •   Search subfolders

  b.   Search for Notepad.exe Record its absolute path.

Step 4   The following are some of the other important folders you'll find in the Windows folder. Select each one to gain more experience using Windows Explorer.

  •   **Cursors**   Windows stores the many different cursors you can use here.

  •   **Fonts**   Windows stores all its fonts in this folder. Note that fonts usually have one of two extensions, .FON or .TTF. The .FON files are old-style screen fonts, and the .TTF files are modern TrueType fonts. You can double-click a font icon to see what the font looks like. Some users even print their favorite fonts and keep them in a three-ring binder for later reference.

  •   **Help**   This folder is the default location for all .HLP and .CHM (help) files. Open one to see what program uses it.

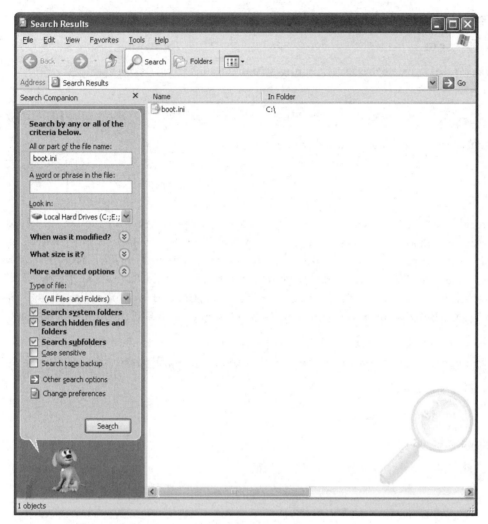

Figure 2-16 The Search utility in Windows XP

- **Media**   This folder is the default location for sounds and audio clips. Double-click a file with a .WAV or .MID extension to hear sounds.

- **System32**   This folder is the heart of Windows. Here you can see the core operating system files. This folder also stores almost all of the .DLL files used by Windows.

Step 5   Collapse the Windows folder, and expand the Program Files folder (see Figure 2-17). This is the default location for applications installed on your system.

Follow these steps:

a.   Open the Windows Media Player subfolder and find the application. Remember to look for the .EXE extension.

b.   Click the .EXE file's icon to start the program.

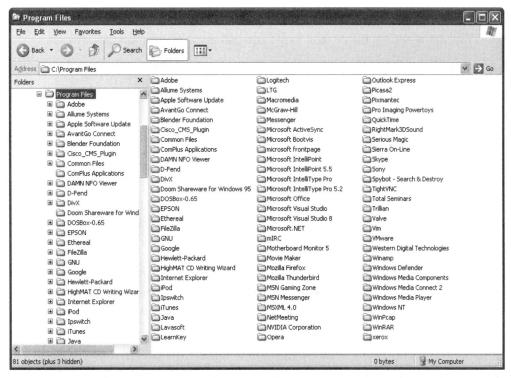

FIGURE 2-17 Exploring C:\Program Files in Windows Explorer

   c.   Close the program you just opened.

   d.   Exit Windows Explorer.

 30 MINUTES

Lab Exercise 2.06: The Windows Control Panel

The Windows Control Panel is the technician's toolbox. It contains the tools you need to do everything from changing the mouse settings to installing new device drivers. This lab exercise won't attempt to examine every tool in the Control Panel, but it will help you become familiar with many of them. Some Control Panel programs—known as *applets*—are specific to particular hardware, while others are used for software configuration. Windows initially sets up defaults that work for most installations, but as a technician, you may need to tweak some of the settings. Also, not all Windows features are enabled in a normal installation, so you may need to enable or disable features according to the needs of a particular user.

✔ Cross-Reference

For a refresher on the Windows Control Panel, refer to the "Control Panel" section in Chapter 2 of *Mike Meyers' CompTIA A+ Guide to 802: Managing and Troubleshooting PCs.*

Learning Objectives

In this lab, you'll practice accessing the Control Panel and making configuration adjustments.

At the end of this lab, you'll be able to

- Navigate to the Control Panel
- Explain the use of some common Control Panel applets

Lab Materials and Setup

The materials you need for this lab are

- A working computer running Windows XP, Windows Vista, or Windows 7

Getting Down to Business

The Control Panel is the toolbox, and one of the key tools in the Control Panel is the Device Manager. Device Manager lists all your system hardware. From there, you can load drivers, set resources, and configure other aspects of your hardware devices. You'll now get familiar with both.

Step 1   As a technician, you'll access the Control Panel and Device Manager often. You really do need to know the path to these important tools in each version of Windows. The CompTIA A+ 220-802 exam has numerous questions about paths to these tools.

> ➜ **Note**
>
> Throughout the rest of this manual, when a lab involves changing settings located in the Control Panel or Device Manager, the directions will assume you know how to get that far, and the steps will begin with the Control Panel or Device Manager already open. Refer to this exercise if you need a refresher on opening the Control Panel.

a.   To open the Control Panel, click on the Start button, then select Control Panel. The Control Panel window opens, as shown in Figures 2-18 and 2-19.

b.   Practice switching between the different views in Control Panel. For Windows XP, on the left pane it says *Switch to Category View*. For Windows Vista, on the left pane it says *Classic View*. For Windows 7, in the upper-right corner of the window it says *View by: Category*. Experiment with each view to see which one fits you the best.

> ➜ **Note**
>
> CompTIA A+ expects you to know both ways of viewing a Windows Control Panel, no matter the operating system. For the rest of this lab, we will operate out of Classic View (also called Icon View).

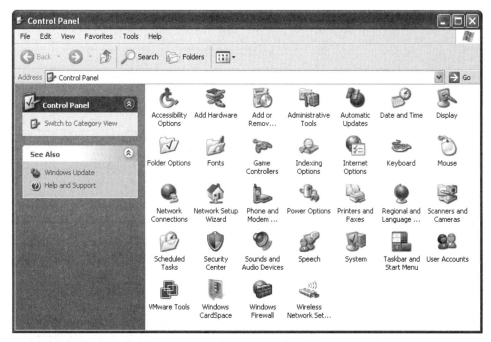

FIGURE 2-18 The Control Panel (Classic View) in Windows XP

FIGURE 2-19 The Control Panel (Classic View) in Windows Vista

c.   List six Control Panel applets that you think are vital to troubleshooting a PC.

_____   _____

_____   _____

_____   _____

d.   Open the System applet. The System applet is the gateway to many important tools and utilities you will use as a PC technician. You will also notice that the System applet in Windows XP is very different from the Windows Vista/7 System applet. What kind of information do you see when looking at the System applet?

_____

e.   Is your operating system type 32-bit or 64-bit?

_____

f.   If you are on a Windows Vista/7 computer, click on Device Manager in the left pane. If you are on a Windows XP computer, click the Hardware tab and then click the Device Manager button.

g.   Device Manager is arguably one of the most important utilities in Microsoft Windows. From here you can see the status and condition of all the devices in your system. Record any irregularities indicated by Device Manager, such as devices with an exclamation point in a yellow field, devices with a red ×, or devices with a down arrow. If Device Manager has none of these symbols, your system is working like a champ; write "devmgmt.msc is the greatest!"

_____

→ Note

Devmgmt.msc is the command-line tool to bring up Device Manager. Remember, it's always good to know multiple paths to get to the same thing.

h.   Close Device Manager and the System applet.

Step 2   Now examine some other applets in the Control Panel.

a.   In Windows XP, double-click the Display icon. This is the same applet you see if you right-click the desktop and select Properties. Windows Vista uses the Personalization applet for many of the same functions. Windows 7 uses both the Display and Personalization applets, splitting the responsibility between the two. In Windows 7, the Display applet adjusts your video resolution and monitor settings, and the Personalization applet changes the look and feel of your desktop interface. According to your OS, find the appropriate Control Panel applet to change your system's video resolution. What is your current resolution?

_____

b.   In Windows XP/Vista, use the slider bar to lower the resolution to the lowest value. In Windows 7, open the drop-down menu and use the slider to lower the resolution to the lowest value. What is the lowest resolution that can be set?

_____

c.   Click Apply. What happens to your desktop interface?

_____

d.   Either let the timer expire to change back to the previous setting, or manually change the setting back to its defaults when you are finished.

✖ Warning

Clicking the Advanced button in the Display applet can give you access to many special features of your particular monitor/video card, including the refresh rate. Be sure you know what you're doing before you change these settings!

✔ Hint

If you click the Apply button instead of the OK button after making a change, the Display applet will remain open after the change takes effect; this can be useful when you need to experiment a bit.

e.   Return to the Control Panel and double-click the Sounds and Audio Devices icon in Windows XP or the Sound icon in Windows Vista/7 to open the applet.

f.   Tabs line the top of the applet. Explore each one, and become familiar with what each does. In Windows Vista/7, click on the Playback tab. In Windows XP, click on the Audio tab, and then click the drop-down menu for Sound playback. List the devices your PC has for playing sound.

_____

g.   Reset all of your changes, if you made any, and close the applet.

Step 3 Keyboard and mouse settings are a matter of personal preference. Be careful to tell the user if you make any changes to these settings. If you need to speed up the mouse while you use someone else's PC, for example, remember to slow it down again when you finish.

To adjust the keyboard settings:

a.   Double-click the Keyboard icon in the Control Panel. In Windows 7, make sure you are on the Speed tab.

b.   Change the Repeat delay and Repeat rate settings and click Apply. Keep the Keyboard applet open and open Notepad or WordPad. Test your changes by pressing and holding individual keys on the keyboard. Based on your findings explain repeat rate and repeat delay.

Repeat rate: _____

Repeat delay: _____

✔ **Hint**

The Mouse applet can have many different looks, depending on whether the system uses a default Windows driver or special drivers for the particular mouse. You may have to explore your applet to find these settings.

---

c.   Double-click the Mouse icon to open the Mouse applet.

d.   Look through the tabs of the Mouse applet. Find the settings for left-handed mode. Set your mouse to left-handed mode. Try it out. Does that make your brain hurt? Well, then, change it back. (Ahhh, that's better!)

e.   Change the double-click speed. Slow it down a bit. Is that easier? Slow it down more. Do you find that annoying? Now speed it up. Can you click fast enough?

f.   Change the mini-icons that represent your mouse pointer, such as the arrow, hourglass, and so on. Try a couple of different sets. Can you think of situations where some of these alternate icon sets might be useful?

_____

_____

g.   Change the pointer options. Change the speed at which the pointer travels across your screen. Everyone has his or her own sweet spot for this, so experiment to find yours. Turn on pointer trails. Do you find them cool or annoying? If you have a Snap To option, turn that on. Now open a dialog box and watch the pointer jump to the active button. Is this convenient, or too much help? Turn off any features you don't want to keep.

h.   Close the Mouse applet.

Step 4   The CompTIA A+ 220-802 exam includes questions about user accessibility. You need to know which settings you can change to accommodate the hearing and visually impaired, and where to find those settings.

  a. In Windows XP, open the Accessibility Options applet (see Figure 2-20). In Vista and 7, choose the Ease of Access Center applet (see Figure 2-21). Notice that you have all the previously mentioned options, plus many more!

  b. Select the Display tab in Windows XP, or click *Make the computer easier to see* in Windows Vista/7.

  c. In Windows XP, check the Use High Contrast checkbox and click Settings (see Figure 2-22). In Windows Vista/7, check the box to enable the High Contrast key combination and then click *Choose a High Contrast theme*.

  d. Choose a scheme you like and click OK.

  e. In Windows XP, click Apply in the Accessibility Options applet to see how it looks. In Windows Vista/7, you have to press LEFT ALT-LEFT SHIFT-PRINT SCREEN to activate High Contrast mode.

  f. Turn off the Use High Contrast option by repeating the key combination, and then click Apply and click OK.

  g. Close the Accessibility Options/Ease of Access Center applet.

Step 5   Finally, let's look at the Date and Time applet.

 Open the Date and Time applet in the Control Panel. This applet has been around since the dawn of time, more or less, when computers didn't automatically adjust themselves for Daylight Saving Time.

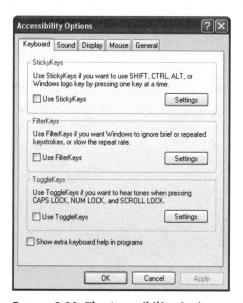

FIGURE 2-20 The Accessibility Options applet in Windows XP

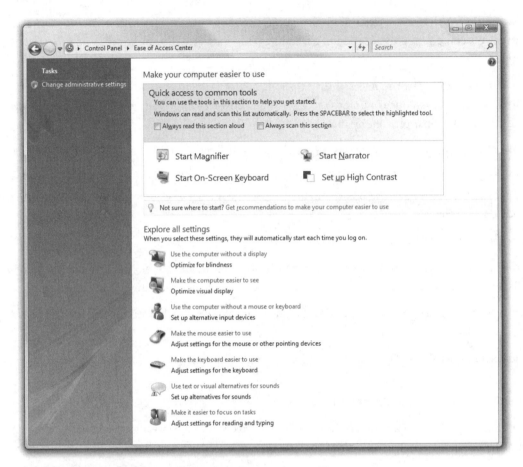

FIGURE 2-21 Ease of Access Center applet in Windows Vista

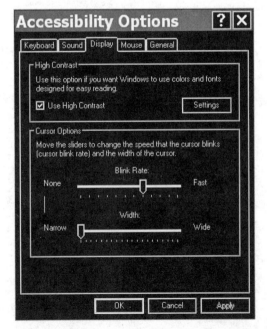

FIGURE 2-22 Setting the High Contrast option for the visually impaired

Adjust the date and time. Notice that you can do this either by scrolling with the arrows or by highlighting the fields and typing in the time on your keyboard. This feature can come in handy if you travel and want to change the time zone on a portable computer.

a.   Click on the Internet Time tab. Record the server your PC connects to in order to receive the correct time.

_____

b.   If you are using Windows 7, click the Additional Clocks tab. Add more clocks to your notification area. How many total clocks can you have (not including Gadgets)?

_____

 30 MINUTES

Lab Exercise 2.07: The Windows Microsoft Management Console (MMC) Toolbox

You're about to learn how to customize your Windows toolkit! Almost every profession requires a set of tools to get the job done. Some of these tools are necessary, and some are luxuries. If you were a carpenter, you might have a toolbox in which you keep your hammer, saw, screwdrivers, pliers, and so on. You could then buy new tools ("I really needed this pneumatic nail gun, and it was on sale!" is a common excuse) and add them to your toolbox—but you'd need to keep it all organized, or risk not being able to find the tool you need when you need it.

To help organize all of your PC technician's utilities, Microsoft created a handy toolbox: the Microsoft Management Console, or MMC. The MMC not only organizes all of those useful tools, but also provides a consistent look and feel between different systems and even different operating systems, which makes it easier to use them.

✔ **Cross-Reference**

For details on working with the MMC, refer to the "Microsoft Management Console" section in Chapter 2 of *Mike Meyers' CompTIA A+ Guide to 802: Managing and Troubleshooting PCs*.

Learning Objectives

In this exercise, you'll learn how to create an MMC. You'll also create a desktop icon that you can use to access this customized software toolkit whenever you need it.

At the end of this lab, you'll be able to

- Create an MMC

- Add tools (snap-ins) to the MMC

Lab Materials and Setup

The materials you need for this lab are

- A working computer running Windows XP, Windows Vista, or Windows 7

Getting Down to Business

The MMC is a shell program that holds individual utilities called snap-ins. The first time you create an MMC, you get a default blank console. A blank MMC isn't much to look at—like any new toolbox, it starts out empty.

Step 1   To create your MMC, select Start | Run in Windows XP, or use the Start menu Search bar in Windows Vista/7, type **mmc**, and then press ENTER. Voilà! You've created a blank console (see Figure 2-23).

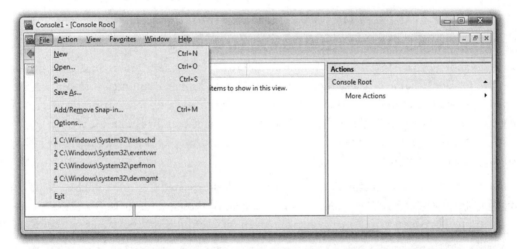

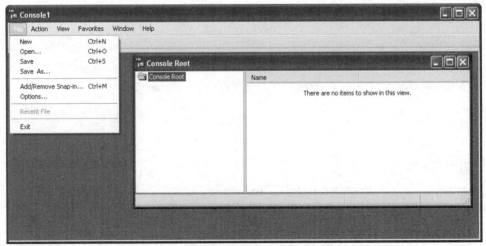

FIGURE 2-23 Blank MMCs in Windows XP (bottom) and Vista (top)

You'll notice that the name in the upper-left corner is Console1. In Vista/7, you'll also notice a panel called Actions, which contains a list of actions that are available to users as you add snap-ins and select them.

Before you actually configure an MMC, you need to understand a few points. First, you can have more than one MMC; successive consoles will be given default names such as Console2, Console3, and so on. Second, you can rename the consoles that you create. Third, you can choose where to save the consoles, so that you can easily find them again. Finally, once you've created an MMC, you can modify it by adding or removing tools—just like your toolbox at home.

Follow these steps to practice working with MMCs:

a. Click File | Save As and fill in the boxes as follows:

- **Save in**   Desktop

- **File name**   *Your Name's* MMC

- **Save as type**   Microsoft Management Console Files (*.msc)

b. Click Save to continue. (Don't exit the MMC!)

c. Notice in the upper-left corner of the open window that the name has changed.

d. Find the new icon that's been created on the desktop. This icon, which bears the same name as your new MMC, enables you to access the MMC in the future with just a double-click of the mouse.

Step 2   When you add snap-ins, they'll show up in the Add/Remove Snap-in dialog box (see Figure 2-24).

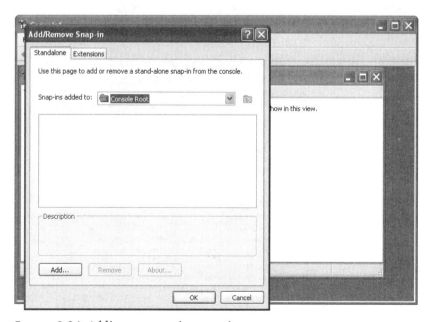

FIGURE 2-24 Adding or removing snap-ins

You'll now add some snap-ins to your MMC:

a.   Click File | Add/Remove Snap-in.

b.   Click Add, and let the fun begin (see Figure 2-25). List five available snap-ins.

_____

_____

_____

_____

_____

c.   Add the Device Manager as your first tool. Select Device Manager from the list and click Add.

✔ **Hint**

When you add a snap-in, you have a choice of adding it for either your local computer or another computer. With the proper access permissions, in other words, you can look at Device Manager on a networked system. More than likely, you don't have the necessary permissions to do this, so stick with the local option for now.

d.   Select Local Computer and click Finish.

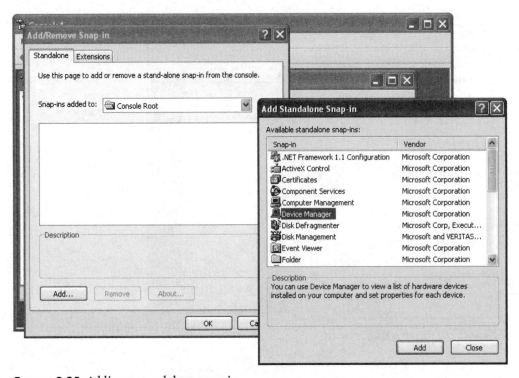

Figure 2-25 Adding a standalone snap-in

✖ **Warning**

I can't emphasize strongly enough that the best way to get a systems administrator mad is to go snooping around on the network. As a technician, your main concern is to do no harm. If you accidentally find your way to an unauthorized area, it's your duty to report it to an administrator.

While you're here, you'll add one more snap-in: Event Viewer. Adding it here will provide an alternate way to access this tool.

    e.   Select Event Viewer from the list.

    f.   Select Local Computer and click Finish to close out the wizard.

    g.   Click Add to close the list window, and click OK to close the Add/Remove window.

    h.   Your MMC should now show two snap-ins.

    i.   Be sure to save your MMC.

    j.   You now have a toolbox with quick access to Device Manager and Event Viewer. You can use these tools in the same way as if you navigated to them through the conventional methods. Have your instructor view your MMC to see if everything works correctly. If you don't have an instructor available, ask a knowledgeable technician that you know to glance at your screen.

        Instructor Check: _____

Step 3 If everything has worked correctly up to now, continue with this step (if you had problems creating your MMC, review the instructions or ask your instructor for assistance):

    a.   Double-click the desktop icon for *Your Name's* MMC.

    b.   Device Manager and Event Viewer are now available directly from your desktop (see Figure 2-26).

✔ **Hint**

I've only scratched the surface of creating an MMC here. Your customizing options are limited only by the number of snap-ins available and your imagination. Try creating different groupings of tools to organize similar tasks—maybe all the disk management tools together, or all the user, group, and resource tools. Be creative!

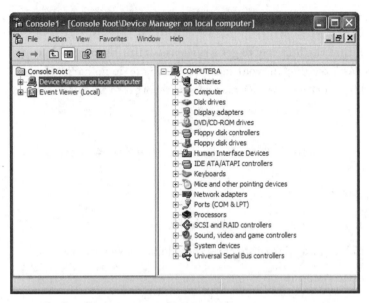

FIGURE 2-26 Accessing Device Manager from a custom MMC

Lab Analysis Test

1. Your friend Brian calls you and asks why his Windows 7 Ultimate desktop interface looks different from other computers he has looked at recently. He elaborates by telling you that he used to be able to see through his window panes, but now they are just solid colors. What is Brian having issues with and how can he go about fixing it?

2. What's the purpose of the MMC? What is the added feature in Windows Vista/7?

3. Your network administrator wants you to set up a lab full of Windows XP computers. He doesn't want the users to mess with important settings, so he wants you to remove the Run command from the Start menu. Give a detailed explanation of how to do that.

4. One of your clients using Windows Vista called your help desk because he's experiencing difficulties using the mouse. He says his mouse moves too fast, and icons don't respond when he double-clicks them. What's wrong? Where would you direct him to go to fix this problem? Give the complete path.

5. A Windows 7 user on your network has just downloaded an important attachment from a colleague, but he is unsure whether the document he downloaded is a .DOCX file or a .DOC file. Give a detailed description of how you can reveal the extensions to known files.

Key Term Quiz

Use the following terms to complete the following sentences. Not all terms will be used.

Aero

Classic View

Control Panel

Device Manager

DirectX 9

Display

Ease of Access Center

Flip3D

Glass

Microsoft Management Console (MMC)

notification area

Recycle Bin

Shake

Snap

snap-ins

Start button

taskbar

Transparency

1. Pressing WINDOWS KEY-TAB in Windows 7 will showcase the _____ feature.

2. The System, Display, and Mouse applets are found in the _____.

3. The various tools in the MMC are known as _____.

4. The area that holds all of your open applications and allows you to pin icons to it in Windows 7 is known as the _____.

5. You can take advantage of Windows _____ as long as you have a _____ compatible video card with 128 MB of video memory installed in your computer running Windows 7.

Chapter 3
Troubleshooting Essential Hardware

Lab Exercises

Your PC includes five core components that it can't live without: a CPU, RAM, the BIOS, a motherboard, and a power supply. If any of these pieces fail, your computer won't work. A bad CPU might cause unexpected shutdowns or system lockups, but these problems might also be caused by bad RAM or a failing power supply. You'll need to determine which component is causing the problem and fix it (or replace it, as is often the case with these sorts of components). Your best course of action is to test each component, one at a time, and replace the faulty one if necessary. Try testing your RAM, for example. If you see something suspicious, replace it. If that doesn't fix the problem, move on to the CPU or the motherboard.

In this chapter, you'll learn how to look for CPU, RAM, and power supply issues. Since there's no clear way to test for a failing motherboard, you'll need to know how to replace it and try a different one. Since the BIOS rarely fails, you'll focus instead on the biggest problem people encounter when trying to interact with CMOS: passwords.

 30 MINUTES

Lab Exercise 3.01: Testing CPUs with CPU-Z

When a CPU goes bad, you'll know it, because your computer won't turn on. But just because it works doesn't mean it's working as well as it should. If you have a super- fast Intel Core i7 CPU that runs as slow as a PC from the 90s, you've got a problem. Admittedly, this is rarely a CPU issue—try shutting down some programs or adding some RAM. But you could have a bad core or a CPU that's not able to run at the right clock speed—it's possible! To check out the specifications of your CPU, you'll use a handy tool called CPU-Z. This utility reads the specifications of different PC components from information embedded in those components.

Learning Objectives

In this lab exercise, you'll identify various CPU specifications.

At the end of this lab, you'll be able to

- Run the CPU-Z utility
- Recognize key characteristics of CPUs

Lab Materials and Setup

The materials you need for this lab are

- Access to a working computer with Internet access to facilitate downloading and running the CPU-Z utility

- A notepad and pencil to document the specifications

- Optional: A word processor or spreadsheet application to facilitate the documentation

This lab is more informative if you have access to different types of systems with different classifications of CPUs.

Getting Down to Business

In the following steps, you'll download a reference utility known as CPU-Z and use it to further explore the characteristics of your CPU.

Step 1   Log on to a computer with Internet access and point your browser to the following Web site: www.cpuid.com. Follow the directions to download the current version of CPU-Z (version 1.60 at the time of this writing). Unzip the file and launch CPU-Z.

Step 2   The CPU-Z utility displays a number of tabs across the top of the window (see Figure 3-1). At this time, you are concerned only with the CPU and Caches tabs.

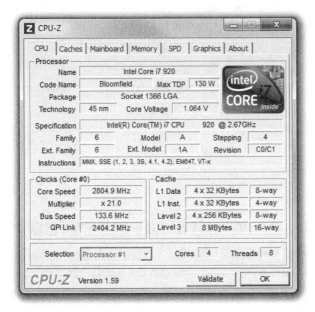

FIGURE 3-1 The CPU-Z utility

Using the data gathered by CPU-Z, record some of the pertinent information here:

Name: _____

Code Name: _____

Package: _____

Core Speed: _____

Multiplier: _____

Bus Speed: _____

L2 Cache: _____

L3 Cache: _____

→ **Note**

The code name is used by the manufacturers to refer to different revisions of a chip. For instance, the Core 2 Duo line of CPUs has three main revisions: Conroe, Allendale, and Wolfdale. Core 2 Quad CPUs include Kentsfield and Yorkfield.

✔ **Hint**

Because of variations in CPUs, chipsets, BIOS, and motherboards, CPU-Z may not be able to display all of the information about your CPU. In some cases, the information may actually be erroneous. The CPUID Web site has good documentation on some of the common incompatibilities.

Step 3   If possible, launch CPU-Z on various machines to compare the characteristics of different CPUs. Save the utility for use in future lab exercises.

 10 MINUTES

Lab Exercise 3.02: Testing RAM with MEMTEST86+

Windows Vista and Windows 7 include the powerful memory-testing tool called the Windows Memory Diagnostic Tool, but Windows XP users are out of luck. Fortunately, you can use a great, free third-party tool called MEMTEST86+ instead. For the purposes of this lab exercise, you should try downloading it and using it even if you have Windows Vista or Windows 7.

MEMTEST86+ cannot be installed into Windows. You must make a bootable optical disc by downloading the ISO file from the memtest.org Web site, or you can make a bootable USB drive by downloading a different installation file, also available on their Web site.

Learning Objectives

In this lab exercise, you'll use two methods to create bootable MEMTEST86+ media.

At the end of this lab, you'll be able to

- Create a bootable MEMTEST86+ optical disc

- Create a bootable MEMTEST86+ USB drive

- Start the MEMTEST86+ process

Lab Materials and Setup

The materials you need for this lab are

- A working Windows PC

- An optical drive capable of burning an optical disc

- A writeable optical disc (512 MB or larger)

- A USB thumb drive

Getting Down to Business

Memory testers like MEMTEST86+ cannot function while Windows is running, so you need to make some kind of boot media to run the program when you turn on the PC.

Step 1   Go to the www.memtest.org Web site. Scroll down the page until you find the Download section. Find and download the following files:

- Download - Pre-Compiled Bootable ISO (.zip)

- Download - Auto-installer for USB Key (Win 9x/2000/XP/7)

Step 2   Using whatever tool you prefer, burn the ISO file to a writeable optical disc. If you're using Windows XP and don't have another tool, try ISO Recorder by Alex Feinman (www.alexfeinman.com/isorecorder.htm) or Active@ ISO File Manager (http://www.ntfs.com/iso_file_manager.htm).

After burning the optical disc, restart your system. Use the CMOS setup program to ensure that your boot order checks the optical media drive first. When you boot the system, MEMTEST86+ should load.

Step 3   You can also use a USB thumb drive to boot to MEMTEST86+. Insert a thumb drive into a USB port and run the MEMTEST86+ USB installer program. Keep in mind that any data on the USB drive will be wiped out, so double-check that you don't have any important data stored on that drive.

Step 4   Reboot the computer and open the CMOS setup program. Change the boot order so that your PC looks for USB drives first. Save your changes and exit the CMOS setup program. When you boot the system, MEMTEST86+ should start testing automatically. You may get a notice onscreen asking which version you'd like to run, so just select the current version and it'll start.

Step 5   When MEMTEST86+ is done, if all goes well, it will give you no errors and you can remove the optical disc, boot into Windows, and continue computing content with the knowledge that your PC is working as intended. If you get errors, though, it's time to replace that RAM!

 30 MINUTES

Lab Exercise 3.03: Configuring and Clearing CMOS Setup Program Passwords

In many professional environments, the IT department doesn't want users to fool with any of the PC's settings—especially with detailed items such as the BIOS settings. The IT manager may even devise a password to prevent entry to the CMOS setup program by unauthorized users. Unfortunately, in your organization, the IT manager has resigned and was not very thorough about documenting these passwords.

When a CMOS setup program has been password protected and its password has been subsequently lost, the typical way to clear the password is to shunt a jumper on the motherboard that clears either the password or the entire contents of CMOS.

Learning Objectives

In this lab exercise, you'll learn how to configure CMOS setup program passwords and how to clear the contents of the password and CMOS using the onboard CMOS-clear jumper.

At the end of this lab, you'll be able to

- Set a password using the CMOS setup program
- Locate the CMOS-clear jumper on the motherboard
- Clear passwords and CMOS settings using the CMOS-clear jumper

Lab Materials and Setup

The materials you need for this lab are

- A working PC whose BIOS settings you can change, with access to the CMOS-clear jumper on the motherboard
- An anti-static mat/wrist strap
- A notepad

Getting Down to Business

In the following steps, you'll reboot your PC and access the CMOS setup program. You will then navigate to the password or security menu and configure a CMOS setup program password. You'll verify the password by rebooting the machine and entering CMOS setup. Finally, you'll open the case and reset the CMOS settings by physically shunting the CMOS-clear jumper.

✖ Warning

Any time you remove the cover from your PC, remember to follow all proper safety and electrostatic discharge (ESD) avoidance precautions.

Step 1   Reboot your system and use the appropriate key or key combination to enter the CMOS setup program.

Step 2   Once you've entered the CMOS setup program, navigate to the security or password menu (see Figure 3-2). Select the supervisor password and enter a four- to eight-character password. Save changes and exit CMOS setup.

Record your password here: _____

✔ Hint

Typically, two types of passwords can be set in CMOS, but a third is now appearing.

The *supervisor* password restricts access to the CMOS setup program so that only authorized personnel can change or modify BIOS settings. Organizations, especially schools, usually configure a supervisor password to keep curious users from causing system errors.

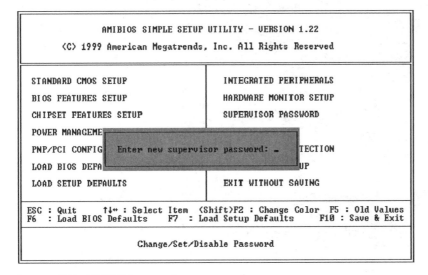

FIGURE 3-2 AMIBIOS supervisor password setup

The *user* or *system* password restricts access to the PC itself and is required every time the system boots (before an operating system is even loaded). This type of password is often used when an individual's PC is located in a public area.

The *hard drive* password is the third and newest password you'll find on some CMOS setups. Hard drive passwords prevent users from accessing a hard drive unless they know the password.

Step 3 Reboot the PC and press the key or key combination required to enter the CMOS setup program. If you completed Step 2 correctly, you should be prompted to enter a password. Enter the password you configured in Step 2 and press ENTER. The main menu of the CMOS setup program will appear.

Discard changes and exit the CMOS setup program.

✖ Warning

The next step will erase all CMOS settings! While you are in the CMOS setup program, take the time to write down important settings such as the CPU settings, boot order, which integrated peripherals are enabled/disabled, and the power management setup. Although the system should run fine using the default settings, taking notes now will help you get back to any custom settings that may have been configured.

Step 4 Shut down the PC and unplug the power cord from the PC and the wall outlet. Remove the case from the PC and, referring to the PC or motherboard documentation, locate the CMOS-clear jumper. Follow the instructions included with the documentation and move the jumper (see Figure 3-3) to clear CMOS.

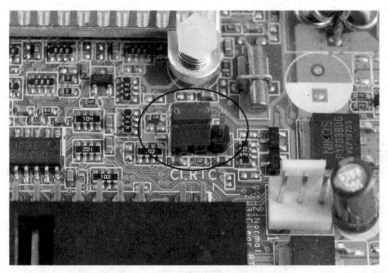

FIGURE 3-3 The CMOS-clear jumper on a motherboard

A less elegant alternative to using the CMOS-clear jumper is to remove the onboard battery for at least 30 seconds. Does your system have an onboard battery? Can it be removed easily?

Step 5 Replace the PC case cover, plug the system back in, and start the system. Press the appropriate key(s) to enter the CMOS setup program.

Were you prompted for a password? _____

Do you need to configure any of the other settings? _____

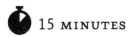 15 minutes

Lab Exercise 3.04: Removing a Motherboard

The best way to test for a bad motherboard is to try out a different one and see if it works better. Techs will tell you that motherboard removal is the exercise that separates the geek from the meek and the true PC tech from the wannabe, but don't let that intimidate you! Motherboard removal is completely straightforward and simple.

Learning Objectives

In this lab exercise, you'll remove your PC's motherboard.

At the end of this lab, you'll be able to

- Remove a motherboard safely and correctly

Lab Materials and Setup

The materials you need for this lab are

- A non-production or lab computer
- A Phillips-head screwdriver
- An anti-static mat and an anti-static wrist strap
- A large anti-static bag

Getting Down to Business

Take all precautions to avoid ESD. Put on an anti-static wrist strap, clip it to your PC case, and dig in.

Start with your PC turned off. Disconnect everything, including the power cable, from the front and back of your PC. If you haven't already, open up your PC case using whatever method your case requires. Because you want to remove the motherboard from the case, you first need to disconnect (almost) everything from the motherboard. You've already learned how to remove RAM and CPUs. I'll quickly outline how to disconnect the remaining cables and expansion cards.

Step 1 If you have any expansion cards installed, first unscrew them from the case. You'll find the screw holding them near the back of the case where the ports are located. After unscrewing the card, gently pull it up and out of the slot without rocking it from side to side. Some PCI Express (PCIe) cards use a latch at the opposite end of the card, farthest from the screw. Simply press down on the tab attached to the motherboard, and the card should be released.

Step 2 You should also have several power and data cables attached to the motherboard. None of these are difficult to remove, though it may take a bit of force to disconnect them. Disconnect each cable until there are none left.

You can leave your storage devices where they are—they should not get in the way of removing your motherboard.

Step 3 Locate and remove the screws holding the motherboard to the frame of the case. There are most likely six to nine screws, which may also have small washers. Be sure not to lose these washers because they help prevent over-tightening the screws during installation. Some systems may use small plastic or metal supports called *standoffs* between the motherboard and the frame. Remove these and store them in a labeled container.

> ✖ **Warning**
>
> Remember to handle the motherboard as you would any printed circuit board: gently, by the edges, as if you were holding a delicate old photograph.

Step 4 Carefully remove the motherboard from the PC case and place it on your anti-static mat. You should place the motherboard in a large anti-static bag for the best protection.

 30 MINUTES

Lab Exercise 3.05: Installing a Motherboard

Now you get the real test of your tech skills: installing the new motherboard and reconnecting everything so that the computer works again! Don't be intimidated, though. Everything you need to install a motherboard (in your case, probably the motherboard you just removed in Lab Exercise 3.04) is right in front of you.

When you remove and replace a motherboard in a system, you interact with almost every component of the computer system. In the field, you must not only successfully disassemble/assemble the hardware, but also verify that the system powers up and operates properly afterward. Many competent techs, when installing a new motherboard, will check for proper operation along the way. Here's a good checkpoint: After you've installed the CPU and RAM, configured any jumpers or switches, and installed the motherboard in the case, insert the power connections and test the system. A POST card is a real timesaver here, but you can also connect the PC speaker, a graphics card, a monitor, and a keyboard to verify that the system is booting properly.

Learning Objectives

In this lab exercise, you'll install a motherboard. You can use the motherboard and system you disassembled in Lab Exercise 3.04.

At the end of this lab, you'll be able to

- Install a PC motherboard and connect all its associated components

Lab Materials and Setup

The materials you need for this lab are

- A working system from which the motherboard has been removed

- Components and cables previously connected to the removed motherboard

- The motherboard book or online documentation for the motherboard

- An anti-static mat and anti-static wrist strap

- A notepad and pen

Getting Down to Business

Physically installing the motherboard itself is mostly a matter of being careful and methodical. The more complex part of the task is reattaching all the cables and cards in their proper places.

✖ Warning

Motherboards are full of delicate electronics! Remember to follow the proper ESD avoidance and safety procedures.

> ✔ **Hint**
>
> When installing a motherboard, it's handy to use your notepad to check off assembly steps as you go along.

Step 1 Carefully line up the motherboard inside the PC case and secure it in place with the mounting screws. Be sure to use the washers and plastic/metal standoffs, if supplied.

Step 2 Insert the front panel control wires in their appropriate places. These should include your power button, reset button, front panel LEDs (power, hard disk activity, and so on), system speaker, and so on. Refer to the labels and your motherboard documentation for the proper connections.

Step 3 Connect all power cables to the hard drive, optical disc drive, floppy disk drive (for older systems), CPU fan, main motherboard, and so on.

Step 4 Connect data cables to the hard drive, optical disc drive, and floppy disk drive (if applicable), as well as the sound cable and USB connector dongles, if applicable. If you removed the RAM or CPU, reattach them now.

Step 5 Double-check all of your connections and cards to make sure that they're properly seated and connected where they're supposed to be. If something is wrong, it's definitely better to discover it now than to smell smoke after you've hit the power switch!

Step 6 Replace the case cover on your PC. Then plug the keyboard, mouse, and monitor back in, plug the power cable back in, and finally turn on the PC. Assuming you've done everything correctly, your system will boot up normally.

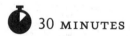 30 MINUTES

Lab Exercise 3.06: Testing Power Supply Output

Power supplies, annoyingly, tend to fail slowly over time. As their power output dies, you'll notice your PC spontaneously reboot for seemingly no reason. If you suspect a bad power supply, you'll want to test each of the power cables to make sure you are getting good power.

Learning Objectives

At the end of this lab, you'll be able to

- Identify the connectors of a PC power supply

- Measure the output of a PC power supply

Lab Materials and Setup

The materials you need for this lab are

- An ATX power supply

- A multimeter

- A PC power supply tester

- Optional: A working PC with an ATX power supply

Getting Down to Business

There are two ways to determine whether a power supply is providing the proper voltages to the components of the computer. One is the traditional method, using a multimeter to measure the actual voltages. Another method growing in popularity is the use of a PC power supply tester.

In the following steps, you'll measure direct current (DC) voltage coming from the PC power supply. The three places to measure power supply output are at the Molex power connectors, the serial ATA (SATA) power connectors, and the motherboard power connectors. Molex power connectors plug into devices that need 5 or 12 volts of power. These include parallel ATA (PATA) hard drives and PATA optical drives. SATA power connectors connect to SATA hard drives and optical drives. On most recent systems, the power supply will provide two motherboard power connectors: the 20- or 24-pin P1 and the smaller P4 (see Figure 3-4). Both of these power connectors are used on motherboards requiring an additional 12-V power supply.

You'll then plug the P1 power connector into a PC power supply tester and verify that the readings you measured with the multimeter are within tolerance. The power supply tester has LEDs that will glow green for each of the voltages that it passes.

FIGURE 3-4 Motherboard power connectors: P1 (left) and P4 (right)

✖ **Warning**

Although the power coming out of the PC power supply is considerably less lethal than that coming directly out of the electrical outlet, you should still take all appropriate safety precautions before taking measurements.

Step 1   Set the multimeter to read DC voltage. Find a Molex connector that's not being used for a device. If no Molex connectors are unused, turn the system off and disconnect the one from the optical drive, and then turn the PC back on.

Do you have a free Molex connector? _____

If not, which device did you unplug? _____

Step 2   Referring to Figure 3-5, place the black probe into either one of the holes on the Molex connector that is aligned with a black wire. Now place the red probe into each of the other three holes of the Molex connector in turn, first the other black wire, then the red, then yellow, and record your findings.

Black wire to black wire: _____ V

Black wire to red wire: _____ V

Black wire to yellow wire: _____ V

Figure 3-5 Measuring the voltage in a Molex connector

Step 3 Measuring the voltage from the motherboard connector is a little trickier. Leave the power connector plugged into the motherboard and push the probes into the end of the connector that the wires run into. You must push the probe deep enough to touch the metal contact pins, but be careful not to push too deeply or you might push the pin out of the connector.

Push the black probe into the motherboard connector alongside any black wire and leave it there. Insert the red probe into each of the other wires and record your findings. Depending on your motherboard connector, you may not have all of these wires.

Black wire to red wire: _____ V

Black wire to yellow wire: _____ V

Black wire to purple wire: _____ V

Black wire to white wire: _____ V

Black wire to black wire: _____ V

Black wire to blue wire: _____ V

Black wire to green wire: _____ V

The voltages generated by the power supply must be within a tolerance (range) level; readings outside these ranges mean the power supply should be replaced. The 5-V connections have a tolerance of ±2 percent (4.9 to 5.1 V is okay), and 12-V connections have a tolerance of ±6 percent (11.25 to 12.75 V is okay).

✔ **Hint**

A single reading from your power supply may not be enough to pinpoint a power-related problem. Sometimes a power problem becomes evident only when the power supply is placed under a heavier-than-normal load, such as burning a CD-ROM or DVD. Also, some RAM-related errors mimic a failing power supply.

The other method to verify that the power supply is operating properly and supplying all the voltages within tolerance is to use a power supply tester. There are many styles of power supply unit (PSU) testers on the market, so make sure you follow the specific directions included with your tester as you complete the steps.

Step 1 Starting with the P1 connector, follow the directions for connecting it to your specific PSU tester. Verify that all of the voltages provided through the P1 connector are acceptable. (Usually an LED will light to verify voltage present and within tolerance.)

Did it light up or display an acceptable voltage? _____

✔ **Hint**

When connecting and disconnecting the power supply connectors, always take care to insert the connector with the proper orientation. Most power connectors are keyed to make it difficult to install the connector backward, but if you use excessive force, you may be able to insert the connector improperly. This applies to powering the motherboard, plugging in devices, and even using the PSU tester.

Step 2   Now, depending on your tester and power supply, plug the 4-pin, 6-pin, or 8-pin auxiliary connector into the appropriate socket on the PSU tester and verify the voltages provided through this connector. Once they are verified, remove the connector from the socket.

Did it light up or display an acceptable voltage? _____

Step 3   Plug the Molex connector into the PSU tester and verify the voltages provided through this connector. Once they are verified, remove the connector from the socket.

Did it light up or display an acceptable voltage? _____

Step 4   Plug the SATA HDD power connector into the appropriate socket and verify the voltages provided through this connector. Once they are verified, remove the connector from the socket.

Did it light up or display an acceptable voltage? _____

Step 5   Finally, plug the mini floppy drive power connector into the PSU tester and verify the voltages provided through this connector. Once they are verified, remove the connector from the socket and remove the P1 from the socket.

Did it light up or display an acceptable voltage? _____

Lab Analysis Test

1. What can you do in a pinch to clear the CMOS settings if you are unable to find the CMOS-clear jumper?

2. Joanna called you to say that ever since you installed her new CPU, the PC experiences intermittent problems when it runs. Sometimes it just quits and freezes up. What could possibly be wrong?

3. John's system has 1 GB of PC4200 DDR2 SDRAM. He recently installed an additional 1 GB of DDR2 SDRAM that a coworker gave him. He tells you that his system now boots up correctly and shows the correct amount of RAM, but then it freezes after several minutes. He notes that if he removes the new RAM, the system runs fine. What could be a possible reason for this?

4. Your assistant technician calls you and says he suspects a bad power supply in one of your client's systems. He said the multimeter readings are 12.65 volts and 4.15 volts. What should he do?

5. Ryan is working on an older Core 2 Duo system. What key or keys should he press to enter the CMOS setup program?

Key Term Quiz

Use the following terms to complete the following sentences. Not all terms will be used.

beep codes

Blue Screen of Death (BSoD)

bootable disk

bootstrap loader

burn-in failure

catastrophic failure

component failure

general protection fault (GPF)

non-maskable interrupt (NMI)

page fault

POST card

power good

power-on self test (POST)

preboot execution environment (PXE)

system disk

1. A _____ can help you troubleshoot boot problems that occur before anything is displayed onscreen by displaying different codes that tell you which step of the boot process your PC is freezing on. Computers without one of these can use _____ to troubleshoot the same problems.

2. A disk containing an operating system is called a _____ or a _____.

3. A _____ can result from many different errors, from catastrophic hardware failure to a poorly written program.

4. After the power supply tests itself, it sends a signal down the _____ wire to awaken the CPU.

5. The _____ is little more than a few dozen lines of BIOS code whose job is to find the operating system.

Chapter 4
Implementing Hard Drives

Lab Exercises

Once you've installed a new drive on a PC and it has been recognized by the system, you have two more steps to complete before you can start storing data: partitioning and formatting.

✔ **Hint**

The tasks of partitioning and formatting have really become automated into the installation of the operating system (and the tools included in the operating system). Many of the steps are now completed in sequence, blurring the line between partitioning and formatting. Make sure you're clear on the distinction between partitioning and formatting, because you must do them in the proper order. Partitioning the disk simply means defining physical sections that are used to store data. Formatting the disk means *configuring the partition* with a file system.

In the early days of DOS, Windows 3.*x*, and Windows 9*x*, your hard drive had to be partitioned and formatted before you could run the installation setup routine. Windows now incorporates these disk-preparation steps into the installation routine itself. However, it's still important for you to be able to perform these tasks from scratch as part of your basic PC tech repertoire.

You have a number of tools at your disposal for performing partitioning and formatting tasks. If you are working with a fresh hard drive, you need to get to these tools without necessarily having an operating system installed. (This may be the first disk in the system, and you are preparing it for the OS installation.) The first of these tools is the Windows installation media. A number of third-party utilities are available for partitioning and formatting, such as Avanquest's Partition Commander, EaseUS Partition Master, and the open source Linux tool Gnome Partition Editor, affectionately known as GParted. These specific tools are beyond the scope of the CompTIA A+ exams; however, a good tech should develop skills in the use of these tools. The second tool you'll explore in this chapter is a live CD of GParted.

Once you have an operating system up and running, you should have some type of partitioning and formatting tool that you can run from the GUI. Windows uses a tool known as the Disk Management utility. Disk Management enables you to create, modify, and format partitions. You can also format partitions from within My Computer/Computer on the Windows desktop.

After looking at how to create and format partitions using the Windows installation media and the live CD of GParted, you'll start up Windows to look at how to accomplish these tasks using the built-in tools. Next, you'll use the Disk Management utility to convert basic disks to dynamic disks and implement a RAID 0 stripe set. Then you'll look at the procedures for performing regular hard drive maintenance and troubleshooting tasks.

✔ **Hint**

The following exercises walk you through the basic management of hard drive storage available on your system. If you have only one drive installed, you will need to install the operating system after the first few exercises to perform the later exercises. I recommend that you use a machine with two hard drives for all of the implementation labs (being careful not to partition or format the first drive, which should contain the operating system). Not only will this enable you to practice creating and deleting partitions and formatting and reformatting those partitions, it will also enable you to verify the partitions and file systems with the Disk Management tool in Windows.

 30 MINUTES

Lab Exercise 4.01: Creating and Formatting Partitions with the Windows XP and Vista/7 Installation Media

You have just worked with a number of donated machines, physically installing and configuring multiple hard drive technologies, primarily PATA and SATA hard drives. Once these drives have been recognized in CMOS, you are only halfway to your goal of using the drives for data storage. You must now partition each drive into usable space (even if only one partition uses all of the available drive space) and then format each partition with a file system.

In this lab, you will use the Windows installation media to partition and format hard drives in your system. You will be left with blank partitions, one of which needs an operating system. In the labs for Chapter 5, you will complete the process of installing the operating system.

✔ **Cross-Reference**

For details about partitioning and formatting drives with the Windows installation disc, refer to the "Partitioning During Windows XP Installation" and "Partitioning During Windows Vista/7 Installation" sections in Chapter 4 of *Mike Meyers' CompTIA A+ Guide to 802: Managing and Troubleshooting PCs, Fourth Edition (Exam 220-802)*.

Learning Objectives

In this lab exercise, you'll use the Windows installation media to partition a hard drive and format the partition for use.

At the end of this lab, you'll be able to

- Set up a primary partition on a hard drive

- Format the partition with the NTFS file system

Lab Materials and Setup

The materials you need for this lab are

- A PC with a primary hard drive that holds your Windows OS and two blank hard drives that you can partition and format to your heart's content

- Optional: A system with one hard drive that you can safely erase

- The Windows XP or Vista/7 installation media

✖ Warning

Partitioning and formatting a hard drive destroys any data on it! Practice this lab using only drives that don't store any data you need.

Getting Down to Business

In this exercise, you'll start the system by booting from the Windows installation media. (You will have to configure your system CMOS to boot from the optical drive or, if available, a USB device.) You'll partition a portion of one of the hard drives and format it with NTFS, as if you're preparing to install the operating system.

The instructions for Windows XP are first, followed immediately by the instructions for Windows Vista/7.

Step 1 Enter the CMOS setup program and configure the boot order, selecting the optical drive as the first boot device. Also make sure that the setting called "Boot Other Device" (or something similar) is enabled; otherwise, your system may not recognize the optical drive as a bootable drive.

Step 2 Place the Windows installation CD in the optical drive tray and boot the machine. Windows Setup copies a number of files and then presents you with the screen shown in Figure 4-1. Press ENTER to set up Windows now.

Step 3 Press F8 to accept the license agreement and enter the main partitioning screen.

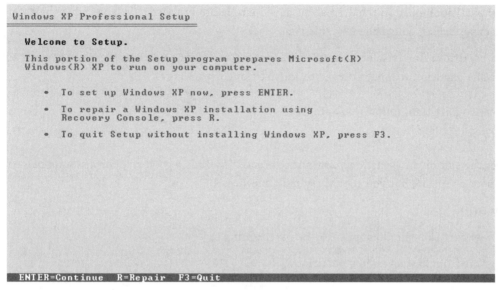

FIGURE 4-1 The first Windows XP Setup screen

✔ **Hint**

If Windows XP has been installed on one of the drives in the system, Setup asks if you would like to repair this installation and advises you to press ESC if you want to install a fresh copy. Press ESC to progress to the next step—partitioning the drive.

The screen displays the installed drives and any partitions and/or file systems that have been configured on the drives prior to this session (see Figure 4-2).

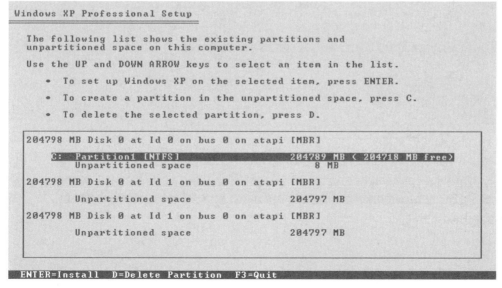

FIGURE 4-2 Partitioning screen

Step 4   If any partitions exist on the drives you have installed to practice this lab (and if the data on these drives is expendable), delete them at this time.

To delete a partition, simply select the partition, press D to delete, and then press L to commit the delete process. The partition will be returned to unpartitioned space.

Step 5   To create a partition, follow these steps:

a.   Press C.

b.   Select the size of the partition you want to create. (10 GB is a good size for a system partition or a boot partition, but you should try multiple sizes.)

c.   Press ENTER.

d.   The new partition should appear in the partitioning screen.

Congratulations! You have created a partition.

Step 6   Press ENTER to see a list of file system options, as shown in Figure 4-3. Choose a file system (NTFS is the default) and indicate whether you will perform an exhaustive formatting process or the "Quick" formatting process.

Press ENTER. Windows formats the partition and proceeds with the operating system installation. You can shut down the PC once this step is completed.

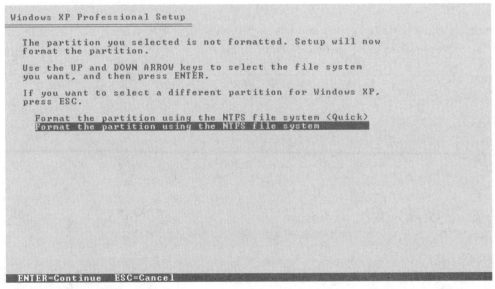

Figure 4-3 Format screen

Step 7 Reboot the machine and allow your Windows OS to boot. Then use the Disk Management tool to verify the partition(s) you have created with the installation CD. Alternatively, you can verify the partitions you created and the file systems you configured when you use the GParted tool in the next lab.

Step 8 Practice deleting, creating, and formatting different combinations of partitions and file systems to become comfortable with the tools used in this exercise. Have fun!

Here are the same instructions, but for Windows Vista/7.

Step 1 Enter the CMOS setup program and configure the boot order, selecting the optical drive (or, if necessary, a USB device) as the first boot device. Also make sure that the setting called "Boot Other Device" (or something similar) is enabled; otherwise, your system may not recognize the optical drive as a bootable drive.

Step 2 Place the Windows installation media in the optical drive tray and boot the machine. Set your language and regional preferences on the first screen, and then click Next.

Step 3 Click the large Install Now button on the next page. Setup will then ask for a product key, but you do not need to enter one right now. Click Next to move on.

Step 4 Pick the edition of Vista/7 you wish to install. Your product key will only activate the edition that you purchased. Click Next to continue, and then agree to the license agreement on the next page.

Step 5 Click the Custom installation button on the following screen. The screen displays the installed drives and any partitions and/or file systems that have been configured on the drives prior to this session (see Figure 4-4).

Step 6 If any partitions exist on the drives you have installed to practice this lab (and if the data on these drives is expendable), delete them at this time.

To delete a partition, simply select the partition, click on *Drive options (advanced)*, and then click Delete. The partition will be returned to unpartitioned space.

Step 7 To create a partition, follow these steps:

    a. Click the *Drive options (advanced)* button.

    b. Click New.

    c. In the Size field, type **50000** and click Apply to end up with a 50-GB partition.

Step 8 Click the Format button. The installer will automatically set up an NTFS file system for the partition and proceed with the operating system installation.

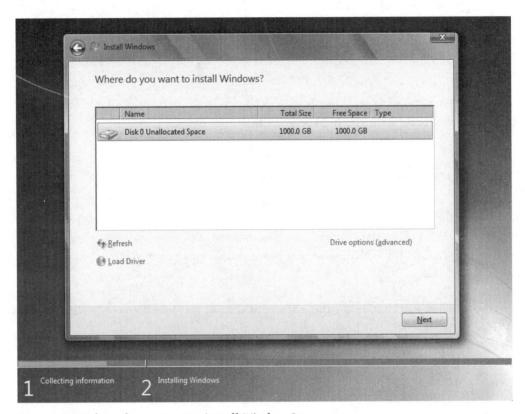

FIGURE 4-4 Where do you want to install Windows?

Step 9   Reboot the machine and allow your Windows OS to boot. Then use the Disk Management tool to verify the partition(s) you have created with the installation disc. Alternatively, you can verify the partitions you created and the file systems you configured when you use the GParted tool in the next lab.

Step 10   Practice deleting, creating, and formatting different combinations of partitions and file systems to become comfortable with the tools used in this exercise. Enjoy!

 30 MINUTES

Lab Exercise 4.02: Creating and Formatting Partitions with Gnome Partition Editor (GParted)

As a competent tech, you want to keep up with the newest methods for accomplishing old tasks. Using the donated computers as an example, you might want to partition and format all of the machines before installing an operating system and deploying the machines to users. To accomplish this task, it might be easier to use a standalone partitioning/formatting tool such as the open source Gnome Partition Editor (GParted). Gnome is one of the many versions of the Linux operating system. GParted uses a basic, bootable version of Gnome with disk management tools built in. This method is somewhat beyond the scope of the CompTIA A+ exams, but the skills and techniques you will practice in this lab are valuable to a real-world tech and can help you gain a deeper understanding of partitioning and formatting hard drives.

✔ Tech Tip

Many techs, and specifically techs employed by the IT departments of small to large businesses, often use one of the popular drive-imaging tools such as Symantec's Norton Ghost. Drive imaging is used to roll out the operating system and applications on multiple machines expediently. This method creates the partition and copies the OS, applications, and user profiles onto the file system that was used to make the image, all in one step.

In this exercise, you will use the live CD of GParted to partition and format the two additional hard drives installed in your lab system. If you are working in a classroom setting, the instructor should be able to provide copies of the GParted live CD to you for this exercise.

✔ Cross-Reference

For additional details about the GParted live CD, refer to the "Third-Party Partition Tools" section in Chapter 4 of *Mike Meyers' CompTIA A+ Guide to 802: Managing and Troubleshooting PCs, Fourth Edition* (*Exam 220-802*).

Learning Objectives

In this lab exercise, you'll use the GParted live CD to partition a hard drive and format the partition for use.

At the end of this lab, you'll be able to

- Set up primary and extended partitions on hard drives
- Format the partitions with various file systems

Lab Materials and Setup

The materials you need for this lab are

- A PC with a primary hard drive that holds your Windows OS and two blank hard drives that you can partition and format to your heart's content

- Optional: A system with one hard drive that you can safely erase

- A GParted live CD

✖ Warning

Partitioning and formatting a hard drive destroys any data on the drive! Practice this lab only on drives that don't store any data you need.

Getting Down to Business

In this exercise, you'll start the system by booting from the GParted live CD. (You will have to configure your system CMOS to boot from the CD.) You'll then partition a portion of one of the hard drives and format it with the file system of your choice.

Step 1   Enter the CMOS setup program and configure the boot order, selecting the CD-ROM drive as the first boot device. Also make sure that the setting called "Boot Other Device" (or something similar) is enabled; otherwise, your system may not recognize the CD-ROM drive as a bootable drive.

Step 2   Place the GParted live CD in the optical drive tray and boot the machine. GParted displays an introduction screen, as shown in Figure 4-5. Press ENTER to boot; Gnome Linux should begin to load.

FIGURE 4-5 The Gnome Partition Editor initial screen

As the system loads, you will be queried a number of times for settings related to boot options, language, keyboard, screen depth, and resolution. Unless told to do otherwise by your instructor, select the defaults for these settings by highlighting OK and pressing ENTER.

GParted should finish booting and arrive at a screen displaying various menu items, icons, and the current drive focus with strange Linux names such as /dev/hda1, /dev/hda3, and so forth. Notice the item at the far right of the menu bar; here, you can click the drop-down arrow to select which physical drive the GParted screen is focused on (see Figure 4-6).

Step 3   Now change the focus to the second or third drive installed on your system. This will probably be labeled /dev/hdb or /dev/hdc in the drop-down list of hard drives.

✔ **Hint**

If you are using a machine where Windows has been installed on one of the drives in the system (most likely the first drive), when GParted first launches, the screen focus will be on this drive and the label will probably read /dev/hda1. Make sure that you select one of the drives that has been set up to be partitioned and formatted, or you'll find yourself reinstalling Windows.

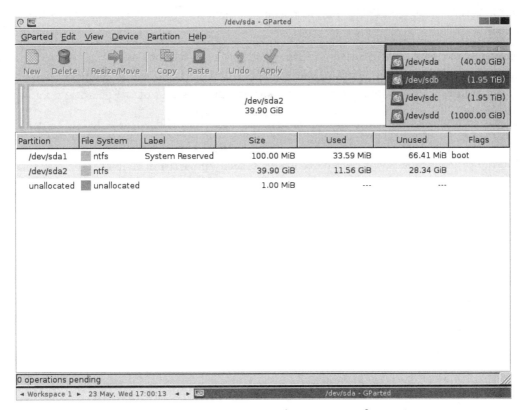

FIGURE 4-6   Selecting a drive on the main GParted partitioning/formatting screen

The screen now focuses on the drive you've selected and shows any partitions and/or file systems that have been configured on that drive prior to this session. If any partitions are displayed, highlight the partition, right-click, and select Delete.

Step 4 GParted requires that you commit any changes that you make to the partitions on the disk, so after deleting the partition, you must click the Apply button to apply the settings and actually delete the partition.

When you click Apply, GParted applies the pending operations. You should now have a drive visible with all of the available space denoted as unallocated space.

Step 5 Select the unallocated space, right-click, and select New. Then follow these steps:

a. Enter the size of the partition in megabytes; either type a number or use the up and down arrows to select a size. For the purposes of practice, 4000 MB (4 GB) to 10,000 MB (10 GB) is a good size for the partition.

b. Select Primary Partition or Extended Partition; primary is a good choice for the initial partition on the drive.

c. Select NTFS.

d. Click the Add button. The new partition with the formatted file system should appear on the screen.

e. Click Apply to create the formatted partition. A message box will pop up, asking you to confirm that you want to apply the pending operations. Click Apply again, and then watch as the *Applying pending operations* dialog box appears, shows you the status of the operation, and then disappears.

f. Click Close.

Congratulations! You should now have a drive with a formatted partition visible in the main screen (see Figure 4-7).

Step 6 There is one last step, which depends on whether you plan to use this partition to boot the machine with an OS (active partition) and which file system you have selected.

With the partition highlighted, right-click the partition and select Manage Flags. A small window appears in which you'll see a number of flags that you can set (see Figure 4-8). Many of these apply to operating systems other than Windows, but one of them must be set if you are to use the partition in

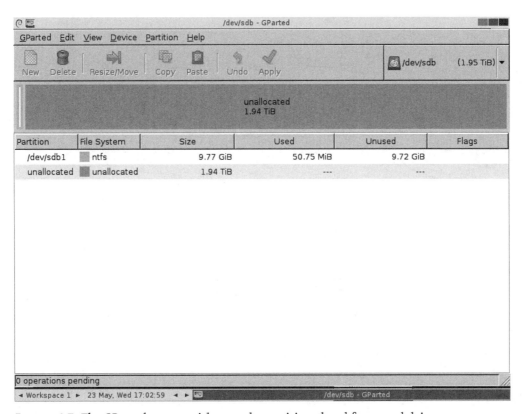

FIGURE 4-7 The GParted screen with a newly partitioned and formatted drive

Windows: boot. This flag must be set if the partition is to be the active partition in the system. (This is usually the first partition on the first hard drive in the system.)

Set the appropriate flags for your partition and file system and close the *Manage flags* window. Notice that you will not have to apply changes, as the settings take effect immediately.

Step 7   Reboot the machine and allow your Windows OS to boot. You can then use Disk Management to verify the partition(s) you have created with GParted.

Step 8   Practice deleting, creating, and formatting different combinations of partitions and file systems to become comfortable with the GParted program.

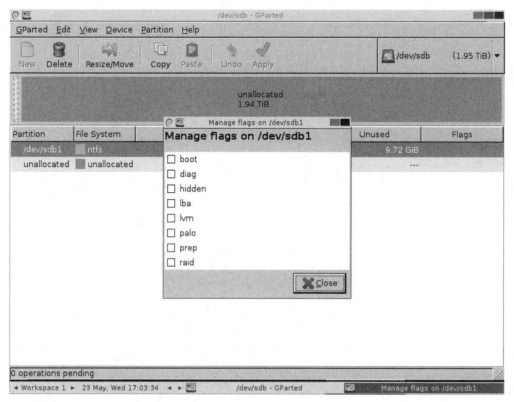

FIGURE 4-8 The Manage flags window in GParted

 30 MINUTES

Lab Exercise 4.03: Using Windows Tools to Create and Format Partitions

Once you have all of the donated machines' drives configured, partitioned, and formatted, and you've installed Windows, working with hard drive storage becomes much more intuitive. Windows includes tools that enable you to create, modify, and format partitions "on the fly" from within Windows. One of these utilities is called Disk Management.

✔ Cross-Reference

For details about creating and formatting partitions using Disk Management, refer to the "Disk Management" section in Chapter 4 of *Mike Meyers' CompTIA A+ Guide to 802: Managing and Troubleshooting PCs, Fourth Edition (Exam 220-802)*.

This lab exercise assumes that you want to create a partition on the second or third hard drive installed on the Windows lab system and then format that partition with a file system. Disk Management will enable you to format the partition right away; however, you can also use another Windows utility that you should be intimately familiar with by now: My Computer/Computer. Follow the steps in this lab exercise to create and format a new partition.

✔ **Hint**

Each version of Windows can read from and write to the FAT16, FAT32, and NTFS file systems. However, only Windows XP can be installed to a FAT16 or FAT32 partition—Windows Vista/7 must be installed on an NTFS partition.

Learning Objectives

In this exercise, you'll use the Disk Management program to partition a hard drive and format the partition with a file system.

At the end of this lab, you'll be able to

- Set up a primary, active partition on a hard drive

- Set up an extended partition and logical drives in that partition

- Format partitions with various file systems

Lab Materials and Setup

The materials you need for this lab are

- A PC with a primary hard drive that holds your Windows installation and two blank hard drives that you can partition and format

---

✖ **Warning**

Partitioning a hard drive destroys any data on it! Practice this lab only on drives that don't contain any data you need.

Getting Down to Business

The steps for partitioning drives and formatting partitions in each version of Windows are very similar.

Step 1   Right-click the My Computer/Computer icon and select Manage to open a Computer Management window. Under the Storage node, click Disk Management.

Step 2   As in prior lab exercises, if there are any existing partitions on the second or third drive, highlight the partitions and either right-click and delete the partitions or simply press DELETE.

Step 3   Start the process of creating a partition by right-clicking an unpartitioned section of drive space and, in Windows XP, selecting New Partition (see Figure 4-9). In Vista/7, select New Simple Volume. This will start the New Partition Wizard or the New Simple Volume Wizard, depending on the OS.

Step 4   Click Next, and, in Windows XP, select Primary Partition. (In Windows Vista/7, you will not have to select Primary Partition.) At the next screen, enter the size of your new partition in megabytes.

Step 5   You can now assign a drive letter or mount the partition to an empty folder. For now, go with the default drive letter assignment and click Next again.

Step 6   The next screen offers you the option to format the new partition with a file system. Select a file system: FAT, FAT32, or NTFS. (Note that Windows will not allow Disk Management to create a FAT16 partition larger than 4 GB or a FAT32 partition larger than 32 GB.) Then enter a volume label if you want and click OK. Figure 4-10 shows this selection screen in the Disk Management utility.

Step 7   The utility warns you that formatting will erase all data on the drive. Click OK to begin formatting.

Step 8   You can also format partitions in My Computer/Computer, but generally speaking you'll use this method only to format removable media such as USB thumb drives.

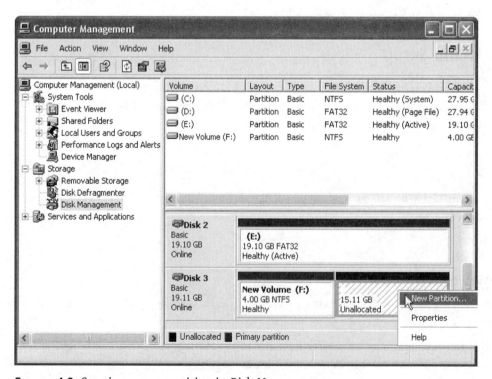

FIGURE 4-9 Creating a new partition in Disk Management

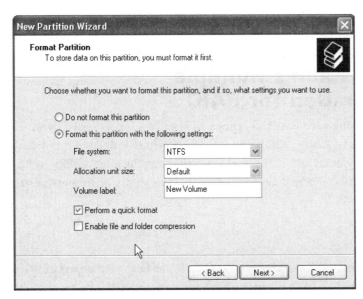

FIGURE 4-10 Formatting a partition in Disk Management

Right-click a drive icon in My Computer/Computer and select Format to open the Format New Volume dialog box (see Figure 4-11). Now proceed as in Step 6.

Step 9 Practice deleting, creating, and formatting different combinations of partitions and file systems to become comfortable with the Disk Management utility.

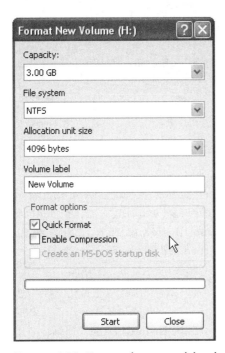

FIGURE 4-11 Formatting a partition in My Computer

 30 MINUTES

Lab Exercise 4.04: Installing Multiple Hard Drives in Preparation for RAID

While RAID setups do a great job of keeping your data safe, they can require a lot of hard drives. A RAID 1 configuration only needs two drives, but a RAID 5 setup requires three or more. Keep in mind that a lot of these drives are for copies or parity data, and it becomes clear that storing a lot of data in RAID means lots of hard drives. Fortunately, most modern motherboards include plenty of connections to install multiple hard drives.

Learning Objectives

In this lab exercise, you will install additional hard drives—PATA, SATA, or both—in an existing system. You will access CMOS to verify that all of the drives have been recognized by the system. You will then use your motherboard's RAID controller to configure a RAID array.

At the end of this lab, you'll be able to

- Install multiple hard drives in computer systems

- Verify multiple drives in CMOS

- Configure a hardware RAID array

Lab Materials and Setup

The materials you need for this lab are

- A working PC with PATA or SATA interfaces and Windows XP Professional, Windows Vista, or Windows 7 installed

- At least two (preferably three) additional, system-compatible hard drives—PATA or SATA, as appropriate

Getting Down to Business

Even though you haven't been reminded during the past few exercises, you know that you should always take the proper anti-static precautions when opening the system case and working with the delicate components inside. Take those precautions now and get ready to install a few extra hard drives into your system. In this exercise, you'll make sure these drives are recognized by the system; in the next chapter's labs, you'll configure them.

Follow these steps to install an additional PATA drive.

Step 1 Determine on which controller, and in which order, you will be installing the drives.

Step 2   Set the jumpers properly for both the master and slave drives. (Usually, the boot device is the master drive on the primary controller, whereas the optical drive is the master drive on the secondary controller, so the new drive is likely to be a slave to one of those drives.)

Step 3   Physically install the second drive, connecting the power and data cables properly.

Follow these steps to install additional SATA drives.

Step 1   Determine which controller you will use for the first additional drive and connect the SATA data cable to the controller on the motherboard.

Step 2   Physically install the first additional drive and connect the SATA power and data cables to the new drive.

Step 3   Determine which controller you will use for the second additional drive and connect the SATA data cable to the controller on the motherboard.

Step 4   Physically install the second additional drive and connect the SATA power and data cables to the new drive.

Follow these steps to verify the drives in CMOS.

Step 1   After installing all of the hard drives, plug the power back in and boot the machine.

Step 2   Press the appropriate key(s) to enter CMOS setup and navigate to the configuration screen for installed devices.

Step 3   Perform autodetection, if required, and confirm that all of the installed devices are present. If any of the devices are missing (and you remembered to reboot the machine if your system requires it), power the machine down, disconnect the power, and double-check all of the cables and drive settings.

Follow these steps to implement RAID.

→ **Note**

Your motherboard must support RAID in order to complete the following section of this lab. Check your motherboard manual to ensure you can do RAID! If not, you'll still configure a software RAID setup in Lab Exercise 4.06.

Step 1   Enter the CMOS setup program and find where you can enable the RAID controller on your motherboard. Usually this is in the same place where you disable your PATA and SATA controllers. Save your configuration and exit.

Step 2   Watch the boot screens. A new screen should appear now that you have enabled RAID in CMOS. If the screens go by too fast, press the PAUSE/BREAK key to pause the screen during boot-up. To enter the RAID setup utility, press the key combination required by your motherboard, similar to the key you press to enter CMOS. Which button must you press to enter your RAID setup utility?

_____

Step 3   Once you are in the RAID setup utility, set up different styles of RAID that your motherboard supports. Every configuration screen is different. As in the CMOS setup program, each setting should have an explanation to help you figure out what to do. Because you are using hard drives with no important data (right?), feel free to experiment. Remove drives once you have set up a particular RAID, such as RAID 0, 1, or 5. What are the results?

_____

_____

_____

Step 4   Once you have completed the RAID configurations, return to the CMOS setup program and reset it to the original settings.

 30 MINUTES

Lab Exercise 4.05: Converting Basic Disks to Dynamic Disks with Disk Management

In the previous lab exercise, you configured two additional hard drives in a system to facilitate a software implementation of RAID. Windows XP Professional, Windows Vista Business/Ultimate/Enterprise, and Windows 7 Professional/Ultimate/Enterprise require that a disk be converted to a dynamic disk to allow the implementation of RAID. In this lab, you will prepare the two additional drives to be used in the next lab exercise by using Disk Management to perform the simple, nondestructive conversion from basic disks to dynamic disks.

✔ **Cross-Reference**

To learn more about dynamic disks, refer to the "Dynamic Disks" section in Chapter 4 of *Mike Meyers' CompTIA A+ Guide to 802: Managing and Troubleshooting PCs, Fourth Edition (Exam 220-802)*.

Learning Objectives

In this lab exercise, you'll use the Disk Management utility to convert basic disks to dynamic disks.

At the end of this lab, you'll be able to

- Convert basic disks to dynamic disks

Lab Materials and Setup

The materials you need for this lab are

- The PC from Lab Exercise 4.04 with a primary hard drive that holds your Windows installation. (Converting to dynamic disks requires Windows XP Professional, Windows Vista Business/ Ultimate/Enterprise, or Windows 7 Professional/Ultimate/Enterprise.)

- The two blank hard drives that you will convert to dynamic disks

Getting Down to Business

The steps to convert a basic disk to a dynamic disk are really quite simple.

Step 1   Open the Disk Management utility as in the previous exercise.

Step 2   Select the first drive to be converted. Position the mouse pointer over the left-hand drive icon, right-click, and select Convert to Dynamic Disk (see Figure 4-12).

Step 3   Follow the wizard's instructions to complete the dynamic disk conversion. Reboot the PC (if necessary), and then open Disk Management again. The disk should now be labeled as a dynamic disk instead of a basic disk (see Figure 4-13).

Step 4   Repeat Steps 2 and 3 on the third drive in the system. (You will need two dynamic disks to implement a RAID 0 stripe set.) Next, proceed to Lab Exercise 4.06.

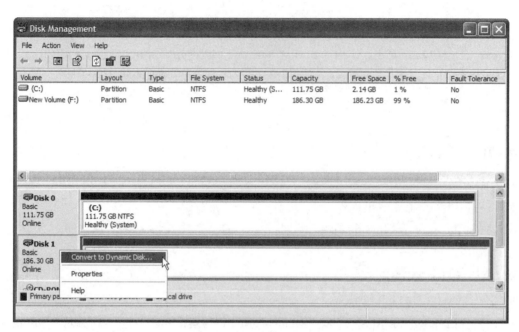

Figure 4-12 Selecting Convert to Dynamic Disk in the Disk Management utility

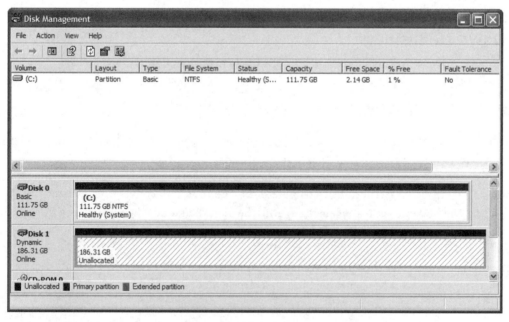

Figure 4-13 Disk Management showing basic and dynamic storage

> **→ Note**
>
> You can also convert master boot record (MBR) disks—the most common basic disk format—to GUID partition table (GPT) disks. GPT supports larger hard drives and more partitions. The instructions are identical to converting a basic disk to a dynamic disk, except that you select Convert to GPT Disk from the hard drive's context menu.

 30 MINUTES

Lab Exercise 4.06: Implementing Software RAID 0 with Disk Management

Now it's time to flex your software RAID muscles. Windows XP Professional, Windows Vista Business/Ultimate/Enterprise, and Windows 7 Professional/Ultimate/Enterprise allow you to configure software RAID implementations using Disk Management and multiple hard drives. At the end of this lab, you will have configured a stripe set using two disks.

> **✔ Cross-Reference**
>
> Additional information on RAID 0, 1, and 5 may be found in the "Dynamic Disks" section in Chapter 4 of *Mike Meyers' CompTIA A+ Guide to 802: Managing and Troubleshooting PCs, Fourth Edition* (*Exam 220-802*).

This lab exercise guides you through the creation of a RAID 0 stripe set using free, unpartitioned space on the second and third hard drives installed on the Windows lab system. These are the same disks that you converted from basic disks to dynamic disks in the prior exercise. Disk Management allows you to configure simple volumes, spanned volumes, and striped volumes on dynamic disks.

Learning Objectives

In this lab exercise, you'll use the Disk Management program to configure a RAID 0 striped volume.

At the end of this lab, you'll be able to

- Create and configure a RAID 0 striped volume

Lab Materials and Setup

The materials you need for this lab are

- The PC from Lab Exercise 4.04 with a primary hard drive that holds your Windows installation (Windows XP Professional, Windows Vista Business/Ultimate/Enterprise, or Windows 7 Professional/Ultimate/Enterprise) and the two blank hard drives that have been converted to dynamic disks

✖ **Warning**

Partitioning a hard drive destroys any data on the drive! Practice this lab only on drives that don't contain any data you need.

Getting Down to Business

You're in the home stretch now! Once you've worked with the Disk Management tool and converted basic disks to dynamic disks, it's just a matter of using the Disk Management New Volume Wizard, choosing the size allocated to the striped volume, and formatting the striped volume.

Step 1   Launch the Disk Management utility and right-click the unallocated space on the first disk of the planned striped volume. Select New Volume, and then select Striped (see Figure 4-14).

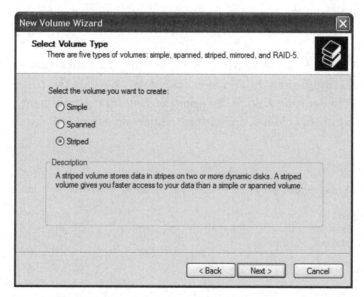

Figure 4-14 The Select Volume Type screen of the New Volume Wizard

Step 2   The wizard asks you to select at least one additional dynamic disk for the striped volume. You will then select the size of the volume you want to create and decide what file system to use to format the striped volume.

Are there any restrictions on the size of the volume? _____

Step 3   Disk Management now allocates the space on the drives and formats them with the file system you've selected. You should now have a healthy, formatted, striped volume.

Step 4   Practice deleting and creating various sizes of striped volumes using various file systems. Can you format a striped volume with FAT? Why or why not?

 45 MINUTES

Lab Exercise 4.07: Troubleshooting Hard Drive Installations

The newest tech in your office has had trouble installing hard drives properly. In fact, he's tried it on four different machines with eight different drives and succeeded only once! You've been tasked to troubleshoot his failed installations and patiently explain the proper installation process to him. What fun!

Learning Objectives

This lab exercise walks you through the errors new techs typically make on hard drive installation, particularly with PATA drives. The lab also addresses the main problems with SATA drives—usually faulty hardware—and how to address this in the field.

At the end of this lab, you'll be able to

- Troubleshoot hard drive installation problems effectively
- Explain the proper installation techniques for PATA and SATA drives

Lab Materials and Setup

The materials you need for this lab are

- Access to a PC system with PATA and SATA interfaces
- At least one PATA or SATA hard drive (preferably two or more)

Getting Down to Business

It might seem odd to mess up a hard drive installation deliberately, but you can't hurt anything, so give it a whirl. Seeing how the PC responds to mistakes when you know specifically what's wrong can help you when you run into similar situations later in the field.

Step 1   You must have a properly functioning PC for this lab to be effective, so verify first that you have a system up and running with one or more hard drives installed.

Step 2   Power down the system. Disconnect the data cable for the hard drive used to boot the system, and then power up the system. What happens? Will the PC autodetect the drive?

It is difficult to imagine not connecting the data cables to hard drives, but many times to add RAM or new devices we have to disconnect the cables to gain access to the component. It is easy to miss reconnecting one of the cables after installing the new device.

Disconnecting the cable also simulates a broken IDE or SATA cable. These cables are somewhat delicate and can fail after a sharp crease or a crimp from the system case. If you're having unexplained problems with your drive, check the cables prior to replacing the drive.

Step 3   Power down the PC and put the cable back on properly.

Step 4   On a PATA drive, change the jumper for the primary master hard drive to slave, and then power on the PC. What happens? Will the PC autodetect the drive? How should the jumper be installed?

Step 5   Power down the PC and put the jumper back on properly.

Step 6   Install a second PATA drive onto the primary controller and set the jumpers on both drives incorrectly. Try variations: both as master; both as standalone; both as slave; and both as cable select. Power on the PC and test each variation. What happens? Will the PC autodetect the drives? How should the jumpers be set for two PATA drives to work properly on the same controller?

 60 MINUTES

Lab Exercise 4.08: Maintaining and Troubleshooting Hard Drives

Of all the devices installed in a PC, hard drives tend to need the most attention. Maintaining and troubleshooting hard drives is one of the most common tasks you'll undertake as a PC tech, but also one of the most important.

After all, the loss of other components such as video cards or NICs is inconvenient, but hardly disastrous. The loss of a hard drive, on the other hand, means the loss of data. This data might be as trivial as your favorite bookmarked Web pages or a saved Half-Life 2 game. But it could be as important as your business records, family photos, or the 1200-page novel that you've spent the last two years writing! Unless you want to spend valuable time and money trying to retrieve data from a damaged or corrupted hard drive, you should familiarize yourself with the built-in Windows drive maintenance tools. These tools include

- **Error-checking** This GUI tool enables you to examine the physical structure of the drive and retrieve data from bad clusters. The command-line utility that performs the same duties is called chkdsk.

- **Disk Defragmenter** This tool reorganizes disorganized file structures into contiguous clusters.

- **Disk Cleanup** This tool reclaims wasted space on the hard drive by deleting unneeded files and compressing files that are rarely accessed.

Learning Objectives

At the end of this lab, you'll be able to

- Use error-checking to scan for and fix physical errors on the hard drive

- Use the Disk Defragmenter utility to reorganize the hard drive's file structure

- Use the Disk Cleanup utility to reclaim wasted disk space

Lab Materials and Setup

The materials you need for this lab are

- A fully functioning Windows PC

Getting Down to Business

Performing regular maintenance on your hard drives can keep them running more smoothly and efficiently. If you're getting obvious disk-related errors (such as error messages indicating that your disk has bad clusters or cannot be read) or if files are missing or corrupt, a tune-up is in order. Another sign that your drive needs maintenance is excessive disk activity, or disk "thrashing." It's also a good idea to do some maintenance after a serious system crash or virus infection by scanning your drive for damage or fragmentation.

✔ Tech Tip

In a computer system, the hard drive wins the prize as the most critical storage device and for having the most moving parts of any of the components. For this reason, it is extremely important that you not only perform routine preventive maintenance (error-checking, defragmentation, and disk cleanup), but also regularly back up critical data.

Step 1 To scan a hard drive for physical problems, open My Computer/Computer and right-click the drive's icon. Select Properties, and then select the Tools tab, shown in Figure 4-15. Click Check Now to start the Error-checking utility.

In the Check Disk dialog box, you can opt to fix file system errors automatically, scan for and attempt to recover bad sectors, or both. When you've made your selections, click Start.

✔ **Hint**

The Error-checking utility must have *exclusive* access to the drive to finish scanning it. If you have services or applications running in the background, the utility will halt. In most cases, the utility will ask you if you want to check the hard disk for errors the next time you start your computer.

Step 2 To launch Disk Defragmenter, click Defragment Now on the Tools tab. The Windows XP version of Disk Defragmenter is shown in Figure 4-16.

Disk Defragmenter offers you a choice: You can click Analyze to examine the disk to see if a defragmenting operation is needed, or simply click Defragment to start the process without first analyzing the drive.

Step 3 Click the General tab, and then click Disk Cleanup. Disk Cleanup calculates the space you'll be able to free up and then displays the Disk Cleanup dialog box, shown in Figure 4-17.

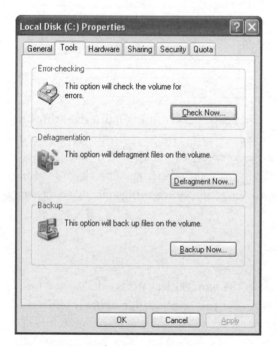

FIGURE 4-15 Disk Properties Tools tab

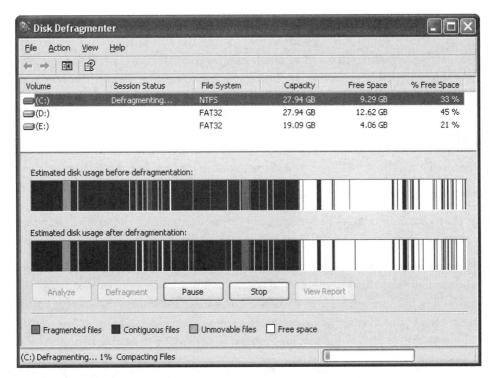

FIGURE 4-16 Disk Defragmenter

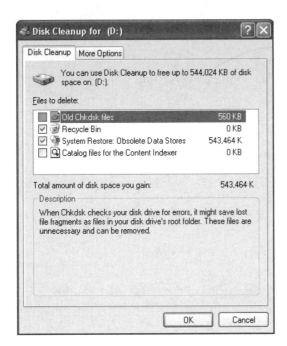

FIGURE 4-17 Disk Cleanup

Near the top of the dialog box, you can see how much disk space (maximum) you could free up using Disk Cleanup. But look carefully! Depending on which categories in the *Files to delete* list are checked, the actual amount of disk space you'll gain could be much smaller than the estimate at the top. As you select and deselect choices, watch this value change. Disk Cleanup can remove Recycle Bin files and temporary Internet files, and can also compress old files.

Lab Analysis Test

1. Name at least two indicators that you should perform maintenance on your hard drive.

2. What is the command-line version of the Windows Error-checking utility?

3. Amanda argues that a hard drive must be formatted before you can set up the partitions. Samantha says the drive must be partitioned first. Who is correct and why?

4. Kyle is running out of disk space on his hard drive on a Windows XP Professional system. He has installed and configured a third hard drive in the system to increase the total storage. He is planning on converting his current drive to dynamic storage and extending the storage space to the newly installed drive (also dynamic storage). Pablo argues that the conversion is destructive and that Kyle would not be able to extend the volume anyway. Is Kyle going to be able to make this work?

5. Sean has created a RAID 0 array using three drives on a Windows 7 Professional system. After running the system for a couple of years, he arrived at work one day to find one of the three drives had failed. He thought that if only one drive failed, he would still be able to access his data. What facts about RAID 0 did Sean misunderstand?

Key Term Quiz

Use the following terms to complete the following sentences. Not all terms will be used.

basic disk

chkdsk

defragment

Disk Cleanup

Disk Management

dynamic disk

Error-checking

format

GParted

partition

volumes

Windows installation media

1. To partition and format a hard drive when no operating system has been installed, you may use either _____ or _____ to boot the system and run disk setup utilities.

2. Use a(n) _____ tool to fix noncontiguous file clusters on a hard drive.

3. The _____ tool enables you to partition and format drives in Windows.

4. Microsoft supports two types of storage configurations now; the _____ uses partitions, whereas the _____ uses _____.

5. If your hard drive is running out of free space, you should use the _____ utility.

Chapter 5

Installing and Upgrading Windows

Lab Exercises

As a PC technician, you'll spend a lot of time installing and upgrading operating systems. For this reason, it's important that you become familiar with the tasks involved; otherwise, you might find yourself in a tight spot when Windows won't install on the laptop that your boss needs for a presentation this afternoon.

A number of different operating systems are in use today, including Apple Mac OS X, several different flavors of Linux, and of course the Microsoft Windows family. Because the CompTIA A+ certification focuses primarily on Microsoft products—and because Microsoft products represent the majority of the market—these lab exercises are dedicated to the installation of Windows.

Just about anyone can install software if everything goes right and no problems come up during the process; plenty of people with minimal software knowledge have upgraded Windows without the slightest incident. Even an experienced technician may have problems, though, if the system has incompatible expansion cards, broken devices, or bad drivers. As a PC technician, you'll need to handle both the simple installations—the ones with only new, compatible components—and the more complex installations on older and more problematic systems.

Installing and upgrading Windows requires more than just popping in the installation disc and running the install program. You need to plan the installation thoughtfully, check for component compatibility, and thoroughly understand the installation options and how to configure them. Good planning up front will give you the best chances for a successful installation or upgrade.

Be sure to have everything you need before you start, from the installation disc to the discs containing your device drivers. Remember the old adage, "Measure twice, cut once." Believe me, it's no fun to start over on an installation or upgrade if you mess it up! Do it right the first time—you'll be glad you did.

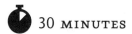 30 MINUTES

Lab Exercise 5.01: Installing/Upgrading Considerations

Your client has asked you to upgrade his system to Windows 7 Professional 64-bit. He's currently running Windows Vista Business 64-bit, and everything works fine. He has the documentation that came with his system, which states that it has an ASUS P5E Deluxe motherboard. He isn't sure how fast the processor is, but he does know that the system has 1 GB of memory. Where do you start the planning process?

✔ **Cross-Reference**

To review the details of pre-installation planning, refer to the "Preparing for Installation or Upgrade" section of Chapter 5 of *Mike Meyers' CompTIA A+ Guide to 802: Managing and Troubleshooting PCs.*

Learning Objectives

In this lab exercise, you'll become more familiar with using the Internet to help answer pre-installation questions.

At the end of this lab, you'll be able to

- Access the Microsoft Support Web site
- Determine the minimal requirements for a system installation
- Determine whether to perform an upgrade installation or a clean installation

Lab Materials and Setup

The materials you need for this lab are

- A working PC
- Internet access
- A notepad and pencil

Getting Down to Business

The first step in a successful Windows installation or upgrade is to determine whether the hardware meets the requirements of the new operating system. Your first stop in this process is the Microsoft Support Web site, found at http://support.microsoft.com/findsolutions/.

Microsoft has invested massive amounts of energy and time in building its Support Web site. Digging through all of the articles on the huge number of Web pages can be overwhelming, but I'm a firm believer in this site's usefulness. When I have a question that directly concerns a Windows operating system (or any Microsoft product, for that matter), I check this site first, and I'm rarely disappointed. In fact, while searching for the answer to a problem or question, I usually learn two or three new, sometimes unrelated, things just by reading through the search results. Also, my search techniques improve with each visit. I consider the Microsoft Support Web site an invaluable tool and resource.

Step 1　You'll first need to make sure that your client's computer is capable of running Windows 7 Professional 64-bit. To do this, you will need to attain a copy of the Windows 7 Upgrade Advisor. Go to www.microsoft.com/download/en/details.aspx?id=20 and click the DOWNLOAD button, which will take you to the actual download page. Microsoft will suggest other applications to download with the Upgrade Advisor, but you can ignore these and click Next. Depending on your Web browser, you will either be asked to save the file to your hard drive or the download will begin automatically.

✔ Hint

Web sites change or disappear all the time—especially Microsoft Web sites. If the Microsoft Web site should change significantly from the time this book was printed to the time you're reading this, and you find that a link listed here is no longer valid, a quick search with Google for "Windows 7 Upgrade Advisor" should get you where you need to be.

Figure 5-1 A Windows 7 Upgrade Advisor scan's results

When the file is downloaded, double-click it to start the installation process, and then follow the onscreen prompts to install the Upgrade Advisor. When it's finished installing, it should start up automatically, so just click the Start Check button and wait for it to complete.

Once the scan completes, it will show you detailed results of the scan (see Figure 5-1). This will tell you whether or not your system is Windows 7-capable. Further down the page, you can click on a set of links to view details about the system requirements, device compatibility, and program compatibility.

Step 2   Once you've seen the scan's results, answer the following questions:

a.   What version of Windows 7 does the Anytime Upgrade allow you to migrate to?

_____

b.   What's the minimum CPU speed requirement?

_____

c.   What's the minimum amount of RAM?

_____

d.   How much available hard drive space is required?

_____

e.   Does your graphics adapter support Aero?

_____

f.   List a few devices or programs that the Upgrade Advisor says are "Not Compatible":

_____

_____

➔ **Note**

At the time of this writing, the Windows 8 Consumer Preview has been released to the public. The guys here at Total Seminars installed it on a computer that was previously running Windows 7 Professional 64-bit and it ran without a hitch. As I type this, there is no separate Windows 8 Upgrade Advisor. Microsoft plans to include it directly inside the Windows 8 installation process.

Step 3   Now you know whether or not your client's computer can run Windows 7 Professional 64-bit, and, if not, what you need to upgrade in order to get it to run. Next, you need to find out whether you can do an upgrade installation, where the new OS is installed on top of the old one, or a clean installation, where the drive is erased before installation of the new OS.

Doing an upgrade installation is based both on the version of Windows Vista you're upgrading from and the edition of Windows 7 that you're upgrading to, so it's a fairly complicated subject. In order to find out the possible upgrade paths, you'll need to do a bit of searching.

Go to www.microsoft.com and do a search for **Windows 7 Upgrade Paths**. The first search result should give you the information you need, but if not, search around a little. This sort of research will make up a substantial part of your life as a tech, so get used to it!

Step 4 When you've found information about Windows 7 upgrade paths, answer the following questions:

a. Can you do an upgrade installation from Windows Vista Business 64-bit to Windows 7 Professional 64-bit? _____

b. Can you do an upgrade installation from Windows XP to Windows 7 Professional? _____

c. Can you do an upgrade installation from Windows Vista Business 32-bit to Windows 7 Professional 64-bit? _____

d. Can you do an upgrade installation from Windows Vista Business 32-bit to Windows 7 Home Premium 32-bit? _____

✔ **Cross-Reference**

For a refresher on the considerations that come into play when you install or upgrade Windows, refer to the "Deciding What Type of Installation to Perform" section of Chapter 5 of *Mike Meyers' CompTIA A+ Guide to 802: Managing and Troubleshooting PCs*.

 30 MINUTES

Lab Exercise 5.02: Using Windows Easy Transfer

You're about to upgrade a client's computer from Windows XP to Windows 7, but the client doesn't want to lose any of her important data. She doesn't have a lot of data to transfer, just a gigabyte or so, but that data is absolutely essential to the operation of her business. Fortunately, you're a savvy tech and you know that Windows Easy Transfer will enable you to back up her documents onto a flash drive and then transfer them to her new OS after it's installed.

Learning Objectives

You'll learn how to use Windows Easy Transfer effectively to back up files and transfer them to a new operating system.

At the end of this lab, you'll be able to

- Use Windows Easy Transfer to back up files onto a USB thumb drive

- Use Windows Easy Transfer to transfer files onto a new OS installation

Lab Materials and Setup

The materials you need for this lab are

- A PC running Windows XP or Windows Vista

- A PC running Windows 7

- Internet access

- A USB thumb drive (1 GB or more)

Getting Down to Business

Microsoft's Windows Easy Transfer has made moving data to a new computer as easy as it could be, but it's still a somewhat complicated program. In this lab, you'll learn all the necessary steps you need to take to move a customer's data from one computer to another. If you ever work as a tech in a retail store, this sort of information will be vital when trying to convince customers to upgrade their PCs.

Step 1   The first thing you need to do to use Windows Easy Transfer, of course, is to get a copy of Windows Easy Transfer for Windows XP. Microsoft offers Windows Easy Transfer as a free download, so go to www.microsoft.com/downloads and do a search for **Easy Transfer** to locate the specific version for the OS from which you are upgrading. Click the search result and then download the program to your hard drive. I'd give you the direct link to the download page here, but it's Microsoft's Web site, so it'll probably change in six months.

→ **Note**

You can also perform this exercise using Windows Vista, though some of the screens may differ.

After you've downloaded a copy of Windows Easy Transfer to your XP machine, run it and follow the onscreen prompts to install the program. Once it's installed, run it from the All Programs menu. (It should be listed as Windows Easy Transfer for Windows 7.) The first screen (see Figure 5-2) gives you information about the transfer process, so once you've read all of that, click the Next button.

Step 2   The next screen (see Figure 5-3) offers you several different options from which to choose how you want to transfer the files and settings to your new computer, whether by Easy Transfer Cable (a special USB cable sold by Microsoft), by a network connection (useful if you're transferring between two computers on a local area network), or by an external hard disk or USB flash drive. Since you're using a USB flash drive, a type of removable media, select the third option.

Once you've selected the removable media option, the wizard asks you which computer you are using now (see Figure 5-4). The only option you have is *This is my old computer*. Makes sense, right? You can't use Easy Transfer to migrate *to* Windows XP, only *from* Windows XP. Click on *This is my old computer*.

On the next screen, you can pick which account's files and settings you want to move to the new Windows 7 computer (see Figure 5-5). After it finishes scanning, choose all of them by selecting the checkboxes and then click Next.

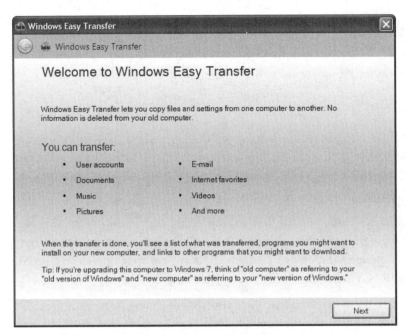

Figure 5-2 Running Windows Easy Transfer

The next page enables you to enter a password to encrypt your data for added security (see Figure 5-6). After adding a password that you can remember, click Save.

Save your Easy Transfer file to your flash drive. Depending on the size of the files belonging to each user account, this can take some time. Once all the files have been saved, Windows Easy Transfer will prompt you. Click Next, and then click Close. It's time to go to the new Windows 7 computer!

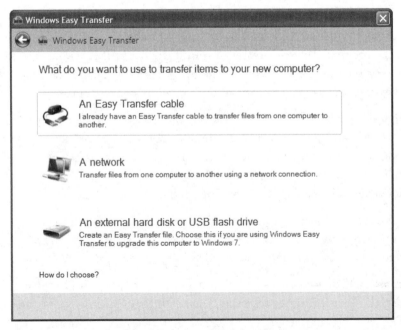

Figure 5-3 How do you want to transfer your files?

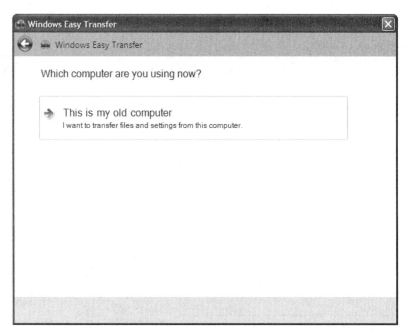

FIGURE 5-4 Which computer are you using now?

Step 3   Once you've transferred all your files onto your USB thumb drive, you can remove the drive and move it to your PC running Windows 7. If you don't have a PC with Windows 7 already installed, skip to Lab Exercise 5.04 and then come back when you're finished with it. Once you are on your Windows 7 PC, open Windows Easy Transfer by going to Start | All Programs | Accessories | System Tools | Windows Easy Transfer.

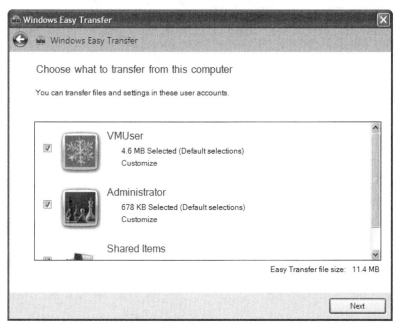

FIGURE 5-5 Choose what to transfer from this computer

FIGURE 5-6 Password protection

When the wizard starts, you can once more click Next past the welcome screen. The next screen will present you with the same options as before. Your choices are an Easy Transfer Cable, a network, an external device, or a USB flash drive. Since you've backed up the files from the old computer onto a flash drive, select *An external hard disk or USB flash drive.*

The next screen asks which computer you are using right now. Since you are now on the Windows 7 computer, choose *This is my new computer* (see Figure 5-7).

Next, the wizard will ask you if Easy Transfer already saved the files from your old computer to an external hard disk or USB drive. Yes it did! Choose the correct path to the file saved on your flash drive and open it.

You will then need to enter the password you created back on the Windows XP computer to access your content. Then click Next.

Windows Easy Transfer will then take a moment to scan the file. Eventually, it will display a screen for you to select which account's files and settings you want to transfer to the new PC. Select all of them if they aren't already selected (see Figure 5-8).

Finally, click the Transfer button, and all of your information from the Windows XP computer will be transferred to the Windows 7 computer.

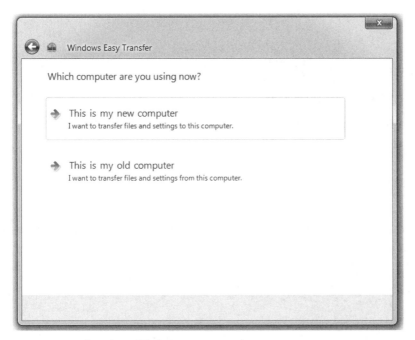

FIGURE 5-7 Choosing This is my new computer

FIGURE 5-8 Choose what to transfer to this computer

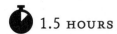 1.5 HOURS

Lab Exercise 5.03: Upgrading a Windows Operating System

A client running Windows Vista Home Premium decides to modernize by moving to a more recent OS. He asks you to upgrade his system to Windows 7 Home Premium. You agree to upgrade the system for him.

Learning Objectives

You need to perform at least one complete upgrade, both for practice and to prepare for questions asked on the CompTIA A+ 220-802 exam.

At the end of this lab, you'll be able to

- Upgrade an operating system

✔ Cross-Reference

To refresh your memory about the ins and outs of performing a Windows upgrade, read the "Installing or Upgrading to Windows XP Professional," "Installing or Upgrading to Windows Vista," and "Installing or Upgrading to Windows 7" sections in Chapter 5 of *Mike Meyers' CompTIA A+ Guide to 802: Managing and Troubleshooting PCs.*

Lab Materials and Setup

The materials you need for this lab are

- A working Windows Vista Home Premium PC with a hard drive that you can write to without negative consequences (make sure it can also run Windows 7)

- A Windows 7 installation disc

✔ Hint

A Windows Vista installation disc has every edition of Windows Vista on it, and you can install any edition you want on your computer for a 30-day trial without a product key. Each edition of Windows 7, however, has its very own installation disc.

Getting Down to Business

You'll need quite a bit of time to complete this lab; most of that time will be spent waiting for Windows to install files. The exercise will walk you through upgrading a Windows Vista Home Premium system to Windows 7 Home Premium. Depending on the systems and software licenses you have available, you may not be able to do this lab exactly as it's laid out here. The important thing is that you actually perform a Windows upgrade, to see the questions that are asked during the installation, and to become familiar with the process so that you're prepared for the CompTIA A+ 220-802 exam.

Step 1   You've completed the compatibility exercise in the earlier labs, and you know whether or not your system can handle Windows 7. Since you won't actually be *using* Windows 7, just installing it, the main consideration for performing this installation is hard drive space. Make sure you have at least 40 GB of hard drive space available on the computer you're upgrading.

The first step to doing an upgrade installation to Windows 7 is to make sure your computer is booted into Windows Vista. Because an upgrade installation is meant to be installed on a computer with a preexisting OS, Windows 7 will not allow you to do an upgrade installation unless you start the installation while booted into another Windows OS. So, with your computer booted up, insert the Windows 7 installation disc, wait until the Setup program starts, and click *Install now*.

Step 2   When asked whether or not you want to download the latest updates for installation, choose the second option, *Do not get the latest updates for installation*. Ordinarily, you would agree to do this, but it can take a long time to complete this download, and you'll be updating this computer in Lab Exercise 5.05, so you don't need to bother right now.

Step 3   The next screen is the End User License Agreement (EULA), shown in Figure 5-9. This document enumerates the deal made between you and Microsoft that you agree to by installing their software. EULAs typically contain a great deal of legalese, and are generally quite lengthy, and the Windows 7 EULA is no exception. You are certainly free to read through it if you like, but you don't have to. When you're done, check the box that says *I accept the license terms* and click Next.

Step 4   The next screen enables you to choose either an upgrade installation or a custom installation. For this lab, you're doing an upgrade installation, so select Upgrade. This option may or may not be available to you based on the version of Windows Vista that you're starting with and the edition of Windows 7 you're installing to, as you saw in the first lab in this chapter. The Windows 7 installer may give you an error at this point, and if it does, follow any instructions it gives you and start the installation process again. If there are no errors, click Next.

Step 5   Wait around for a while as Windows installs itself.

Step 6   Wait some more.

Step 7   Twiddle your thumbs. Did you know that Windows 7 can be installed from a thumb drive? Use another computer to go online and search for **Windows 7 USB tool**. This tool will take the contents of your Windows 7 disc and place it on your thumb drive. That might speed up this process (for the next time you install Windows 7, at least).

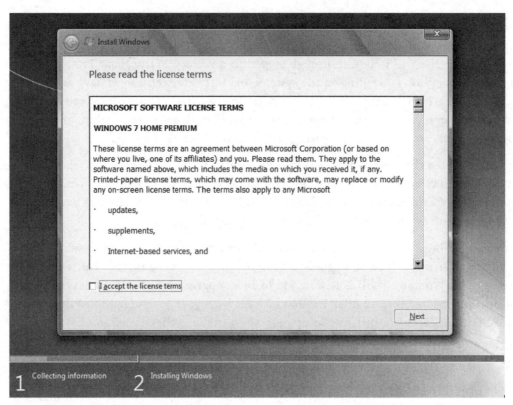

Figure 5-9 Windows 7 EULA agreement screen

Step 8   Why does it have to copy files and then "gather" them? What does that even mean?

Step 9   Oh, hey! It finished! Once the installer's done copying files, it will need to reboot the computer to continue setting up Windows 7.

Step 10   If you have a legitimate Windows 7 product key, enter it on the next screen (see Figure 5-10). If not, just click Next and then answer No to the dialog box that pops up asking you if you want to enter your product key.

Step 11   On this next screen you will decide how you want the operating system to interact with Windows Update. I suggest clicking on *Use recommended settings* in order to keep your computer fully patched from vulnerabilities.

Step 12   Now you're asked to set your time zone, the time, and the date. Make sure all the settings are correct and click Next.

Step 13   If your computer has network access, the installer will ask you whether you are on a home, work, or public network. Answer appropriately.

Step 14   You're done! Type in your credentials to log on. Click Start and enjoy the Windows 7 experience. After installing Windows 7, you will have 30 days to run the Windows Activation Client to activate Windows, or else the OS will stop functioning, so keep that in mind, especially if you didn't enter a product key.

FIGURE 5-10 Product key screen

 60 MINUTES

Lab Exercise 5.04: Performing a Clean Installation of Windows 7

Your boss has traditionally ordered new workstations already assembled and loaded with the desired Windows OS. She recently decided that with her great in-house techs, she should be buying PC parts from a wholesaler instead and having you and your team build the systems. You've enjoyed choosing the various hardware components and building these custom machines, but now it's time to bring your creations to life! You need to load Windows 7 Professional onto these new machines that have never seen the light of day.

Learning Objectives

You should complete at least one clean Windows installation, both for the experience and to prepare for questions asked on the CompTIA A+ 220-802 exam.

At the end of this lab, you'll be able to

- Install a Windows operating system on a blank hard drive

Lab Materials and Setup

The materials you need for this lab are

- A working PC with a blank hard drive, or with a hard drive that you can write to without negative consequences

- A Windows 7 installation disc

Getting Down to Business

In this exercise, you'll be putting an operating system onto a hard drive that doesn't currently have one. Even if the hard drive has an operating system on it, doing a clean installation will format that drive and erase all its data, so be sure you've backed up any important files!

→ **Note**

> This lab was designed for installing Windows 7, but you can very easily perform this lab exercise using Windows Vista. The order of some of the screens will change, such as when you put in the license key, but other than that, it should be a similar experience.

Step 1   Insert the Windows 7 installation DVD into the optical drive, close the tray, and reboot your PC. If prompted, press any key to boot from the DVD. Wait for the Install Windows screen to appear. Windows 7 will first ask you to select your preferred language (see Figure 5-11). After you do so, click Next. Then, click *Install now*.

✔ **Hint**

> If you notice that it takes what feels like forever during the wait for the Install Windows screen to appear, go into your CMOS setting and disable the floppy drive. It will dramatically improve the speed for a Windows Vista or Windows 7 installation.

Step 2   This process is almost identical to the upgrade installation, with a few key differences, so if you start to feel a sense of déjà-vu, just stick with it. Here are the steps for performing a clean installation of Windows 7:

   a.   The next screen is your old friend, the End User License Agreement (EULA). When you're done reading it, check the box that says *I accept the license terms* and click Next.

   b.   The next screen, shown in Figure 5-12, is the fork in the Windows 7 installer's road. You've already tried the Upgrade, so go ahead and click Custom (advanced) to do a clean installation.

   c.   The next screen is the disk partitioning page, where you can select which drive to install Windows 7 on to, as well as how to partition that drive. You should already be familiar with partitioning drives using this screen, but that's not important for now. Simply select the drive you wish to install to and click Next.

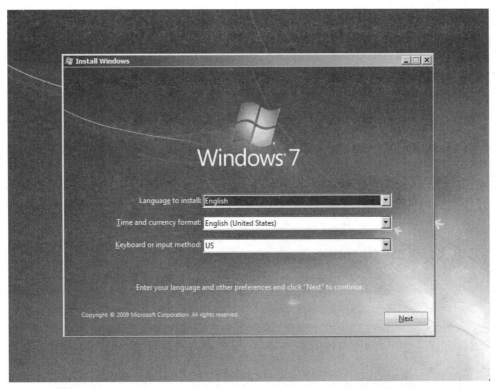

FIGURE 5-11 Language selection screen

d. Wait, once again, for Windows 7 to install itself.

e. Once the installer is done copying files, it will need to restart the computer.

f. Once the computer finishes restarting, type in your name. This will be the user name for the computer. Next, type in a computer name. If you want to, you can choose to keep it set as the default, but you also have the option of changing how your computer appears on the network. When you are finished, click Next.

g. Type in a password for your user account that you can remember, and give yourself a hint. Click Next. You have the option of skipping this step and going without a password. Doing so can be a huge security risk.

h. If you have a legitimate Windows 7 product key, enter it in the appropriate box. If not, just click Next and then answer No to the dialog box that pops up asking you if you want to enter your product key.

i. Now you're back in familiar territory, at the screen asking how you want to set up Windows Update. Generally, there's no reason not to select the first option, *Use recommended settings*, so click that now.

j. Now you're asked to set your time zone, the time, and the date. Make sure all the settings are correct and click Next.

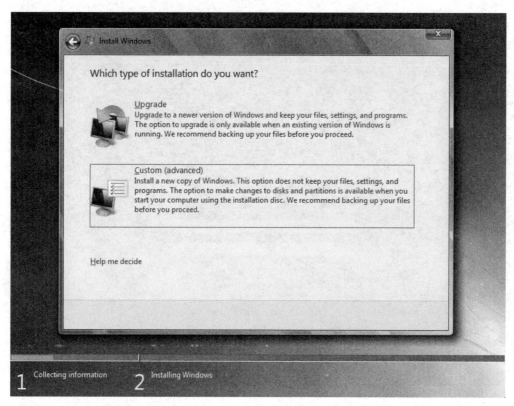

FIGURE 5-12 Installation selection

k. If your computer has network access, the installer will ask you whether you are on a home, work, or public network. Answer appropriately. If you select home, you will be prompted with the option of setting up a homegroup. For now, skip this step.

l. You're done! Click Start and enjoy the Windows 7 experience.

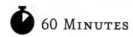 60 MINUTES

Lab Exercise 5.05: Performing a Clean Installation of Windows XP

You work for a school and you have just received some old computer equipment from a few local businesses. These computers don't meet the minimum requirements for Windows Vista or Windows 7, so you have no option but to load the longest running operating system that Microsoft ever released, good ol' Windows XP.

Learning Objectives

You should complete at least one clean Windows installation, both for the experience and to prepare for questions asked on the CompTIA A+ 220-802 exam.

At the end of this lab, you'll be able to

- Install a Windows operating system on a blank hard drive

Lab Materials and Setup

The materials you need for this lab are

- A working PC with a blank hard drive, or with a hard drive that you can write to without negative consequences

- A Windows XP Professional Edition CD-ROM with a valid product key

Getting Down to Business

In this exercise, you'll be putting an operating system onto a drive that doesn't currently have one. If the hard drive that you plan to use currently has data on it (even data that no one needs), then you must wipe that drive clean before you begin the exercise. Once you have a clean hard drive, you can proceed as directed.

Step 1 Turn on the computer and insert the Windows XP CD-ROM into the optical drive, close the tray, and boot from the optical drive. Ensure that your boot order is correct in CMOS.

Step 2 The Windows setup will begin in text mode, which means you won't have any mouse support and everything feels like the old days of the command-line interface. It is at this point you will notice a bunch of text cycling through at the bottom of your screen. These are drivers being loaded. During this process, you will have the option to press F6 to load third-party drivers. This is essential if you are installing Windows XP on an SCSI drive or on a RAID setup. If you are installing Windows XP onto a SATA hard drive with an installation disc that has a pre–Service Pack 1 version of Windows XP, you will need to press F6 to load SATA drivers.

Step 3 You will then see the Welcome to Setup screen. Press ENTER to set up Windows. Read the EULA (End User License Agreement) and agree to it by pressing F8.

Step 4 When the Setup program prompts you to partition your drive, set up a single NTFS partition that uses all the available drive space. Then you'll simply need to wait and watch while the Setup program does its magic and reboots the computer.

Step 5 When the computer has rebooted, work through the graphical portion of the installation process by carefully reading each screen and filling in the appropriate information. Be sure to enter the product key correctly, as you won't get past that screen with an invalid key.

Step 6   When you come to the Networking Settings screen, ask your instructor (if you're in a classroom setting) whether to choose Typical settings or Custom settings, and what specific information to use. If you're not in a classroom setting, select Typical.

Step 7   Click Next. Your computer will reboot one more time. You'll need to adjust your display settings by following the prompts.

Step 8   The Welcome to Microsoft Windows screen appears. Press Next to continue.

Step 9   Click the option to protect your computer by having it pull down updates from Microsoft's Web site.

Step 10   Next, you have the option to register your copy of Windows XP. Keep in mind that registration is completely optional.

Step 11   Who will use this computer? Type in the names that identify as many users as you would like (up to five users during the setup of Windows XP).

Step 12   Click Finish. Welcome to Windows XP!

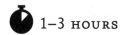 1–3 HOURS

Lab Exercise 5.06: Post-Installation Tasks: Drivers and Updates

As a tech, you will run into countless well-meaning, industrious, but ultimately hopeless customers who have taken their OS installation into their own hands, only to find that some critical piece of hardware doesn't work properly post-installation. Because of this, you absolutely must become well versed in the art of finding and installing hardware drivers and Windows updates.

Imagine, then, that you have a friend who has been happily using Windows XP Professional on his custom-built PC for a few years. The PC recently grew unstable, so your friend decided to do his own migration to Windows 7, which seemed to go pretty well. Now, however, his wireless networking card doesn't work. And his graphics card seems to be acting kind of funny. And he can't hear any sound. And ... you get the picture. Because you're an excellent tech, you instantly recognize the problem, and you graciously let him know that the problem is a result of his not properly following up his Windows installation with the appropriate driver installations. Then, of course, you offer to help him out.

✔ **Cross-Reference**

To review the process of installing drivers and updates, refer to the "Post-Installation Tasks" section in Chapter 5 of *Mike Meyers' CompTIA A+ Guide to 802: Managing and Troubleshooting PCs*

Learning Objectives

In this exercise, you'll learn how to finish up an installation by installing hardware drivers and operating system updates.

At the end of this lab, you'll be able to

- Find and install the correct hardware drivers for your operating system
- Install updates to the operating system

Lab Materials and Setup

The materials you need for this lab are

- A working Windows 7 PC
- Internet access
- A notepad and pencil
- Possibly a second PC and a thumb drive or other removable media

Getting Down to Business

The first thing you should do post-installation is to update your operating system, so you'll learn how to do that before you move on to finding and installing drivers.

Step 1   When you install Windows 7, it installs basic drivers for a wide range of products, so it's highly likely that Windows 7 will immediately have Internet access. If that isn't the case, you will have to use another computer to find network drivers for your Windows 7 PC, and then use a thumb drive or other removable media to transfer them over. For more information on how to do that, see the next step of this lab.

Once you have Internet access, click Start | All Programs | Windows Update. Over the years, Microsoft has made this a fairly painless process, so all you have to do is click the *Check for updates* button and wait.

When Windows Update has finished finding updates for your OS, click the *Install updates* button to begin the installation process. If you're curious about the updates being installed, you can click the *View available updates* button for more information.

After clicking the *Install updates* button, you may be asked to agree to further license agreements, which you should agree to. Then, Windows 7 will download and install any updates it found. Note that for a just-installed OS, this can take a long time, so you may have to be patient for this step.

Once the updates have all been downloaded and installed, you will be asked to restart your computer. Do so, and you're done. Sometimes, it's a good idea to run Windows Update again after updating, just to make sure it got everything, but that's really up to you.

Step 2   Once you've got your operating system updated (or if you need drivers to access the Internet), it's time to install hardware drivers. On a custom-built PC, this step can be pretty intimidating, since you can't just go to, say, Dell's Web site and download all the drivers in bulk. Instead, you have to track down drivers for each and every component in your system. This can be a time-consuming process, but there are a few tools that all good geeks should know about that can drastically reduce the frustration of this process.

The first thing to do when looking for drivers is to check Device Manager to get an idea about what drivers you should be looking for. To get to Device Manager in Windows XP, right-click My Computer, go to Properties, select the Hardware tab, and click Device Manager (in Vista/7, just open the Start menu, type **Device Manager** into the Search bar, and then click the Device Manager icon).

If you see "Video controller (VGA compatible)" listed in Device Manager with a yellow question mark next to it, you know you need to look for graphics drivers. If you see "Ethernet controller" listed, you know you need to look for drivers for your network interface card, and so on. Most of the missing-driver descriptions should give you a hint as to what they are for.

To find the drivers, you'll need to know the model name or number of your devices. Shut down your computer, open the case, and look at the motherboard, graphics card, and any other expansion cards the PC may have, like sound cards, TV tuners, and so forth. Often, these parts will have a manufacturer and model number on them somewhere, such as Gigabyte GA-MA790GPT-UD3H written on your motherboard, or NVIDIA GeForce GTX 560 on your graphics card. Write those things down and then do a Google search for them. If you can find the manufacturer, just go to its Web site, look up your product, and follow the link to download drivers.

Sometimes, you're not lucky enough to get a manufacturer or model number, but just about every device out there should have a sticker with some sort of part number or serial number on it. Usually, doing a quick Google search for that number and the word "driver" will get you the results you need. Finding drivers can be pretty frustrating, but keep searching and you're almost guaranteed to find what you're after.

In today's computing world, if you can find your motherboard's chipset drivers, most of the unknown driver icons in Device Manager will go away, so concentrate on finding your motherboard drivers first, and the expansion cards second.

Lab Analysis Test

1.   Phyllis wants to do an upgrade installation from Windows Vista Business to Windows 7 Professional, and the Windows 7 Upgrade Advisor says her computer is eligible for an upgrade installation. When she boots her computer from the Windows 7 installation disc, however, the Upgrade option is grayed out. Why is that?

2.   What's the recommended CPU speed and amount of RAM needed to install Windows 7 Professional 32-bit? How about 64-bit?

3. Dwight wants to upgrade his old Windows XP system to Windows Vista, but he isn't sure whether his hardware is sufficient to support Vista. Since the Windows Vista Upgrade Advisor is no longer available, what would you recommend that he use to check his system?

4. Michael is about to replace his aging Windows XP Home machine with a hotrod PC running Windows 7 Ultimate, but he wants to transfer all his documents to the new computer. What tool can you recommend that he use to do that?

5. What happens if you don't run the Windows Activation Client for Windows 7 within 30 days of installation?

Key Term Quiz

Use the following terms to complete the following sentences. Not all terms will be used.

1 GHz

2 GHz

BD-ROM

CD-ROM

clean installation

DVD-ROM

Easy Transfer

network drive

Upgrade Advisor

upgrade installation

Windows 7

Windows Vista

Windows XP

1. If you plan to install Windows Vista onto a system, it must have a(n) _____.

2. You can start with a blank hard drive to perform a(n) _____ of Windows 7.

3. You can use the _____ to see if your computer is capable of running Windows 7.

4. If you want to migrate your data from a Windows XP or Vista computer to a Windows 7 computer, you can use the _____ tool.

5. _____ can be upgraded to Windows 7.

Chapter 6

Windows Under the Hood

Lab Exercises

While Windows is arguably one of the most accessible operating systems available, Microsoft doesn't plaster your desktop with every single feature and option. In fact, certain options are well hidden so that less technically inclined users don't break anything. As a PC tech, of course, you'll be the one digging up these options and understanding how they work. The Registry rests at the heart of Windows, storing everything there is to know about your computer. The Windows boot files are special files used to load the OS. The Task Manager utility enables you to control programs, processes, services, and more. While all of these tools hide under the hood, they are key to controlling how Windows functions.

 30 MINUTES

Lab Exercise 6.01: The Windows Registry

The Registry stores everything about your PC, including information on all the hardware in the PC, network information, user preferences, file types, and virtually anything else you might run into with Windows. The hardware, software, and program configuration settings in the Registry are particular to each PC. Two identical PCs with the same operating system and hardware can still be remarkably different because of user settings and preferences. Almost any form of configuration done to a Windows system results in changes to the Registry.

> ✖ **Warning**
>
> When changing the Registry, proceed with great care—making changes in the Registry can cause unpredictable and possibly harmful results. To paraphrase the old carpenter's adage: consider twice, change once!

Learning Objectives

Most of the common tools used to modify the Registry are contained in the Control Panel. When you use the Display applet to change a background, for example, the resultant changes are added to the Registry. The Control Panel applets are what you should normally use to configure the Registry. However, there are times—a virus attack, perhaps, or complete removal of a stubborn application—when direct manipulation of the Registry is needed. In this lab, you'll familiarize yourself with the Windows Registry and the direct manipulation of the Registry using the regedit command.

At the end of this lab, you'll be able to

- Access the Registry using regedit

- Export, import, and modify Registry data subkeys and values

- Define the function of the five top-level Registry keys

Lab Materials and Setup

The materials you need for this lab are

- A working computer running Windows XP, Windows Vista, or Windows 7

Getting Down to Business

A technician needs to know how to access the Registry and modify the configuration based on solid support from Microsoft or other trusted sources. As mentioned in the Learning Objectives, your main interface to the Registry is the Control Panel. Changes made through the applets in the Control Panel result in modifications to the Registry settings. To see what's going on behind the scenes, though, you'll explore the Registry directly in this exercise using the regedit command.

✔ **Cross-Reference**

For more details on the Windows Registry and working with regedit, refer to the "Registry" section in Chapter 6 of *Mike Meyers' CompTIA A+ Guide to 802: Managing and Troubleshooting PCs.*

Step 1 You almost never need to access the Registry directly. It's meant to work in the background, quietly storing all the necessary data for the system, updated only through a few menus and installation programs. When you want to access the Registry directly, you must use the Registry Editor (regedit or regedt32).

✔ **Hint**

This lab exercise was written using a system running Windows XP Professional and works in Vista/7. Windows XP and all later versions have combined the two versions of the Registry Editor—regedit and regedt32—into simply regedit (although you can still use either command to open the editor).

To edit the Registry directly, follow these steps:

a. Select Start | Run, type **regedit**, and then click OK (see Figure 6-1) to start the Registry Editor.

b. Note the five main subgroups or root keys in the Registry (see Figure 6-2). Some of these root key folders may be expanded. Click the minus sign by any expanded folders. Do a quick mental review—do you know the function of each Registry key? You should!

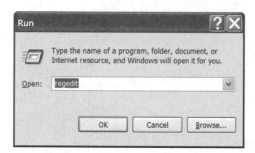

FIGURE 6-1 Starting the Registry Editor

c. Now test your knowledge of the Registry. Referring to the textbook as necessary, match the listed keys with their definitions by writing the definition letter next to the corresponding key:

HKEY_CLASSES_ROOT	
HKEY_CURRENT_USER	
HKEY_LOCAL_MACHINE	
HKEY_USERS	
HKEY_CURRENT_CONFIG	

A. Contains the data for non-user-specific configurations, and includes every device currently in your PC as well as those you've removed

B. Contains the personalization information for all users on a PC

C. Contains additional hardware information when there are values in HKEY_LOCAL_MACHINE such as two different monitors

D. Defines the standard class objects used by Windows; information stored here is used to open the correct application when a file is opened

E. Contains the current user settings, such as fonts, icons, and colors on systems that are set up to support multiple users

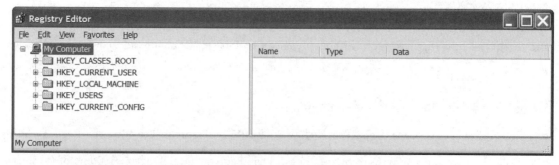

FIGURE 6-2 Viewing the five main subgroups of the Windows XP Registry

Step 2   One of the reasons you might want to edit the Registry directly would be to implement or expand a component of Windows that is not accessible through the Control Panel interface. A favorite of many techs is to enable the Rename function for the Recycle Bin. Expand the HKEY_CLASSES_ROOT key by clicking the plus sign. Notice that there are more subkeys underneath it, some of which have subkeys of their own, and so on. Search down to the CLSID subkey and expand the key by clicking the plus sign. You will see hundreds of long identification codes. Now use the Find utility (CTRL-F) and enter the following string into the text box: **645FF040-5081-101B-9F08-00AA002F954E**. Make sure you enter the numbers correctly. Expand the subkey and click the ShellFolder icon. You should see the information shown in Figure 6-3.

Before you start changing the Registry, it's a good idea to learn how to "back up" the keys by exporting and importing them. This will enable you to reset the subkey to its original state if you make a mistake in your entries.

a.   Highlight the ShellFolder subkey, and then select File | Export to open the Export Registry File dialog box. Save the key in a folder where you can find it again, and give it a useful name that you won't forget.

b.   Highlight the key again, and double-click the Attributes REG_BINARY file. Replace the hexadecimal number 40 01 00 20 with **50 01 00 20** and click OK.

c.   Double-click the CallForAttributes REG_DWORD file. Replace the 40 with **00** and click OK.

d.   Minimize the Registry Editor and find the Recycle Bin on your desktop.

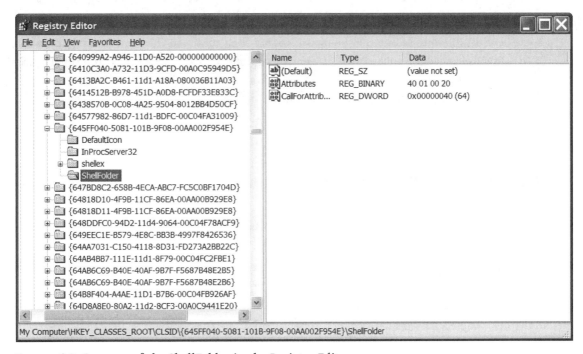

FIGURE 6-3 Contents of the ShellFolder in the Registry Editor

e.   Right-click the Recycle Bin icon. In the drop-down menu there is now a Rename option (see Figure 6-4). Click Rename and change the name of the Recycle Bin. Fun, eh?

f.   To return the Recycle Bin to its natural state, first rename it back to Recycle Bin. Now navigate to your exported Registry file and double-click the file. You will be asked if you are sure you want to add this information to the Registry. Click Yes. You should see a message that the information was successfully added to the Registry.

g.   To confirm that your backup Registry information has taken effect, right-click the Recycle Bin. Can you still rename it? _____

Step 3   Imagine you're in the Control Panel adjusting your mouse settings, and you adjust the mouse double-click speed to the maximum (fastest) and close the window without testing it. When you try to use the system, you can't double-click the mouse fast enough even to get back into the Control Panel to fix it. (This is a bit of a stretch, as you could always use the keyboard to access the Mouse applet, but go with me here to see the Registry in action.) So, what do you do? Follow these steps to view your current Mouse applet double-click speed setting and then use regedit to change it:

a.   Access the Control Panel and open the Mouse applet.

b.   On the Buttons tab, adjust the slider for the double-click speed to the middle position, and test to be sure it works.

c.   Click Apply and then OK. Close the Mouse applet and the Control Panel.

d.   Open the Registry Editor, and make sure that My Computer is highlighted at the top of the left pane.

e.   Select Edit | Find to search for the mouse double-click speed. In the Find What field, type **doubleclickspeed** (be sure to spell it as one word, no spaces). Check the Match Whole String Only box. Click Find Next. You want only the first occurrence it finds. There are other things with that name that you don't want to change.

FIGURE 6-4 The Recycle Bin's newly added Rename option

f.   When regedit finds the file, right-click the word DoubleClickSpeed in the right pane and select Modify.

g.   Change the value to something between 100 and 900 (milliseconds); 100 is very fast. Click OK and then close the Registry Editor.

h.   Reopen the Mouse applet in the Control Panel. Did the slider move from where it was?

_____

i.   For more practice, set your double-click speed to the fastest setting in the Control Panel and go to the Registry to slow it down.

✔ Hint

The Web site www.pctools.com/guides/registry is full of working Registry fixes.

 30 MINUTES

Lab Exercise 6.02: Windows XP Boot Files

In Windows XP, there are important system files that are required for the operating system to load properly. These files are vital to the boot process of any Windows XP–based operating system. Becoming more familiar with their purpose and where they reside on a Windows system can help you when you get in a situation that calls for you to replace corrupted system files.

Learning Objectives

At the end of this lab, you'll be able to

- Locate and understand the different boot files associated with Windows XP

- Make changes to the boot.ini file

Lab Materials and Setup

The materials you need for this lab are

- A working computer running Windows XP

Getting Down to Business

A technician needs to understand the location of important system boot files on a Windows XP system so that he or she can troubleshoot any corrupted files quickly and efficiently.

→ Note

This exercise was done on a computer with a clean installation of Windows XP Professional. Although the edition of your Windows XP operating system will not affect this lab, having multiple operating systems installed could alter the results you see in your lab environment.

Step 1 By default, Microsoft hides important system files. This is a good thing, because normal users don't need access to these files. However, we aren't normal users!

    a. To see all the files that Microsoft hides, click on Start | My Computer. Click Tools | Folder Options.

    b. Click on the View tab. In the Advanced settings area, select the *Show hidden files and folders* radio button.

    c. Uncheck *Hide protected operating system files (Recommended)*.

    d. Finally, uncheck *Hide extensions for known file types* so that you can see the files in all of their glory. Click OK. Windows will ask if you are sure you want to reveal everything. Click OK again to confirm.

Step 2 You should now see many new files in your C: drive, as shown in Figure 6-5.

FIGURE 6-5 Windows XP C: drive showing hidden and system files

a.   There should be about eight freshly revealed system files on your screen. Pick five of these files (not folders) and give a short description of each.

_____

_____

_____

_____

_____

b.   All of these files are important for the booting of Windows XP. Some are extremely relevant and some are meant for backward compatibility with legacy operating systems.

c.   List the four files that are kept around for legacy operating systems.

_____

_____

_____

_____

d.   Double-click on the boot.ini file. Given your first impression of the boot.ini file, describe its function and purpose. Notice that the boot.ini file is just a text file. Close the file when you are finished.

_____

Step 3   Next, let's find another way to view the boot.ini and how your system boots up.

a.   Open the System Properties applet by pressing WINDOWS KEY+PAUSE/BREAK. Click on the Advanced tab. Under Startup and Recovery, click Settings. This will open the Startup and Recovery dialog box. The first section is all about system startup.

b.   Click Edit. Now that should look familiar! Pretty cool, eh? Close out of the boot.ini file to return to the Startup and Recovery dialog box.

c.   Change the _Time to display list of operating systems_ setting to 15 seconds. Click OK.

d.   Return to the Startup and Recovery dialog box by clicking Settings again. Click Edit to view the boot.ini file again. Your new timer of 15 seconds should be listed. Your boot.ini file should look something like the one shown in Figure 6-6.

e.   Now, let's really go to town on the boot.ini file. First, we need to save a backup on the C: drive. Use File | Save as and name it **bootini.bak**. Close Notepad.

f.   Click on Edit to open the original boot.ini file again.

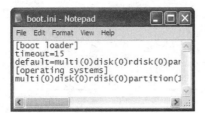

FIGURE 6-6 Boot.ini showing a 15-second timeout

✔ **Cross Reference**

If you want more clarity on the syntax used in the boot.ini file, refer to the "The Windows XP Boot Process" section in Chapter 6 of *Mike Meyers' CompTIA A+ Guide to 802: Managing and Troubleshooting PCs*.

g. This is an example of what your boot.ini file should look like:

```
[boot loader]
timeout=15
default=multi(0)disk(0)rdisk(0)partition(1)\WINDOWS
[operating systems]
multi(0)disk(0)rdisk(0)partition(1)\WINDOWS="Microsoft Windows XP Professional" /
fastdetect /NoExecute=OptOut
```

h. Change your boot.ini file to say this:

```
[boot loader]
timeout=20
default=multi(0)disk(0)rdisk(0)partition(2)\WINDOWS
[operating systems]
multi(0)disk(0)rdisk(0)partition(1)\WINDOWS="Microsoft Windows XP Professional"
multi(0)disk(0)rdisk(0)partition(2)\WINDOWS="I Love Lamp"
```

i. Save your settings. Close out of boot.ini. Reboot the computer.

j. Give a detailed description of what happens.

_____

_____

_____

_____

Step 4 Reboot the computer and this time choose to enter Microsoft Windows XP Professional instead of I Love Lamp.

Log on to the computer and delete the boot.ini file that you altered during the lab exercise. Restore the original that you created by renaming it from bootini.bak to **boot.ini**.

 30 MINUTES

Lab Exercise 6.03: Windows Vista/7 Boot Files

Just like in Windows XP, there are important system files that are required to get the operating system to load when a computer is turned on for Windows Vista/7. These files are essential to the Windows Vista and Windows 7 boot process. Becoming more familiar with their purpose and where they reside on the system can help you when you need to replace corrupted system files.

Learning Objectives

In this lab, you will practice locating the Windows Vista/7 boot files and using the bcdedit program.

At the end of this lab, you'll be able to

- Locate and understand the different boot files associated with Windows Vista/7

- Use bcdedit.exe

Lab Materials and Setup

The materials you need for this lab are

- A working computer running Windows Vista/7

Getting Down to Business

Just like in Windows XP, the boot files in Windows Vista/7 are hidden to protect them from users. A technician, though, needs to know where to find them and how to fix them if there are any problems. Unfortunately, just because Windows Vista and Windows 7 use the same files to manage the boot process doesn't mean that they store them in the same location.

Step 1   Where are my boot files? Well, the answer isn't easy. It really depends on your operating system and the motherboard you are using. To figure it all out, let's do a series of "If-Then" statements—if this, then that. Follow along and it will all make sense.

a.   If your computer is a Windows Vista computer, then all of your important system boot files will be stored in the following path:

C:\Boot\

b.   If your computer is a Windows 7 computer using a motherboard with a traditional BIOS, then your computer will have a special 100-MB system partition. You can view the contents of this partition by going to Disk Management and mounting the 100-MB partition with any drive letter you want. The path will be the same as above, except you need to replace "C:" with the drive letter you chose to assign to the tiny system partition.

→ **Note**

In order to see any of these files, you need to go to the Folder Options dialog box and select the *Show hidden files, folders, and drives* radio button and uncheck the *Hide protected operating system files (Recommended)* checkbox. You can reach these options from any Windows Explorer view in Windows Vista/7. Click Organize | Folder and search options, and then click on the View tab.

c.   If your computer is a Windows 7 computer using a motherboard with an EFI/UEFI BIOS, your computer will still have that same 100-MB system partition. For security reasons, however, you will not be able to access the contents of the system partition through the Windows GUI. If you really want to—I don't recommend it—you can mount the drive letter by opening a command prompt with elevated privileges and typing **mountvol /s**. This command mounts the EFI/UEFI system partition to a drive letter of your choosing. Unfortunately, you still can't access this drive letter from the Windows GUI. With a little more command-line interface knowledge, you might stand a chance to navigate your way around the EFI/UEFI system partition. Good luck!

→ **Note**

To determine if you have an EFI/UEFI motherboard, go to Disk Management. If the system partition is labeled "EFI," you have an EFI/UEFI motherboard. You can also check if your motherboard supports EFI/UEFI by looking at the box it came in or the manual.

Step 2   In order to see some of the important system files in action for a Windows Vista/7 system, we are going to have to venture into the realm of the command-line interface.

a.   Open the Start menu and type **cmd** in the Search bar. Don't press ENTER. Right-click on cmd.exe and select *Run as administrator*. You will then be presented with a confirmation from UAC. Click Yes.

b.   At the command prompt, type **bcdedit**. It will take a few moments to load completely.

c.   What would happen if you ran the command bcdedit without choosing *Run as administrator* in Step 2a?

_____

d.   You use the bcdedit utility to edit the BCD. Describe, in your own words, the BCD.

_____

_____

e.   The bcdedit screen can be overwhelming. Fill in the following values based off the Windows Boot Manager section of bcdedit. If the values don't exist on your PC, then skip them.

Identifier   _____

Devices   _____

Path   _____

Description _____

Timeout   _____

f. You should also have a section in bcdedit called Windows Boot Loader. You may have one or more sections depending on how your system is configured. Pick one of the listings and fill in the following values.

Identifier   _____

Devices   _____

Path   _____

Description _____

Osdevice   _____

g. Make a backup copy of the BCD by exporting it. To export the BCD, type in the following command:

bcdedit /export "C:\backup\bcdbackup"

h. This command will export the BCD into the path of your choice. In this case, we chose C:\backup\ bcdbackup. Browse to your C:\backup folder that you just created to ensure that it created the backup file. List the size of the file in the space provided.

_____

i. Close all open windows and command prompts to return to your desktop.

 30 MINUTES

Lab Exercise 6.04: The Task Manager

All Microsoft operating systems include a utility that enables you to view all of the tasks running on your system. Since the days of Windows NT, Windows has used the Task Manager to accomplish this. The Task Manager is arguably one of the most important troubleshooting utilities included in Windows. The Task Manager enables you to start, view, and end tasks. You can also see the resources being used by each running task. This lab exercise will show you how to best use the Task Manager, as well as introduce you to a third-party tool that makes the Task Manager look like a child's toy by comparison.

Learning Objectives

In this lab, you'll learn how to use the Task Manager and Process Explorer to work with running applications and processes.

At the end of this lab, you'll be able to

- Locate and use the Task Manager
- Download and run Process Explorer

Lab Materials and Setup

The materials you need for this lab are

- A working computer running Windows XP, Windows Vista, or Windows 7

Getting Down to Business

Your friend Max just bought a new computer. He's loaded it up with new games and applications, but after he finished installing everything, he noticed his computer slowing down. He has no idea what could be causing this and needs help! Assist Max by using the Task Manager and a third-party tool called Process Explorer.

Step 1   Opening the Task Manager can be done in a variety of ways on a Windows computer. Try each of the following:

- CTRL-ALT-DEL

→ **Note**

If you are on a PC with the Welcome screen disabled, you will need to click on Select Task Manager (Windows XP) or Start Task Manager (Windows Vista/7).

- CTRL-SHIFT-ESC
- Right-click on the taskbar and select Task Manager (Windows XP) or Start Task Manager (Windows Vista/7)

Step 2   The first screen you will see is the Applications tab. This shows you the currently running programs on your system. This list should comprise any open applications on your taskbar.

a.   With the Task Manager still open, open Notepad.

b.   Notepad should now be listed as a task in the Task Manager. The Status column should list it as Running. This is good—we like it when applications (or tasks) are running. If you ever see an application listed as Not Responding, the application is having issues.

c.   With Notepad selected in the Task Manager, click End Task. Describe the results.

_____

Step 3   Open Windows Media Player. Then open the Task Manager (if you closed it). You should now see Windows Media Player listed in the tasks under the Applications tab.

a.   Sometimes, using the End Task button doesn't end the task. The application might feel stuck and won't close. When this happens, we need to turn to the Processes tab. Right-click on the Windows Media Player task in the Applications tab and select Go To Process. This opens the Processes tab with the appropriate process selected.

b.   Record the process that is associated with Windows Media Player as well as how much memory is allocated to it.

  •   Process name: _____

  •   Mem Usage: _____

c.   Right-click on the process name and click End Process. Describe what happens.

_____

→   **Note**

If you ended the process and Windows Media Player didn't go away, then you ended the wrong process. Whoops!

d.   You may have also noticed the End Process Tree option next to the End Process option. This ends the process as well as any processes it started.

Step 4   With the Task Manager open, click on the Performance tab. This is another great area for troubleshooting and diagnosing a Windows PC. You'll notice that you can monitor the CPU and RAM usage from this tab.

a.   Record the following based on your operating system. For Windows XP users, record the Commit Charge. For Windows Vista/7 users, record the Physical Memory percentage. Both of these values are located in the bottom-right corner of the window.

_____

b.   Open 15 instances of Microsoft WordPad. Record the new Physical Memory percentage or Commit Charge.

_____

c.   Close all 15 instances of Microsoft WordPad.

Step 5   Switch back to the Processes tab. Scroll down until you find winlogon.exe. This process is a bit odd because, even on Windows Vista/7, there is no description listed.

a.   Try to end the process winlogon.exe. Record the results.

_____

b.   You might think this process is some type of malware that has infected your system, but before you do anything else, you need to be sure.

c.   Open a Web browser and search for **Process Explorer**. Clicking the first search result should take you to the Windows Sysinternals Web site (see Figure 6-7).

d.   Download the latest version of Process Explorer. Once downloaded, extract the contents of the zipped archive to a folder on your desktop or another location of your choosing.

e.   Open the folder with the extracted files and run the program **procexp.exe**. It should look familiar. Think of Process Explorer as a super-advanced Task Manager.

FIGURE 6-7 The Windows Sysinternals Web site

f. Look around the Process Explorer application. Notice that certain processes branch off of other processes. This is where that End Process Tree option from earlier can come in handy. You can end all the connected processes at once.

g. Scroll down and find winlogon.exe. You'll notice that pretty much every process shows how much RAM is allocated to it, along with descriptions of the process—except for winlogon.exe again! Right-click on winlogon.exe and select Search Online. Give a detailed description of winlogon.exe.

_____

_____

Step 6 It's a good thing we were unable to end that process—looks like Windows needs that one. Take some time to become more familiar with Process Explorer. You'll see that it's more powerful than the Task Manager. You can even use Process Explorer to replace the traditional Task Manager when you press CTRL-ALT-DEL.

a. Click Options | Replace Task Manager.

b. If you want to undo the replacement of the Task Manager, just repeat the previous step.

c. Close out of all the open windows and programs to finish the exercise.

Lab Analysis Test

1. Sally says that her computer runs slowly and that it doesn't respond like it used to. How could you use the Task Manager to check out the problem?

2. Jim receives an error message on startup that says "NTLDR is Missing." What can you tell Jim about ntldr that will help him understand why it is so important to a Windows computer?

3. Why would a user ever want to edit their boot.ini file?

4. Describe the function of the Registry and explain why someone would edit it.

5. John wants to access the Task Manager so he can end some processes. What are the three ways he could open it?

Key Term Quiz

Use the following terms to complete the following sentences. Not all terms will be used.

bcdedit

boot.ini

bootmgr

HKEY_CLASSES_ROOT

HKEY_CURRENT_CONFIG

HKEY_CURRENT_USER

HKEY_LOCAL_MACHINE

HKEY_USERS

ntdetect.com

ntldr

Process Explorer

regedit

Registry

Task Manager

winload.exe

1. The Registry contains all the configuration data and can be accessed directly using
    _____.

2. The _____ file is used to manage the boot process of Windows Vista/7.

3. The _____ is a built-in Windows tool used to start and end processes.

4. _____ is the Registry key that stores the plug-and-play information about your computer.

5. Windows Vista/7 use the _____ tool to view and edit the boot configuration.

Chapter 7
NTFS, Users, and Groups

Lab Exercises

Not every computer is a part of some vast corporate network. Not everyone logs on to a domain and manipulates multiple file servers to carry out their business. Sometimes, a system stands alone. And lest you take pity on this lonely PC—or worse, ignore it entirely—you must still think about its security. Even without a network, a single computer contains plenty of vital data, and it is these very systems that will be accessed by multiple users (because, well, it's the only one). Without taking the necessary security precautions, your data could easily be stolen or destroyed by anyone else who uses that computer. This is why user accounts, permissions, and encryption in Windows are so important.

As a PC tech, you may be called upon to set up a new user account. But simply adding a new user is just the beginning. You will need to keep in mind what sort of powers or permissions you want each user to have—do they need to be able to install new software, or is just being able to open and edit files enough?

But sometimes, the general set of abilities granted by each type of user account isn't specific enough—maybe certain files or folders should be accessed only by certain users, or groups of users. Then there are the files that should only be seen or touched by you, with access granted by your password alone. Or the opposite—maybe you need to share some folders so that everyone on that PC can get to them. This chapter will show you how to implement these security features in Windows so that a single system can have multiple users working with and sharing files securely.

 15 MINUTES

Lab Exercise 7.01: Managing Users in Windows

Any time you access a PC, you do so through a local user account, whether Windows makes it obvious or not. A lot of home PCs have only one user, without a password, so this process becomes transparent. But that would not be the ideal setup for the workplace, unless you want everyone to be able to go through everyone else's bank records, e-mail messages, personal photos, and so on. Having local user accounts provides a means of authentication—making sure that Steve *is* Steve—and authorization—allowing Steve to delete this, but not install that.

Learning Objectives

In this lab, you'll practice creating and managing new users.

At the end of this lab, you'll be able to

- Create and manage a new local user account

- Work with user groups

Lab Materials and Setup

The materials you need for this lab are

- A PC running Windows

Getting Down to Business

Your client is a small business with four employees and one computer. They each need their own user account so that they can keep their personal data private and so that they stop accidentally deleting everything while logged on as an administrator. Adam is the only one with enough knowledge of computers to have a more powerful account. Betsy, Carol, and Dale each need more limited accounts, because they aren't tech savvy and could easily break something.

This exercise works with any version of Windows, but for the sake of instruction, the steps will be repeated for Windows XP, Windows Vista, and Windows 7.

✔ Cross-Reference

For more information on users and groups, refer to the "Managing Users in Windows XP," "Managing Users in Windows Vista," and "Managing Users in Windows 7" sections in Chapter 7 of *Mike Meyers' CompTIA A+ Guide to 802: Managing and Troubleshooting PCs*.

Step 1   Follow these steps to create a new user account for Betsy in Windows XP:

a.   Make sure to sign in as an administrator so that you can create the user account. Then click Start | Control Panel.

b.   If Classic view is not enabled in the Control Panel, enable it now by clicking Switch to Classic View.

c.   Double-click User Accounts. Then click *Change the way users log on or off*. Deselect the *Use the Welcome screen* option (see Figure 7-1). This also disables Fast User Switching. Now each user will have to type in their user name and password at the login screen. Click Apply Options.

d.   Click *Create a new account*. Enter a user name, and then click Next.

e.   For the account type, choose Limited. Then click Create Account (see Figure 7-2).

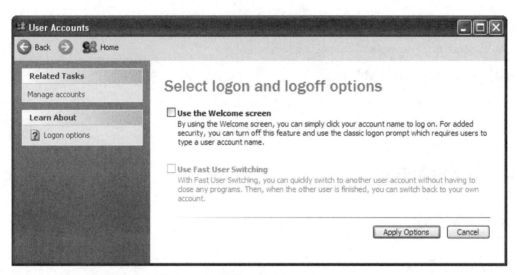

FIGURE 7-1 Disabling the Windows XP Welcome screen

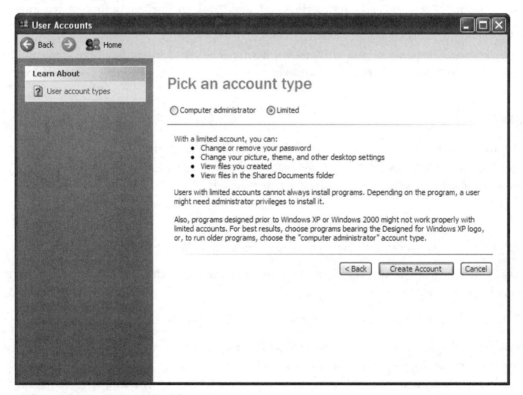

FIGURE 7-2 Choosing Limited for account type

f.   Windows XP creates user accounts without passwords by default, so you need to add the password manually. Select the user you just created by clicking her icon. Then click *Create a password*. Type in a memorable password and confirm it. Then create a hint phrase to remind you of the password if you forget it. *Do not* use the password as the hint phrase, since this makes having a password pointless. Click *Create password*.

Step 3   Follow these steps to create a new user account for Carol in Windows Vista:

a.   Make sure to sign in as an administrator so that you can create the user account. Then click Start | Control Panel. Click Switch to Classic View, and then double-click User Accounts.

b.   Select *Manage another account* (see Figure 7-3). Then click *Create a new account*.

c.   Type in a new account name. Standard user should already be selected. Click Create Account.

d.   Select Carol's user account from the Manage Accounts screen. Click *Create a password*. Type in a memorable password, confirm it, and then create a password hint to remind yourself in case you forget. Click *Create password*.

Step 4   Follow these steps to create a new user account for Dale in Windows 7:

a.   Make sure to sign in as an administrator, so that you can create the user account. Then click Start | Control Panel. Under the link to User Accounts and Family Safety, click on the link *Add or remove user accounts*.

b.   Click on *Create a new account*.

c.   Type in a new account name. Standard user should already be selected. Click Create Account.

FIGURE 7-3 Selecting the Manage another account link

d.   Select Dale's user account from the Manage Accounts screen. Click *Create a password*. Type in a memorable password, confirm it, and then create a password hint to remind yourself in case you forget. Click *Create password*.

Step 5   Now that you have standard users created, your client decides that he really needs another administrator besides Adam. Based on the operating system you are doing this exercise on, choose an account to upgrade to Administrator.

a.   As usual, make sure your account is set to Administrator. Click Start, right-click My Computer/ Computer, and select Manage.

b.   On the left side of the screen, select Local Users and Groups. On the right side, double-click Groups, and then double-click Administrators.

c.   In the Administrators Properties window, click Add. Type the user name in the *Enter the object names to select* box, and then click Check Names. Click OK.

d.   Click OK in the Administrators Properties dialog box. Find the name of the group that the user had been in previously, most likely Users. Double-click it to open the Properties dialog box.

e.   Find the user name in the list, click it, and then click Remove. Click OK. Now the user is an administrator!

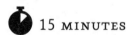 15 MINUTES

Lab Exercise 7.02: Defining NTFS Permissions

Now that you've learned how to set up authentication, it's time to talk about authorization—what a user can do with files, folders, or any other resource. Granting NTFS permissions is a powerful and complex tool that enables you to define precisely who can do what on a system. Depending on your needs, this can quickly become a complicated and sticky web of overlapping settings that you don't want to deal with. But it's important to know how to define these permissions so that each user has the specific powers and limitations he requires. It's best to start thinking about it one folder at a time: who can open it, and who can edit it?

Learning Objectives

In this lab, you'll use NTFS permissions to define which users can access specific files and folders.

At the end of this lab, you'll be able to

•   Set up NTFS permissions for files and folders

Lab Materials and Setup

The materials you need for this lab are

- A PC running Windows XP Professional, Windows Vista Business/Ultimate/Enterprise, or Windows 7 Professional/Ultimate/Enterprise on an NTFS partition

Getting Down to Business

Now that your client has a set of user accounts for his employees, he wants to set up a folder on the C: drive for everyone to use. But there's one text file he doesn't want Dale to touch—he doesn't even want Dale to be able to open it, let alone make any changes. He's asked you to set up the file with the right permissions so that Dale can't access the file.

Setting up permissions for files and setting up permissions for folders are very similar procedures. In this exercise, you'll work with setting up permissions for a text file, but the same procedure will also work with folders.

Step 1   The rest of the steps in this lab will be more straightforward if you first deactivate simple file sharing (in Windows XP only). To do so, open any folder in Windows Explorer, such as My Documents. Select Tools | Folder Options. Switch to the View tab. At the bottom of the list of Advanced settings is the *Use simple file sharing (Recommended)* option. Deselect the box. Click OK.

Step 2   If you haven't done so already, create an account for Dale on your computer using Lab Exercise 7.01. Make sure Dale *isn't* an administrator and *you* are. Then navigate to My Computer/Computer and double-click the C: drive. Right-click an empty area in the right pane of the window and select New | Folder. Rename it **Work**.

Step 3   Open the Work folder you just created. Right-click an empty area again and select New | Text Document.

Step 4   Right-click the text document and select Properties. Then open the Security tab. Click Edit. This opens a more detailed version of the tab you were just looking at. Listed should be several users and groups, but Dale might not be listed. To add him, click Add. Type **Dale** in the *Enter the object names to select* box (see Figure 7-4) and click Check Names. Click OK.

Step 5   Now that Dale is on the list, you can set his permissions. Select Dale from the list of Group or user names. The bottom half of the window shows a list of permissions for Dale. Everything should be set to Allow. Scroll until you see Read. Check the Deny box next to Read. Click Apply. A dialog box will pop up explaining how this will change the permission of this file and how it could affect other files. Choose Yes.

FIGURE 7-4 The Select Users, Computer, or Groups applet

Step 6 Log off of the administrator account and log in as Dale. Go back into My Computer/Computer, double-click the C: drive, and open the Work folder you created. Double-click the new text file.

What happens?

_____

If all goes well, Notepad should open, but Windows should deny you (Dale) access to the text file. Congratulations! You just set a permission!

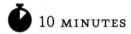 10 MINUTES

Lab Exercise 7.03: Sharing Files and Folders

There are plenty of times when delving into specific NTFS permissions is overkill. Sometimes, you just want to share a folder, one that everyone can freely add to, edit, and so on. Windows makes it incredibly easy to share a folder with multiple local user accounts. Most versions even come with a folder set up for this purpose, like Public Documents in Windows Vista/7. But one shared folder isn't always enough.

Learning Objectives

In this lab, you'll use sharing in Windows to set up a folder that can be accessed by all users.

At the end of this lab, you'll be able to

- Set up a shared folder

Lab Materials and Setup

The materials you need for this lab are

- A PC running Windows XP Professional, Windows Vista Business/Ultimate/Enterprise, or Windows 7 Professional/Ultimate/Enterprise

Getting Down to Business

In the previous lab, you created the Work folder on the C: drive of your computer. But the only account that has complete control of that folder is the one used to create it. Your client wants to make sure that every user on that system has full access to the contents of that folder. The easiest way to accomplish that is to use the share feature of Windows.

This is pretty easy, but to make it clear, the exercise will be divided between Windows XP and Windows Vista/7. You'll need the professional editions of these operating systems (Windows XP Professional, Windows Vista Business/Ultimate/Enterprise, or Windows 7 Professional/Ultimate/Enterprise) because the Home editions of Windows can only use simple file sharing.

✔ **Hint**

Just because you know how to set up sharing in one operating system doesn't mean you shouldn't practice in another. Remember that the CompTIA A+ 220-802 exam isn't just testing you on the OS you already know. Take time to check out all the differences between the Windows versions.

Step 1 Windows makes the basic process of sharing files and folders over a network pretty easy. File sharing in Windows, however, is an incredibly deep and complex topic, and you're only going to scratch the surface in this lab. Entire books have been written about share permissions and proper sharing security. With that said, here are the basic steps for sharing a file over a network with Windows XP:

a. In Windows XP, navigate to the C: drive in My Computer. If you haven't already done so, create a Work folder in the root folder of the C: drive. Then right-click the folder and click Properties.

b. Open the Sharing tab. Select Share This Folder. Then click Permissions. From the choices given, select Everyone. On the bottom half of the window, under Permissions for Everyone, check the Allow box next to Full Control. Click OK. Now you are sharing the Work folder with everyone!

Step 2 The process for sharing folders in Windows Vista/7 has changed significantly. Here are the steps for accomplishing in Vista/7 what you did in XP in Step 1:

a. In Windows Vista/7, navigate to the C: drive in Computer. If you haven't already done so, create a Work folder in the root folder of the C: drive. Then right-click the folder and select Share or Share With, depending on the operating system.

b. Select *Specific people*. From the drop-down menu, select Everyone. Click Add. Then, in the list of Names and Permission Levels below, click Everyone. Open the drop-down menu for the Permission Level and select Read/Write or Co-owner, depending on the operating system. Then click Share. Done!

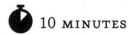 10 MINUTES

Lab Exercise 7.04: Encrypting Important Data

So far, you've gone through several methods of securing data on a machine accessed by multiple users. But these features don't secure the data itself as much as put a wall around it to keep people out. The data inside is (as of yet) defenseless. If a system has two administrator accounts, and one administrator sets up file permissions to keep the other out, the second administrator has the power to undo those permissions and access the data—unless you activate encryption.

When you encrypt a file, it becomes absolutely secure from everyone else but you or, more specifically, your password. If you were to lose your password, or an administrator were to change it for you, that data would be lost forever, because that password is *the only way* to get it back. So be careful!

Learning Objectives

In this lab, you'll use encryption to protect sensitive data.

At the end of this lab, you'll be able to

- Use the Encrypting File System in Windows

Lab Materials and Setup

The materials you need for this lab are

- A PC running Windows XP Professional, Windows Vista Business/Ultimate/Enterprise, or Windows 7 Professional/Ultimate/Enterprise

Getting Down to Business

Your client has several personal documents that she keeps copies of on her computer at work. But she isn't the only administrator on that system, so to fully secure the data, she wants it to be encrypted.

Thanks to the Encrypting File System (EFS) introduced with NTFS, encrypting files in Windows is simple. Be warned, however, that if you lose access to the user account that you used to encrypt the files, you will lose those files forever!

✔ **Hint**

The Home editions of Windows, such as Windows XP Home, Windows Vista Home Premium, and Windows 7 Home Premium, do not include a utility to encrypt data. If you are using one of these operating systems and still want to or need to use encryption, check out TrueCrypt. Open source (and free), TrueCrypt provides advanced encryption features across multiple platforms. Check it out at www.truecrypt.org.

Step 1 Navigate to the files or folder in question (for the purposes of the lab, use the Work folder you already created). Right-click the Work folder and select Properties. Next to the Attributes checkboxes, click the Advanced button. At the bottom of the Advanced Attributes dialog box, check the box for *Encrypt contents to secure data* (see Figure 7-5). Click OK.

Step 2 Now switch to another user, even another administrator. Navigate back to the folder that you just encrypted. Try opening it.

What happens?

FIGURE 7-5 The Advanced Attributes dialog box

 10 MINUTES

Lab Exercise 7.05: Configuring User Account Control

Starting with Windows Vista, Microsoft introduced users to a new feature called User Account Control (UAC). User Account Control was designed to put controls in place to stop malicious code from spreading on a computer. UAC ensures that important changes cannot be made to a Windows Vista/7 computer without the permission of an administrator. When it debuted with Windows Vista, users were less than enthusiastic about this new feature. Many, myself included, turned the feature off almost immediately because of how invasive it was. With Windows Vista, UAC could either be on or off—there was no middle ground. Microsoft fixed this in Windows 7 and has enabled users to choose four distinct levels of how UAC presents itself. Note that this feature is not available in Windows XP Home or Professional.

Learning Objectives

In this lab, you'll learn the effects of the different UAC settings.

At the end of this lab, you'll be able to

- Understand the effects of User Account Control

Lab Materials and Setup

The materials you need for this lab are

- A PC running Windows 7

Getting Down to Business

You have set up a client, Taylor, with a new computer using Windows 7 Home Premium. Taylor has just downloaded and installed a copy of Ventrilo, a popular Voice over IP (VoIP) application used in the world of online gaming. When she clicks on the icon to start Ventrilo, her screen goes dark and a small prompt appears. She is scared and calls you for help!

Step 1   Open your favorite Web browser and visit www.ventrilo.com/. From that page, visit the Download section and download the appropriate client software package for your version of Windows 7 (see Figure 7-6). After you have downloaded the program, install it on your computer.

→ **Note**

We won't actually be using Ventrilo for anything other than testing out the functions of UAC. So after we are finished with this exercise, feel free to uninstall the application.

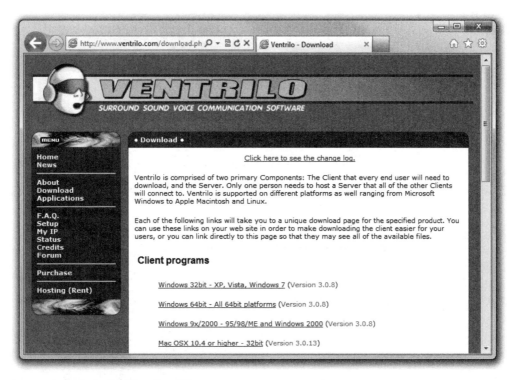

FIGURE 7-6 Downloading Ventrilo

Step 2 Now, before we get crazy checking out how UAC reacts to Ventrilo, let's see what User Account Control looks like and the different settings it offers in Windows 7.

a.   Click Start | Control Panel | System and Security. Under the Action Center section, click on the *Change User Account Control settings* link.

➜ **Note**

Alternatively, you can click Start, type **UAC** into the Search bar, and click on the *Change User Account Control settings* link at the top of the search results. However, even when searching, CompTIA still wants you to know the path of how to find the different utilities in Windows.

b.   You should now be in the User Account Control Settings window. If the default settings aren't being used on this machine, go ahead and switch to the default settings (see Figure 7-7). Give a short description of what the default settings are.

_____

_____

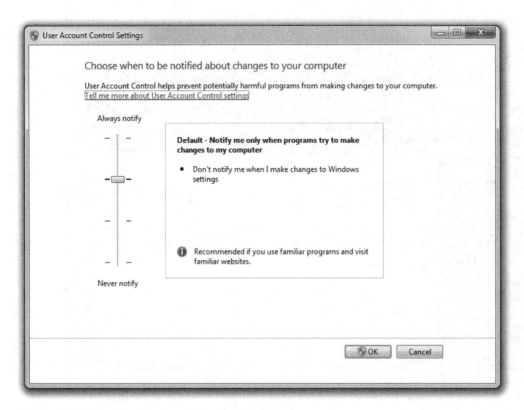

FIGURE 7-7 User Account Control Settings window

c. Click OK to confirm your settings changes, or minimize the UAC window if you made no changes, and open Ventrilo. Describe what happens.

_____

_____

d. Go ahead and click No on the prompt. Return to the User Account Control Settings window as described in Step 2a.

e. Move the slider down one notch, just above Never notify. Click OK to confirm your settings.

f. Open Ventrilo again. Describe what happens this time.

_____

_____

g. Go ahead and click No on the prompt.

Step 3

a.   Click Start | Control Panel | System and Security.

b.   Notice the links to items such as Allow remote access, Device Manager, and Create and format hard disk partitions. What is a similarity between those links and the Ventrilo icon in your Start menu?

_____

c.   Open any of those utilities and record what happens.

_____

d.   This similarity between these items ties directly into how UAC interacts with programs and utilities that are either third-party applications or built directly into the Windows operating system. Return to the User Account Control Settings window as described in Step 2a.

e.   Move the slider bar to the very top for Always notify. Click OK to save the changes. Instantly, you should see the UAC dialog box prompt appear. Click Yes to proceed.

f.   Click on Start | Control Panel | System and Security. Try to click on *Allow remote access*, *Device Manager*, or *Create and format hard disk partitions*. Also, try to open Ventrilo again. Record the results.

_____

_____

Step 4

a.   This exercise was designed to help you become more familiar with UAC. Why do you think this feature is useful in modern computing?

_____

_____

b.   Which level of User Account Control best fits your needs as a user and why?

_____

_____

 10 MINUTES

Lab Exercise 7.06: Using BitLocker To Go with Windows 7

Starting with Windows Vista, Microsoft introduced users to a new feature called BitLocker. BitLocker is drive-level encryption, meaning it enables you to encrypt your entire hard drive so that no one else can access it. BitLocker requires two volumes (partitions) on your disk. This can take a lot of partition resizing and hassle in Windows Vista, but Windows 7 creates a 100-MB system partition during the installation that fills this requirement. You also need a Trusted Platform Module (TPM) chip to store the encryption key. If you do not have a TPM chip, you have the option of using a USB flash drive to store the key.

Windows 7 added a new feature called BitLocker To Go, which enables you to encrypt flash drives and other similar devices, instead of just entire hard disk drives. While Windows Vista Enterprise/Ultimate and Windows 7 Enterprise/Ultimate all support BitLocker, only Windows 7 Enterprise/Ultimate supports BitLocker To Go. Because you can use BitLocker To Go without all of the hassle of multiple partitions, you'll use it here to learn more about drive encryption.

Learning Objectives

In this lab, you'll learn how to use BitLocker To Go.

At the end of this lab, you'll be able to

- Use BitLocker To Go to encrypt a flash drive

Lab Materials and Setup

The materials you need for this lab are

- A PC running Windows 7 Enterprise or Ultimate
- A PC running Windows Vista or Windows XP
- A USB flash drive

Getting Down to Business

Nikki works for a company that has highly sensitive data stored on its servers. The network administrator is concerned about possible data theft when users like Nikki take work home on a flash drive. He wants to train Nikki and users like her to use BitLocker To Go so that lost flash drives won't be readable by any stranger who picks them up.

Step 1 First, you'll use BitLocker To Go to encrypt the flash drive.

a. Go to Start | Control Panel | System and Security. Select BitLocker Drive Encryption (see Figure 7-8).

b. From here you have the ability to turn on BitLocker for your entire hard drive, but we're here for the BitLocker To Go feature. Attach your USB flash drive.

c. You should see the flash drive appear in the BitLocker Drive Encryption window.

d. Click Turn On BitLocker. This will begin the BitLocker To Go wizard (see Figure 7-9).

e. Enter a password that will later unlock the drive. BitLocker To Go also has another way of unlocking the drive besides a password. What is the other method of unlocking the drive?

_____

f. Click Next. This screen asks you where you want to store the recovery key in case you forget the password. What options are available for storing the recovery key?

_____

g. Choose either option available.

h. The last screen begins the encryption process. This can take a while depending on the size of the flash drive.

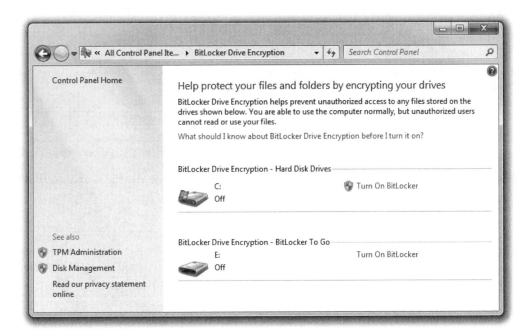

FIGURE 7-8 BitLocker Drive Encryption applet

FIGURE 7-9 BitLocker To Go wizard

> **→ Note**
>
> The time it takes to encrypt your drive is another reason why I had you do BitLocker To Go rather than regular BitLocker. Encrypting an entire hard drive can take hours!

i. Upon completion, you will receive a message stating that the drive has been encrypted. Click OK.

j. Close out of all the open windows and return to your desktop. Click Start | Computer. What is different about the icon of your flash drive?

_____

k. Try opening and working with your flash drive. It should work and act like any other flash drive.

Step 2   To test what happens when you connect to your PC a flash drive encrypted using BitLocker To Go, you'll need to disconnect it from your PC, then reconnect it.

    a.   Remove your flash drive from the computer.

    b.   Wait a minute and then reinsert your flash drive into the computer.

    c.   Immediately you should be prompted with a BitLocker Drive Encryption window to supply your password. Click *I forgot my password* and supply it with the recovery key from Step 1. You can also automatically unlock the drive on this computer from now on. When might you check the option?

    _____

    d.   Click Unlock.

    e.   Once you click Unlock, you will be able to read and write to the drive without any problems.

    f.   BitLocker To Go also gives you the ability to manage your device by right-clicking on the drive and selecting Manage BitLocker.

    g.   List the five options you can choose from while managing BitLocker.

    _____

    _____

    _____

    _____

    _____

    h.   Close the Manage BitLocker dialog box.

➜ **Note**

You will only be able to do Step 3 if you have an available Windows XP or Windows Vista computer.

Step 3 What about other versions of Windows? You know that only Windows 7 Enterprise and Ultimate can configure BitLocker To Go thumb drives. You'll now see what happens when you try to read the encrypted thumb drive on a Windows XP or Windows Vista PC.

 a. Take your BitLocker encrypted flash drive and insert it into your Windows XP or Windows Vista computer.

 b. Click Start | My Computer/Computer. Double-click to open your flash drive. You should notice two files listed. Open the BitLockerToGo file.

 c. Supply BitLocker To Go with your password and click Unlock.

 d. You can now drag and drop the files that are located on your flash drive onto the local computer to view them using BitLocker To Go Reader, which enables Windows XP and Windows Vista machines to read your BitLocker-encrypted files.

 e. Take a file that is on your Windows XP computer and attempt to drag and drop it onto the flash drive. What happens?

→ **Note**

With BitLocker To Go Reader, you can only read files from an encrypted drive. You can't write to it.

Lab Analysis Test

1. Jonas has an administrator account and sets up the permissions for a folder on the C: drive to deny anyone else from accessing it but himself. If another administrator account was created, would the folder still be secure? Why or why not?

2. Reginald needs to set up a folder that can be seen by the administrator and two standard users, but can be edited only by the administrator. How would he make this work?

3. Arnold wants to implement BitLocker on his hard drive at home because he heard a technician from his IT department at work tell him how much it has helped them at the office. Unfortunately, Arnold has no idea what BitLocker is. Explain to him what BitLocker does and what he will need in order to implement it.

4. Nina created several user accounts in Windows Vista for her family, but forgot to give each of them passwords. List the steps to take to add a password to a user account in Windows Vista.

5. What makes EFS a great security feature in Windows?

Key Term Quiz

Use the following terms to complete the following sentences. Not all terms will be used.

administrator

authentication

authorization

BitLocker

BitLocker To Go

BitLocker To Go Reader

group

limited user

NTFS permissions

simple file sharing

standard user

Trusted Platform Module

User Account Control (UAC)

Users group

Welcome screen

1. A(n) _____ cannot install software or delete system files.

2. Typing your user name and password is a means of _____.

3. Windows Vista introduced a new feature called _____. Windows 7 improved on it by adding _____.

4. _____ are used to define specific rules for which users and groups can and cannot access files and folders.

5. _____ prevents a program from running unless a user authorizes it to.

Chapter 8

Maintaining and Optimizing Windows

Lab Exercises

Imagine that your company has just acquired a small architectural firm. One of the principals of the firm informs you that they haven't really had any IT support to speak of in a few years. You visit the new office and determine that the computers are about five years old. They were good machines when they were purchased, and as long as the hardware is not failing, they should be more than adequate for a year or two more. The architects do complain that their machines are running slowly and that it's affecting productivity. You would like to avoid a complete rollout of new PCs, since you're looking at a replacement expense of thousands of dollars. Consequently, you decide it would be worthwhile to spend a day trying to figure out if anything can be done to make the machines run faster.

After checking out a few of the systems, you determine that they could definitely benefit from additional memory, but that's not the only issue—none of the systems have been updated in over three years! Even though most versions of Windows are optimized when they're installed, time and use can alter that fact significantly. It's important, therefore, to be able to take what you know about navigating and manipulating the Windows environment and put it to work figuring out what needs to be fixed, updated, or improved. Sometimes a simple tweak is all it takes to make a sluggish system run like it's fresh out of the box.

One of the first tasks is to make sure that all of the systems have the latest service packs and Windows updates. Before you do that, however, it's recommended that you back up all of the data on the systems, as this can be a pretty major upgrade. Another item that needs to be checked is whether the device drivers are all up to date. Neglected PCs will definitely require updated device drivers.

First, you will learn how to back up and restore your system in preparation for updating and optimizing Windows. You'll then explore the various troubleshooting tools included with Windows. It's time to drop a few sticks of memory into the pilot machines, back them up, run them through the service packs and updates, and get this office back on its feet!

 60 MINUTES

Lab Exercise 8.01: Performing a Backup and Restoration

Windows offers simple backup/restoration utilities that you can use to back up system data and program data and files, and an advanced recovery feature, in case the system becomes so unstable that it won't even boot.

Windows XP introduced the Automated System Recovery (ASR) routine, and Windows Vista/7 uses the Backup and Restore Center (though Windows 7 drops the "Center" part). The ASR creates nonbootable disks with tools to restore a system (along with a backup of the system and boot partitions), whereas Vista/7's Backup and Restore Center will make a full (or partial) backup of your entire system that is restored using the System Recovery Options. It is important to understand—and the CompTIA A+ 220-802 exam expects you to know this—that none of these options are bootable.

This lab introduces you to the ASR process in Windows XP Professional and the Backup and Restore Center in Windows Vista/7.

Learning Objectives

Performing backups of any kind is a critical responsibility of a PC technician. The Windows XP Professional Automated System Recovery and the Vista/7 Backup and Restore Center are excellent representations of the steps required to back up and restore an OS.

At the end of this lab, you'll be able to

- Prepare a backup

- Perform a restoration

Lab Materials and Setup

The materials you need for this lab are

- A working PC with Windows XP Professional, Windows Vista, or Windows 7 installed

- Some form of backup media/device (CD/DVD drive, tape drive, network drive, separate partition)

- A blank, formatted floppy disk (XP only)

- The Windows XP Professional or Windows Vista/7 installation media

Getting Down to Business

The time to prepare a backup is while the system and data are in a state of complete integrity. It's when they crash or get corrupted that you'll need the backup! The following steps create an ASR set and then use that ASR set to restore a Windows XP system to working condition. The steps for the Windows Vista/7 Backup and Recovery Center will follow.

AUTOMATED SYSTEM RECOVERY PREPARATION

Step 1   Launch the Windows Backup or Restore Wizard by clicking Start | Run and typing **ntbackup.exe** in the dialog box. Alternatively, you can click Start | All Programs | Accessories | System Tools | Backup. Click the Advanced Mode text link to bring up the screen shown in Figure 8-1.

Step 2   Launch the Automated System Recovery Wizard and perform the following steps:

a.   Click Next, and in the *Backup media or file name* dialog box, type or browse for the location in which you want the backup to be placed. This backup includes your entire system and boot volumes, which, in most cases, is your C: drive. Your backup media (second hard drive or optical disc) will need to be big enough to hold the contents of that drive.

b.   Name the backup file, being careful to preserve the .BKF file extension. If you are using a second hard drive, for example, you might enter D:\MyASRBK.BKF to create the file on the D: drive.

c.   Click Next and then click Finish to start the backup of your system files.

d.   When the backup completes, the ASR Preparation Wizard instructs you to insert a formatted 1.44-MB floppy disk. Click OK. ASR copies the required files onto the floppy disk.

e.   When instructed, remove and label the floppy disk and then click OK. You have completed the preparation for an Automated System Recovery.

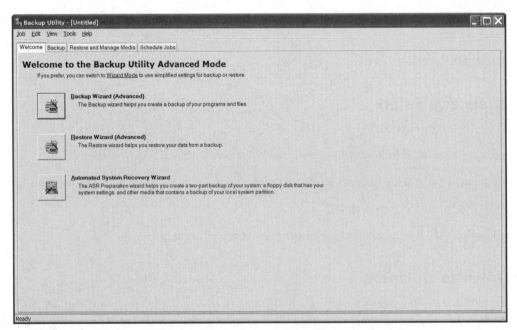

FIGURE 8-1 Windows XP Backup Utility's Advanced Mode screen

→ **Caution**

When you run the ASR restoration, you will format the C: drive. Make sure you've backed up everything you want to keep!

AUTOMATED SYSTEM RECOVERY RESTORE

Step 1   Boot the system using the Windows XP Professional installation CD-ROM.

Step 2   When prompted with *Press F2 to run Automated System Recovery (ASR)*, press the F2 key.

Step 3   Insert the ASR floppy disk and press any key when ready.

Step 4   The Windows XP Installer will copy files to a temporary folder, format the partition where XP will be installed, and prompt you to remove the installation CD-ROM and reboot.

Step 5   After rebooting, the Windows XP installation continues.

   a.   During the installation, you'll be prompted for the location of the ASR backup file.

   b.   Enter the file location or use the Browse button to enter the location and name of the ASR backup file.

   c.   Click OK.

   d.   The installation now completes. All of the Windows XP configuration settings and preferences should be as they were on the original system.

BACKUP AND RESTORE CENTER

Step 1   Open Control Panel. Switch to Classic View (if you haven't already) and double-click Backup and Restore Center (Vista) or Backup and Restore (Windows 7).

Step 2   To set up the backup, decide first whether to back up certain files or the whole computer. (In Windows 7, use the *Create a system image* option to create a complete backup of your system.) The Back Up Files wizard will open. Select where to save the backup and click Next. If you chose only a partial backup, select the file types you wish to back up from the list provided. Click Next. For partial backups, Windows also asks how often you want the backup to be updated. Click *Save settings and start backup*.

Step 3   To restore files, choose whether to restore only certain files or to restore a Windows Complete Backup and Restore image (referred to as a System Image in Windows 7). If you are performing a partial restoration, click *Restore files*. Select whether to restore the latest backup or an older one. Click Next. Then select where to restore the backup files to and click Start Restore. If you are overwriting any files, a window will pop up asking how to resolve the conflict.

→ **Note**

To do a complete restoration, you must reboot your system and open the System Recovery Options from the installation media.

30 MINUTES

Lab Exercise 8.02: Upgrading to Windows Vista SP2 and Configuring Automatic Updates

These systems have been around for some time, so there are probably a number of outdated patches and drivers. Windows Vista went through a major upgrade with Service Pack 2, so this is where you'll start. If you are working with a new installation of Windows Vista, Service Pack 2 should already be incorporated into the cabinet files, but these are old machines, so they will need some attention. Upgrading to Service Pack 2 is imperative to keeping the system up and running, secure, and compatible with new technology. To bring the OS up to date, you will first manually download and install Service Pack 2, and then configure Automatic Updates so Windows will take care of future updates on its own.

Learning Objectives

A competent technician should understand the importance of upgrading an OS with the latest service pack.

At the end of this lab, you'll be able to

- Upgrade Windows Vista to Service Pack 2
- Configure Windows Automatic Updates to update drivers, security patches, and utilities

Lab Materials and Setup

The materials you need for this lab are

- A working PC with Windows Vista (prior to Service Pack 2) installed
- An Internet connection

→ **Note**

The procedures for updating Windows and setting up Automatic Updates are very similar between Windows XP, Windows Vista, and Windows 7. Although this lab describes a Windows Vista upgrade, the concept remains the same for Windows XP and Windows 7.

Getting Down to Business

You will begin by downloading and installing Service Pack 2 for Windows Vista. Then you will learn how to configure Automatic Updates.

Step 1   You will need to procure Windows Vista Service Pack 2. Go to Microsoft's Web site and search for "Vista Service Pack 2," or go straight to http://technet.microsoft.com/en-us/windows/dd262148.aspx. The search should return a page with the title Service Pack 2 for Windows Server 2008 and Windows Vista; follow the directions on this page to download Service Pack 2. (You'll look at getting updates through Automatic Updates next.)

Step 2   Once the download finishes, log on to the system that you want to update. Open the folder where you have placed the files and complete the following steps:

a.   Double-click the setup file you downloaded.

b.   The Windows Vista Service Pack 2 setup wizard welcome screen appears (see Figure 8-2). Click Next to continue.

c.   The End User License Agreement screen displays next. Accept the agreement and click Next to continue.

d.   The setup wizard now inspects your machine, installs files, and upgrades your system. When the upgrade is complete, the wizard informs you that "Windows Vista Service Pack 2 is now installed on your computer" (see Figure 8-3).

e.   Click Finish and let the system reboot.

f.   After the machine reboots for the first time with Service Pack 2 installed, Windows gives you the opportunity to turn on Automatic Updates before it presents the logon screen. Decline this option for now; you will manually configure this in the next step.

Step 3   You will now configure the system to perform automatic updates. Log on to Windows and complete the following steps:

a.   In Windows XP, click Start | All Programs | Accessories | System Tools | Security Center. In Windows Vista, type **Security Center** in the Start Search bar. This opens the Windows Security Center window, where you'll find the configuration utility for Windows' Automatic Updates feature. Click Automatic Updates. In Windows 7, go to Control Panel | Windows Update.

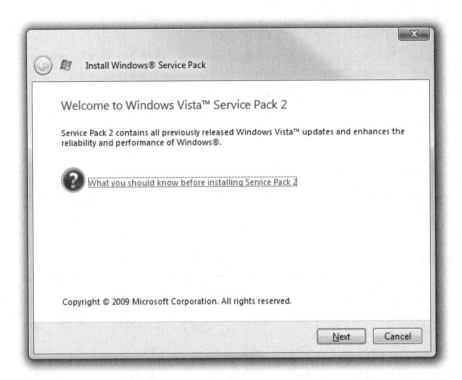

FIGURE 8-2 Welcome to the Windows Vista Service Pack 2 setup wizard

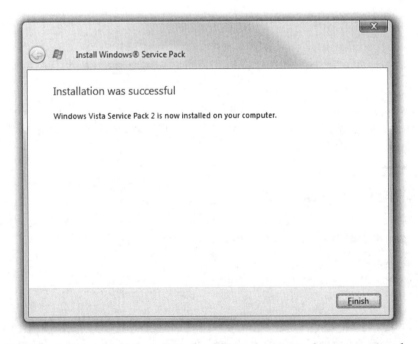

FIGURE 8-3 Completing the Windows Vista Service Pack 2 setup wizard

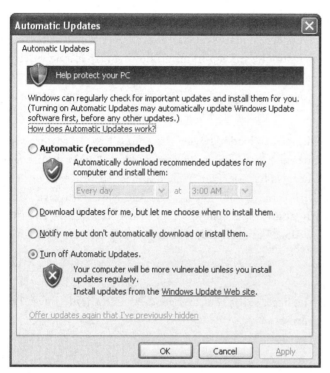

FIGURE 8-4 Automatic Updates configuration screen

✔ **Cross-Reference**

You will have the opportunity to work with antivirus software in Chapter 18.

---

b. This brings up the Automatic Updates configuration screen (see Figure 8-4) in Windows XP.
    Select the Automatic (recommended) option button and then click Apply. In Windows Vista/7,
    click *Change settings*, and then choose *Install updates automatically* from the drop-down menu.

 30 MINUTES

Lab Exercise 8.03: Installing Device Drivers in Windows

Installing new devices under Windows is easier than it has ever been. Assuming, of course, that you
start with compatible hardware, Windows will detect the new device and install the correct driver with
little prompting. If that doesn't work, it is often just a matter of updating the driver or using Roll Back
Driver. It's best to check the Internet for new drivers whenever you install a new device.

Even after a device has been installed, you should check for newer drivers periodically, even for devices that have been working fine. Manufacturers occasionally release new drivers aimed at optimizing the device or enabling it to work with some new technology. Keep in mind, however, that a new driver may cause unexpected problems with your operating system. Because of this, Windows XP introduced a feature that enables you to roll back to the previous (working) driver if something should go wrong with a driver update.

One of two wizards will assist you when you need to load a driver: the Found New Hardware Wizard or the Add New Hardware Wizard. Windows starts the Found New Hardware Wizard when it discovers some new hardware device while booting. If Windows has a driver in its database, it proceeds on its own. If not, the Found New Hardware Wizard will prompt you for one. The Add New Hardware Wizard enables you to add or update hardware manually at any time. There's a lot of overlap in how the two wizards work, so you'll look at just the Add New Hardware Wizard, which you can activate at any time.

Learning Objectives

Loading and removing device drivers is one of the basic skills that any good PC tech should have. The following lab exercise walks you through the process.

At the end of this lab, you'll be able to

- Load a device driver in Windows

- Roll back to a previously working driver

Lab Materials and Setup

The materials you need for this lab are

- A working PC with Windows XP, Windows Vista, or Windows 7 installed

- An Internet connection

Getting Down to Business

This lab covers the steps for installing and updating device drivers. You'll also look at the steps to roll back (uninstall) device drivers that turn out to be incompatible.

> → **Note**
>
> Adding hardware in Windows 7 has become so automated that you can't pretend to install a piece of hardware like you could in Windows XP and Windows Vista (as this lab exercise is about to instruct you to do). In the case of Windows 7, make sure your device is plugged in properly, and the OS will take care of the rest (though you might still need to supply drivers).

Step 1   The first step before you begin installing any new device is to make sure it's compatible with your current Windows OS. Microsoft has removed the Windows XP and Windows Vista Web sites that detail device compatibility with those OSs, but you can find the Windows 7 Compatibility Center at www.microsoft.com/windows/compatibility/windows-7/en-us/default.aspx.

Step 2   Now you'll walk through the process of adding a device using the Add Hardware Wizard:

a.   From the Window XP/Vista Control Panel, double-click Add Hardware. In Windows 7, open the Devices and Printers applet and click *Add a device*.

b.   On the Add Hardware Wizard's welcome screen, click Next. (Windows 7's Add a device wizard skips this step.)

✔ Hint

If the Add Hardware Wizard doesn't find any new hardware, it asks, "Have you already connected this hardware to your computer?" Select Yes or No, and follow the directions.

c.   Select the device you want to install or update by either selecting from the given list or choosing the Add a New Hardware Device item in the list box. In Windows 7, select the device from the list. If it's not on the list, chances are the device is not properly plugged in. (Windows 7 users should stop here.) For Windows XP/Vista users, select the last item in the list—*Add a new hardware device*—and then click Next.

d.   Click the *Install the hardware that I manually select from a list (Advanced)* option button, and then click Next.

e.   Select the type of hardware you're trying to install or update from the list. If your device doesn't fit the descriptions, select the Show All Devices item. When you've made your selection, click Next.

f.   If you chose the Show All Devices item, the wizard displays the *Select the device driver you want to install for this hardware* screen. If you chose a specific type of hardware, you'll be led off into a series of options for that type of hardware.

g.   Choose the Windows driver for your device, or click Have Disk and point to the location of the new driver you want to install. This driver generally is located either on the installation CD-ROM that came with the device, if you have it, or on your hard drive if you downloaded it from the manufacturer's Web site.

h.   Click Next. Windows is ready to install the driver.

i.   Click Next again, and click Finish when the installation is complete.

You should now have a driver that runs your newly loaded device. If the device isn't working properly and you're sure the driver loaded correctly, you can check online and see if there's a newer driver that you can download from the manufacturer's Web site.

Step 3   What if you have a device already installed and you want to update the driver to address a problem, improve performance, or just add a new feature? This step will take you through updating new drivers.

   a.   Begin by locating the updated driver. In most cases, the best way to obtain the updated driver is to search the Internet for the manufacturer's Web site. Search its site for your specific model, and download the most recent driver.

   b.   Go to Device Manager and expand the appropriate device category. Locate the device you want to update.

   c.   Double-click the device.

   d.   Select the Driver tab and click the Update Driver button (see Figure 8-5). This launches a wizard similar to the Add New Hardware Wizard.

✔ **Hint**

In all modern Windows operating systems, you can right-click on the device in Device Manager and update the driver without accessing its properties.

FIGURE 8-5 The Windows Vista Update Driver button

For Windows XP, select *Install from a list or specific location (Advanced)* and click Next. Select *Include this location in the search*, and browse to where you have saved the new driver.

For Windows Vista/7, click *Browse my computer for driver software*. Then choose *Let me pick from a list of device drivers on my computer*. Click the Have Disk button and then click Browse. You can locate the file from there.

You may be wondering, "What if I load a new driver, and my system doesn't work correctly anymore?" Well, you're in luck! Read the next step, and your question will be answered.

Step 4   If a driver is corrupt or if the wrong driver is installed, Windows has a bad habit of stopping dead in its tracks, rendering your PC useless. Windows XP and Vista/7 have a feature that keeps track of the drivers you install on a system and allows you to roll back to a previous one when a new one isn't working as it should.

a.   Go to Device Manager and locate the device you want to roll back.

b.   Double-click the device.

c.   Select the Driver tab. You can revert to the previous driver by clicking Roll Back Driver (see Figure 8-6).

FIGURE 8-6 Windows XP's Roll Back Driver button

Lab Analysis Test

1. Tommy wants to install a service pack for his Windows operating system but is unsure because he doesn't know what a service pack actually is or how to get one. Explain to Tommy what a service pack is and how to install one.

2. Jackie has a Windows 7 Professional computer with thousands of pictures and music files. Needless to say, she is very concerned about losing her data. She heard from a technician at her work that she should create an image of her computer every week and have it saved to her network storage device. Can Jackie's computer do this? If so, how would she make this happen?

3. Tammy has Windows 7 Ultimate 64-bit installed on her PC and is attempting to install drivers for a USB scanner that she was previously using on a Windows Vista Ultimate 32-bit PC. She has not been successful thus far and continues to get errors. She knows the scanner is fully functional. List some plausible reasons for the failure of the scanner installation.

4. Laurie has been given six computers in various stages of disrepair. None of the systems will boot. They are all Windows XP systems. A friend gives her some floppy disks labeled "ASR" and recommends that she boot the machines using these floppies. When she tries it, the machines display the message *Non-System disk or disk error, replace and press any key when ready*. Why?

5. William has been running his Windows XP system for a few days and notices a small yellow shield icon in the system tray/notification area. He calls you to ask what it might be. What do you think it is?

Key Term Quiz

Use the following terms to complete the following sentences. Not all terms will be used.

Add Hardware Wizard

Automated System Recovery (ASR)

Automatic Updates

Backup

Backup and Restore Center

ntbackup

Roll Back Driver

service packs

System Recovery options

Windows 7 Compatibility Center

1. To assist in the recovery of a system crash, Windows XP uses the _____ process, which requires a floppy disk to store critical system files.

2. If you update a driver on your computer for a video card that you have been using for a year and it ends up not working, you could use _____ to restore the original driver.

3. As operating systems age, many of the system files, drivers, and utilities are updated. It is recommended that Windows always has the latest _____ installed.

4. Use the _____ to ensure that your devices will work with Windows 7.

5. In Windows XP, you can use _____ from the command line to make and restore backups.

Chapter 9

Working with the
Command-Line Interface

Lab Exercises

The CompTIA A+ 220-802 exam's objectives stipulate that PC technicians should know some of the basic commands and functions available at the command-line interface in all versions of Windows. Why? Because they still work, and good techs use the command line often. You'll need a solid understanding of several basic command-line commands and a few advanced tasks. Commands such as cd, copy, and attrib, as well as the tasks of starting and stopping services, editing files, and converting file systems, should be part of your PC tech arsenal.

If you have a system crash and are able to gain access to the machine using Windows XP's Recovery Console or Windows Vista's or Windows 7's System Recovery Options menu, you'll really need to know the proper commands for navigating around your drives, folders, and files, and launching utilities that will get your OS up and running again. Also, when you start working with networks, the command-line interface on all Windows systems is invaluable.

✔ **Cross-Reference**

You will further explore the use of the Recovery Console and System Recovery Options in the lab exercises for Chapter 10. You will also have the opportunity to work with additional networking command-line utilities in the lab exercises for Chapter 12.

The command line can often provide a quicker way to accomplish a task than the graphical alternative. In cases where a virus, hard drive failure, or OS problem prevents you from booting to Windows, you need to know how to get around with the command line. The following labs are designed to give you the chance to practice your basic command-line skills so that when the need arises, the command line will be your friend.

✔ **Hint**

As you have worked through the labs in this manual, I have recommended often that you explore features, options, and components not specifically covered in the lab exercises. You have embarked on the journey to become a CompTIA A+ certified technician! Natural curiosity, enthusiasm, and determination will go a long way toward developing the understanding and experience you need to become a competent technician and pass the exam. These qualities are especially important when it comes to working with the command-line interface. As you navigate through the following labs, it is easy to take a left when you should have taken a right and get lost in subdirectories, mistype a command, or delete a file you didn't want to. Don't let it discourage you.

Making mistakes while learning is good, and learning from those mistakes is great! If you get lost, explore ways to get back to where you need to be—you're unlikely to hurt anything. If you really get lost, work with your instructor or a more experienced classmate to determine where you went astray, then work through it again.

 30 MINUTES

Lab Exercise 9.01: Configuring the Command-Line Window

Before you can use the command line, you need to know the basics: ways to access it, manipulate and customize the look of it within the GUI, and close it down properly. This lab covers those basics.

Learning Objectives

In this lab, you'll practice opening, resizing, customizing, and closing a command-line window.

At the end of this lab, you'll be able to

- Open a command-line window from within the Windows operating system

- Resize the command-line window

- Customize the look of the command-line window

- Exit the command-line window

Lab Materials and Setup

The materials you need for this lab are

- A PC with Windows installed

Getting Down to Business

The first thing you'll need to do, obviously, is get to a command line. Spend the next several minutes becoming familiar with accessing the command-line window.

✔ **Cross-Reference**

For details on how to access the command-line interface, refer to the "Accessing the Command Line" section in Chapter 9 of *Mike Meyers' CompTIA A+ Guide to 802: Managing and Troubleshooting PCs.*

Step 1 Turn on your system and wait for the Windows desktop to appear. Then follow these steps:

    a.   In Windows XP, select Start | Run, then type **cmd** (see Figure 9-1). In Windows Vista/7, select Start, then type **cmd** into the Search bar.

    b.   In XP, click OK to open a command-line window. In Vista/7, press ENTER.

Step 2 There are three ways to change the size of the command-line window for better viewing:

- Use the resize arrows along the edges of the windows (this will not work when the window is maximized).

- Use the minimize/maximize button in the upper-right corner of the window.

- Press ALT-ENTER to toggle between the full screen mode and a window.

Step 3 Windows XP's default prompt displays C:\Documents and Settings\username>, while the Windows Vista/7 prompt displays C:\Users\username>.

To the right of the prompt, you'll see a flashing cursor indicating that it's waiting for your input. There's also a scroll bar along the right side of the window. Sometimes your command causes more information to be displayed than the window can hold, and it's really useful to be able to scroll back up and see what messages were displayed.

You'll now execute a few commands for the purpose of exploring the scrolling issue. The change directory command (cd) lets you change the focus of the working directory displayed in the command-line window. The directory command (dir) lists the filename, extension, file size (in bytes), and creation date/time of the files in the current folder.

You are going to change from the current working directory to a subdirectory with hundreds of files. Type **cd C:\Windows\System32** (C:\ is the root directory, Windows is the system folder, and System32 is where many of the system configuration and driver files are stored). You may have to use a different drive letter or system folder name to arrive at the System32 directory.

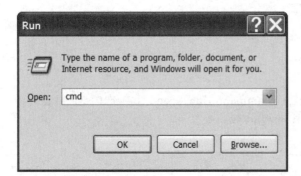

FIGURE 9-1 Opening the Windows XP command-line window

Now type **dir** and press ENTER. The System32 folder contains over 15,000 files, so the command-line window will not be able to display all of the information at once. If there's more than one screen's worth of information, it will keep scrolling out of sight until everything has been displayed. You can use the scroll bar to go back a few screens' worth—give it a try.

If you were actually trying to work with a few of the files in the folder, you'd probably be out of luck, because you can't scroll back more than a few screens. To address this problem, there's a command you can use that forces the information to be displayed one screenful at a time. Type **dir /p** and then press ENTER. Adding the /p switch to the command tells it to pause after each screenful of text. Press the SPACEBAR to display the next screenful. You can't go back if you're too quick with the SPACEBAR, so take a good look at each screen! If you tire of paging through the screens, you can end the command by pressing CTRL-C.

Step 4   Just as with most applications in the Windows environment, if you right-click the title bar and select Properties, you can configure some of the features of the command-line window. The following tabs appear in the Command Prompt Properties dialog box:

- **Options**   Configure the cursor size, command history, display options, and edit options

- **Font**   Select from a limited set of command-line fonts and sizes

- **Layout**   Set the screen buffer size and window size, and position the window on the monitor screen

- **Colors**   Configure the color of screen text, screen background, pop-up text, and pop-up background

> **→ Note**
>
> Some features differ depending on which operating system you are using. For example, Windows Vista does not offer the Display Options panel in the Command Prompt Properties dialog box.

Explore some of the settings you can change, and feel free to set up the command-line window to your personal taste. I grew up on early IBM machines, in the days when owning a color monitor meant that you had an electric green or bright orange character on a black monochrome screen. See if you can re-create this wonderful look!

Step 5   There are two common ways to close a command-line window:

- Click the × in the upper-right corner of the window. This method isn't recommended if the window is actively running a program. You should wait until you see the prompt before clicking the ×.

- Type **exit** at the command line, and press ENTER. I prefer this method, because I can be sure the window is inactive when I quit.

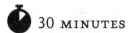 30 MINUTES

Lab Exercise 9.02: Navigating Basic Commands

Before you can really use the command line, you must know the basic commands needed to navigate around a drive to locate and modify files. In this lab exercise, you'll learn more basic command-line commands that you would need to know when troubleshooting your or your client's PC.

✔ **Hint**

For the most part, mistakes such as spelling a command or filename incorrectly won't be disastrous for you. But it is possible to misspell just incorrectly enough to delete the wrong file, or something similar, especially if you're using wildcards (I'll get to those in a bit). Typically, though, if you misspell a command or filename, the command line won't know what you're asking it to do and therefore won't do anything, or won't know what file you're asking to work with, and will return an error message.

Learning Objectives

In this lab, you'll learn or review commands for directory and file management while using the command line.

At the end of this lab, you'll be able to

- Use commands to view, navigate, create, and delete directories using the command line

- Use commands to copy, move, rename, and delete files using the command line

Lab Materials and Setup

The materials you need for this lab are

- At least one working computer running Windows

✔ **Hint**

Any version of Windows will work just fine for this exercise, as long as you understand that the results may appear differently on your screen.

Getting Down to Business

Hundreds of commands and switches are available to you from the command-line interface. Although it is beyond the scope of these exercises to explore every possible command and its associated switches, you should spend the time in this lab exercise working with the specific ones that form the cornerstone of command-line navigation. These are the basic commands you'll use most often when working with the command line.

Step 1 Follow these steps:

a. Launch the command-line interface in Windows XP by typing **cmd** in the Run dialog box and either clicking OK or pressing ENTER. In Windows Vista/7, access the command-line interface through the Start menu Search bar with the same command.

b. When you first open the command-line window, your prompt might not be focused on the root directory. Because you want to focus on the root directory at this time, you must change directories before continuing.

The cd (change directory) command changes the directory the system is focused on. When you use the cd command, you must type the command followed by a space and then the name of the directory you want to view. This is true of all command-line commands. First, type the command followed by a space and then any options. Because you want to focus on the root of C: and the name of the root is the backslash (\), you'd type in the following and press ENTER (assuming that you're in the C: drive to begin with):

```
C:\Documents and Settings\username>cd \
```

Notice that the prompt has changed its focus to C:\> (see Figure 9-2).

Step 2 Probably the most frequently typed command is the request to display the contents of a directory (dir). Because the command-line interface doesn't continually display everything the way a GUI does, you have to ask it to display specific information. The way you display the contents of a directory is to focus on the particular directory or subdirectory, and enter the command **dir**.

Let's take a look at the contents of your root (C:\) directory. You should already be focused there from the previous step in this exercise. Type **dir** at the command prompt and press ENTER.

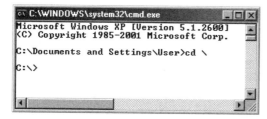

FIGURE 9-2 Changing the command-line focus

✔ **Hint**

From now on, when you see an instruction to type a command, assume that you should press ENTER afterward to complete the request (command). Otherwise, the command line will sit there, waiting patiently until the sun grows cold.

Now here's where it gets a little gray. Because I don't know what's in your root directory, there's no way to predict exactly what your C:\ contents will look like—but it's a good bet that *something* will be different from what I show you here! In theory at least, your display should be similar to Figure 9-3. Windows XP, Vista, and 7 will have the same basic look.

Notice that using the dir command in any Windows operating system gives you the following information:

- Filename

- File extension

- Date and time of creation

- Size in bytes

- Designation as either a directory (<DIR>) or a file

- The number of files in the directory

- The amount of free space on the drive

Look at your particular results and note the mixture of files, which display a size in bytes, and directories, which have the annotation <DIR> after their name. In the preceding examples, AVG7QT.DAT is a file of 12,288,463 bytes, and Windows, Program Files, and Documents and Settings are all names of directories.

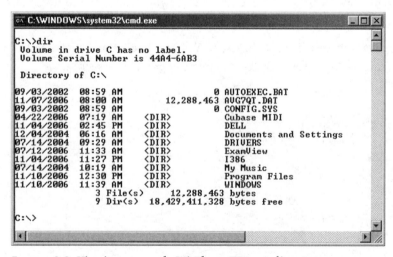

FIGURE 9-3 Viewing a sample Windows XP root directory

Note whether you see the following files or folders in your root (C:\) directory (you won't see them all):

	Yes	No
autoexec.bat		
config.sys		
WinNT		
Windows		
Documents and Settings		
Program Files		

List the names of all the directories you see displayed in your root directory:

_____   _____

_____   _____

_____   _____

_____   _____

_____   _____

_____   _____

Step 3   The biggest challenge when working with the command prompt is remembering what exactly to type to achieve your goal. Learning the commands is one thing, but each command can have switches and options that modify it somewhat. Also, you may have noticed that the screen fills up and scrolls from top to bottom, making it difficult to view all the information you might need. Let's look at a command to clear the screen and another to provide assistance with how to use the commands.

   a.   Type the command **cls**. What happened? _____

   b.   Type the command **dir /?**. What happened? _____

The question mark (/?) is a standard help switch for most commands. Even though I've used these commands for decades, I still use the /? switch occasionally to remember what options are available for a specific command.

✔ **Hint**

Be careful not to confuse the backslash (\) and the forward slash (/). In a command-line world, the path uses the backslash and command switches use the forward slash.

At this point, a huge amount of help information is displayed (see Figure 9-4), so you may feel like you're in command overload! Take comfort in the fact that dir is the most complex command. Other

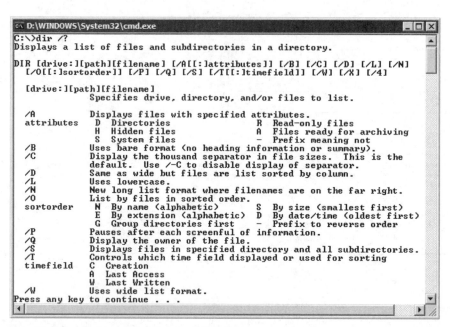

FIGURE 9-4 Viewing the syntax of the dir command

commands are more straightforward with their help. You don't need to know what all the switches are—just know how to use the help switch (/?) to find them! The main thing to learn is the syntax of the commands.

Everything in brackets ([ ]) is optional for the command. Notice that dir is the only mandatory part in that command even though there are several optional switches and parameters. This is the same for all the commands. The system will use defaults if you don't specify a switch or optional parameter. It's the defaults that can cause problems if you're not careful when using these commands. Now follow these steps:

   c. Put a known good disc with files in your optical drive and let it spin up and come to rest. Cancel any windows that automatically open and proceed to the next substep.

   d. Type **dir**, and examine the resulting list of files and folders. Did they change from the previous step? _____

      Do you think it read the disc? Probably not, because your prompt is still focused on the root directory of the hard drive.

   e. Type **dir d:** (replace d: with the appropriate drive letter for your optical drive, if necessary) and examine the resulting list of files and folders. Did they change this time? Aha! The option of [drive:] was needed to change the focus of the dir command to the optical drive.

The [drive:] option will work for any of the drive letters. Optical discs and USB thumb drives are all fair game as well. When you use this option, you can look at those other drives without switching from the directory you're in.

Step 4   Type **dir /?** to look at two more optional switches: /p and /w. The /p switch is used when all the information will not fit on one screen, and /w is used to see a condensed listing of the directory.

Let's focus on a different directory. Remember, the cd command will let you change the directory you want to focus on:

a.   Type **cd \Windows**.

b.   Type **cls**.

c.   Type **dir** at the command prompt. This shows way too much data for the screen to display all at once.

d.   Type **dir /p** at the command prompt. This very useful switch causes the display to stop scrolling (pause) after each screen, waiting until you press the SPACEBAR to show you more. In directories with lots of files, this is a lifesaver!

✔ **Hint**

If you want to stop a process that seems to be running forever, you can press CTRL-C. The process will end, and you'll get the prompt back.

e.   Type **dir /w** at the command prompt. This switch is convenient when you're simply looking to see if a particular file resides in a particular directory, because it shows a "wide" list with filenames but no details.

f.   Now practice moving around in the command window. Right now you're focused on the Windows directory. Go back to the root directory by typing **cd **. To change the focus to another directory, use the **cd** command as you've learned. Use the **dir** command to see what directories you have available in your current folder.

g.   Try going to a subdirectory in another subdirectory and listing the contents. Look back at the list of directories you made previously and select one. Issue the **cd** command followed by a backslash (\) and the name of the target directory. For example, to switch to the Documents and Settings directory in the previous listing, type this:

```
C:\Windows>cd \Documents and Settings
```

Do this using several of the directory names you wrote down previously, and then type **dir** to see what's there. Are there any subdirectories in this directory? Make a note of them.

_____   _____

_____   _____

_____   _____

✔ Hint

After you've changed the prompt focus many times, you may become confused about exactly where you are. You can always get to the root directory from any focus by typing **cd **.

Step 5 A Windows installation creates a Drivers directory, within a directory called System32, under the Windows directory in the root of the C: drive. To go to the Drivers directory, you don't have to do the cd command three times unless you really want to. If you know the path, you can go directly to the subdirectory with one cd command.

Go to the Drivers subdirectory by typing this at the command prompt:

```
C:\>cd \Windows\System32\Drivers
```

Your prompt should now look like Figure 9-5.

Type **dir** to see what's there.

One final navigation hint—you can change directories going back up toward the top level without returning directly to the root. If you want to go up a single directory level, you can type **cd** followed immediately by two periods (sometimes referred to as *cd dot dot*). For example, typing this takes you up one level to the System32 directory:

```
C:\>\Windows\System32\Drivers>cd..
C:\>\Windows\System32>
```

Do it again to go to the Windows directory:

```
C:\>\Windows\System32>cd..
C:\>\Windows>
```

Type the command once more to arrive at the root directory:

```
C:\>\Windows>cd..
C:\>
```

Take a minute and practice using the cd command. Go down a few levels on the directory tree, and then jump up a few, jump back to the root directory, and then jump down another path. Practice is the only way to get comfortable moving around in a command-prompt environment, and a good PC technician needs to be comfortable doing this.

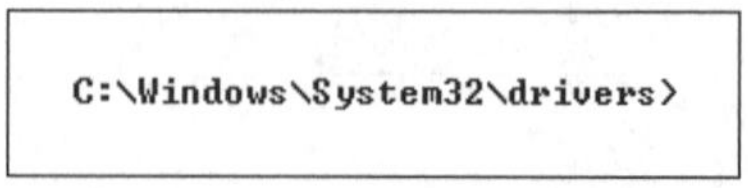

```
C:\Windows\System32\drivers>
```

FIGURE 9-5 Focusing on the Drivers subdirectory

Step 6 Sometimes a technician needs to make a directory to store files on the system. This could be a temporary directory for testing purposes, or maybe a place to store something more permanently (diagnostic reports, for example). In any case, it's important that you know how to create and remove a directory. The CompTIA A+ 220-802 exam will test you on this. Follow these steps:

a. Be sure you're in the root directory. If you aren't there, type **cd ** to return to the root directory, where you'll add a new top-level directory. Actually, you can make a directory anywhere in the file structure, but you don't want to lose track of where it is, so make your new directory in the root. Do this using the md (make directory) command.

b. Type **md /?** to see how the command is structured and view the available options (see Figure 9-6).

c. At the command prompt, type the following:

   C:\>**md Corvette**

d. When the command line just presents a fresh prompt, it means that everything worked correctly. But to verify that the directory was actually made, type **dir** to see your new directory in the list. It's as simple as that!

✖ **Warning**

Be careful—the new directory will always be created wherever the prompt is focused when you issue the command, whether that's where you meant to put it or not.

---

e. Be sure you're in the root directory (type **cd**), and prepare to remove your new Corvette directory.

   Removing a directory requires the RD (remove directory) command and two conditions: First, the directory must be empty, and second, your system must not currently be focused on the directory about to be deleted.

f. Type this command:

   C:\>**rd Corvette**

   The directory has been deleted.

g. Type **dir** to confirm that Corvette has been removed.

```
C:\>md /?
Creates a directory.

MKDIR [drive:]path
MD [drive:]path
```

FIGURE 9-6 Using the md command

✔ Hint

Be *very* careful when you remove directories or delete files in the command line. It isn't as forgiving as Windows, which allows you to change your mind and "undelete" things. When you delete a file or directory using the command line, it's gone. If you make a mistake, there's nothing left to do but pout. So think carefully before you delete, and be sure you know *what* you're deleting before you do it—you'll save yourself a great deal of agony. Also pay attention to the directory you're currently focused on, to ensure that you're in the correct one.

Step 7   Sometimes you know the name of the file you want to use, but you don't know in which directory it's located. In this case, working with files and directories can become quite tedious. To help you locate files more easily, here are some switches and wildcards you can use with the dir command:

a.   Look again at the results of the **dir /?** command, and find the /s switch. The /s switch will look for a file(s) in the specified (focus) directory and all subdirectories under that directory.

b.   Windows has a file named xcopy.exe somewhere on the drive. Locate the path to the xcopy.exe file using the **/s** switch.

c.   Start with your command prompt at the root directory (**cd **).

d.   Type this command:

    C:\>dir xcopy.exe

If the file isn't in the root directory, nothing will be displayed.

e.   Now try the new switch you just learned about to search all subdirectories. Type this command:

    C:\>dir /s xcopy.exe

f.   On my system, the file shows up in two places: in the C:\Windows\System32 directory and in the C:\Windows\System32\dllcache directory (see Figure 9-7).

Another way to look for a file is to use a *wildcard*. The most common wildcard is the asterisk character (*), which you can use in place of all or part of a filename to make a command act on more than one file at a time. Wildcards work with all commands that use filenames.

The * wildcard replaces any number of letters before or after the dot in the filename. A good way to think of the * wildcard is "I don't care." Replace the part of the filename that you don't care about with *.

For example, if you want to locate all the readme files on a hard drive and you don't care what the extension is, type the following:

    C:\>dir /s/p readme.*

The result is a list of all the readme files on the hard drive. Notice that I used the /s switch to look in all the directories and used the /p switch so that I can view one screenful of results at a time (see Figure 9-8).

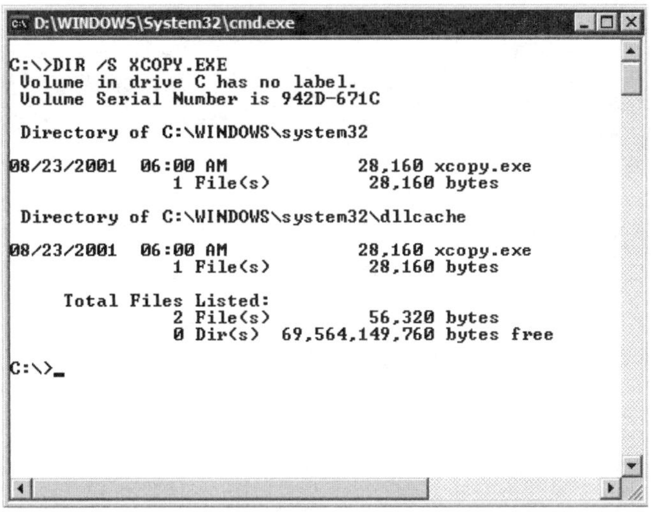

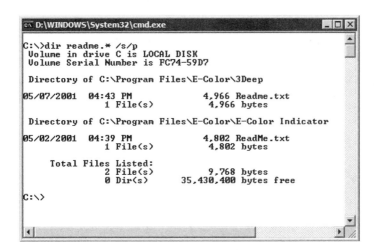

FIGURE 9-7 Locating the xcopy.exe file

You can use the * wildcard for any number of characters. For example, not all companies use readme.txt as the help filename. Some use read.me, and others may use read.

Because read is common to all those variations, let's find all the files with "read" in the filename. You should be prepared to see a long list of every file with "read" in the name, not just the readme files.

Type the following:

```
C:\>dir /s/p *read*.*
```

Figure 9-9 shows the first screenful of results from my system. I found 104 files with "read" somewhere in the filename. How many files and directories did you find with "read" as part of the name?

FIGURE 9-8 Using a wildcard to locate files

```
D:\WINDOWS\System32\cmd.exe - DIR /S/P *read*.*

 Volume in drive C is LOCAL DISK
 Volume Serial Number is FC74-59D7

 Directory of C:\Program Files\E-Color\3Deep

05/07/2001  04:43 PM             4,966 Readme.txt
05/07/2001  04:43 PM             4,966 ReadmeNT.txt
               2 File(s)          9,932 bytes

 Directory of C:\Program Files\E-Color\E-Color Indicator

05/02/2001  04:39 PM             4,802 ReadMe.txt
               1 File(s)          4,802 bytes

 Directory of C:\Work Files

10/20/2001  12:30 PM             6,895 Style Guide Proofreader's and Editor's Sy
mbols.htm
02/21/2003  01:02 PM    <DIR>          Style Guide Proofreader's and Editor's Sy
mbols_files
               1 File(s)          6,895 bytes

Press any key to continue . . . _
```

FIGURE 9-9 Using a wildcard to locate *read*.* files

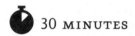 30 MINUTES

Lab Exercise 9.03: Using Command-Line Tools

Commands such as type, copy, move, rename, and delete are used for manipulating files, such as you would be doing while troubleshooting a client's PC. These are more of the commands that every working tech should know by heart.

Learning Objectives

In this lab, you'll use commands for file management.

At the end of this lab, you'll be able to

- View text (.txt) documents from the command-line interface

- Rename files using the command-line interface

- Copy files using the command-line interface

- Move files using the command-line interface

- Delete files using the command-line interface

Lab Materials and Setup

The materials you need for this lab are

- At least one working computer running Windows

Getting Down to Business

You might refer to these as the "second-tier" commands. Once you've used commands such as dir, md, and cd to navigate and create folders, you can use the following commands to manipulate individual files.

→ **Note**

This lab exercise is written assuming you are using Windows XP. However, you can perform the entire exercise in Windows Vista/7 by using C:\Users\%USERNAME%\Documents instead of C:\Documents and Settings\%USERNAME%\My Documents.

Step 1 Open Notepad by clicking Start | All Programs | Accessories | Notepad. Type the following sentence and save the file in the My Documents or Documents folder as **command line test.txt**:

This is a small sentence of text created in Notepad.

Close Notepad.

Step 2 You will now navigate to your My Documents/Documents folder using the command-line interface and verify that the file is there and contains readable text:

    a.   If you don't already have the command-line window open, get to a command prompt.

    b.   Enter the following commands:

```
C:\>cd \Documents and Settings\%USERNAME%\My Documents
C:\Documents and Settings\%USERNAME%\My Documents\>dir /p
```

✔ **Hint**

The variable %USERNAME% (including the preceding and trailing percent signs) in the command-line syntax represents the user name you're currently using. Microsoft has assembled many variables that can be used in this manner, such as %SYSTEMROOT% to represent the system folder (usually named Windows). You may actually use the variable in the command-line syntax to have the system insert your user name (the folder where all of your personal settings and saved documents are) in the path. I have included a generic example of the use of this variable in Figure 9-10.

Do you see the file you created? (It should be called command line test.txt.) _____

FIGURE 9-10 Using an environment variable to insert the user name

Now you will use another command to verify that the file is a text file containing readable text. There are many ways to do this; you'll use one of the simplest methods. The type command displays the contents of a text file, but doesn't allow you to edit or manipulate the text in any way.

   c.   Enter the following (carefully enter the line in the exact syntax as shown, including the quotation marks):

       `C:\Documents and Settings\%USERNAME%\My Documents\>`**`type "command line test.txt"`**

You should see the text that you entered earlier. All of the text should be displayed, although you may have to resize your command-line window to see all of it, and even then it won't be pretty.

The other thing you may have noticed is that to access the text file, you had to add quotation marks to the beginning and the end of the filename. This is because the command line only understands spaces as breaks between commands and operators or switches. Leave the quote marks out of the command line and run the **type** command again. What happened?

You should see something similar to the output in Figure 9-11.

You're going to use this file in the next few steps, and it will be easier to work with if its format conforms to the 8.3 rule. In the early days of MS-DOS, filenames could only be eight characters long, with a three-character extension after the period. The three-character extension has remained throughout all versions of Microsoft operating systems (though there are common exceptions to that rule, such as .docx for Microsoft Word files), but you can now use up to 255 characters (with spaces) as the filename. To make

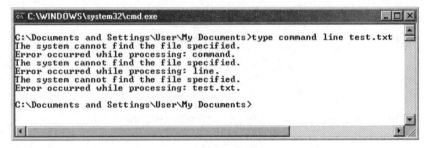

FIGURE 9-11 Results of running type without using quotation marks

this file easier to work with in the command line, you'll use the ren (rename) command to change the filename.

    d.   Type the following command:

```
C:\Documents and Settings\%USERNAME%\My Documents\>ren "command line test.txt"
cmdlntst.txt
```

    e.   Now confirm that this has worked by typing the following command:

```
C:\Documents and Settings\%USERNAME%\My Documents\>type cmdlntst.txt
```

Great! Now you will be able to type the filename more quickly as you complete the rest of the exercise.

Step 3   At the command prompt, type **cd ** to change your focus to the root directory.

You'll now create a new directory called Study in the root so that you can do some copying and moving. The only difference between copying and moving is that copy leaves the original file in the same place (as a backup) with a duplicate made elsewhere, whereas the move command relocates the original file to a new location with no backup available. They're otherwise similar, so once you've learned the copy command, you've pretty much learned the move command too! Follow these steps:

    a.   Make a directory named Study by typing the following:

```
C:\>md Study
```

    b.   Verify that the directory is there by using the **dir** command.

       Now follow these steps for copying your file named cmdlntst.txt to the new Study directory:

    c.   Change the focus of the command prompt to the Study directory:

```
C:\>cd Study
```

    d.   Copy the cmdlntst.txt file to the Study directory:

```
C:\Study>copy "C:\Documents and Settings\%USERNAME%\My Documents\cmdlntst.txt"
C:\Study\cmdlntst.txt
```

Here, copy is the command, "C:\Documents and Settings\%USERNAME%\My Documents\cmdlntst.txt" is the current location and name of the file (notice the use of the quotation marks and the %USERNAME% variable once again), and C:\Study\cmdlntst.txt is the target location and name of the file.

The entire command and response will look similar to Figure 9-12.

FIGURE 9-12 The copy command and response

e. Run the **dir** command to see if you copied the file. If the file isn't there, carefully repeat the previous steps or ask your instructor for help.

f. Change your directory focus back to the My Documents folder (**cd \Documents and Settings\%USERNAME%\My Documents**) and run the **dir** command to see if the original cmdlntst.txt file is still there.

✔ Hint

If you're already in the target directory, you don't need to include the target path in the command. My idea of copying or moving files is to start in the directory to which you want to copy the files. Then you can bring the files to where you are. Each time you copy or move a file, you can run the dir command to see if it's actually there. The other way of sending a file to a directory can be troublesome if you're moving files, because you may accidentally send them to a wrong directory and waste time looking for them.

Another good use of the copy command is to make a backup copy of a file and rename it at the same time, so that the two files can reside in the same directory.

g. To make a backup of the cmdlntst.txt text file, type the following command:

```
C:\Study\>copy cmdlntst.txt cmdlntst.bak
```

You now have three copies of the same file; you will clean these up in the last step.

Step 4 The last two commands you will work with in this step are the move and del (delete) commands. First, you will delete the copy of cmdlntst.txt that you copied into the Study folder in the last step. You will then move the file permanently from the My Documents folder to the Study folder. Follow these steps:

a. Change the focus of the command prompt to the Study directory:

```
C:\>cd Study
```

b. Delete the cmdlntst.txt file from the Study directory:

```
C:\Study\>del cmdlntst.txt
```

c. Run the **dir** command to see if you deleted the file. If the file isn't there, you deleted it.

Now you will follow the steps to move the file from My Documents to the Study folder. You will then verify that the file is in the Study folder and no longer in the My Documents folder.

d. Make sure the focus of the command prompt is still the Study directory.

e. Move the cmdlntst.txt file to the Study directory:

```
C:\Study>move "C:\Documents and Settings\%USERNAME%\My Documents\cmdlntst.txt"
C:\Study\cmdlntst.txt
```

In this case, move is the command, "C:\Documents and Settings\%USERNAME%\My Documents\cmdlntst.txt" is the current location and name of the file (notice the use of the quotation marks and the %USERNAME% variable once again), and C:\Study\cmdlntst.txt is the target location and name of the file.

f. Run the **dir** command to see if you moved the file. If the file isn't there, repeat the previous steps or ask your instructor for help.

g. Change your directory focus back to the My Documents folder (**cd \Documents and Settings\%USERNAME%\My Documents**) and run the **dir** command to see if the original cmdlntst.txt file is still there.

Do you see it? _____

Why or why not? _____

You should now have two copies of the file in the Study directory, cmdlntst.txt and cmdlntst.bak. The file should have been moved from the My Documents directory.

 60 MINUTES

Lab Exercise 9.04: Advanced Command-Line Utilities

In Windows, you can perform many tasks either from the GUI or from the command-line window. The CompTIA A+ 220-802 exam wants you to be comfortable with both methods to accomplish these tasks. To practice your skills with the command-line versions of these tasks, work through the following scenarios and steps to explore the attributes, the Print Spooler service, and the NTFS file system, all with the view from the command prompt.

Learning Objectives

In this lab, you'll work through three scenarios.

At the end of this lab, you'll be able to

- Work with the attrib and edit utilities
- Start and stop services with the net command
- Convert file systems

Lab Materials and Setup

The materials you need for this lab are

- At least one working computer running Windows

- A hard drive with at least 1 GB of unallocated space, or a 1-GB or greater partition formatted with the FAT32 file system

---

✔ **Hint**

If the machines configured with multiple hard drives are still available from Lab Exercise 4.05, "Implementing Software RAID 0 with Disk Management," you can convert these back to basic disks and format them with FAT32 to use in Step 3 of this exercise.

Getting Down to Business

Working through commands as you have in the prior exercises is an excellent method to explore the commands and their usage, but it can seem a little sterile since the commands are isolated and out of context. The next few steps are built around scenarios common in the workplace, requiring you to perform tasks that incorporate both commands you have learned in prior exercises and new commands that will be introduced as needed.

Step 1 In the steps that follow, you will use the attrib command to alter the attributes of a text file.

    a.   Create a new folder in the root directory. Name it **Folder**. Inside that folder, create a new text document and name it **text.txt**.

    b.   Using your favorite method, launch the command prompt and change your focus to the new folder you created.

    c.   To list the files and all of their attributes, use the attrib command:

```
C:\Folder>attrib
```

Because the folder contains one file, the only file that should be listed is your new text document. Notice the *A* to the left of where text.txt is listed. This means that the Archive attribute has been applied. To make this blank text file more secure, we'll add two more attributes: r (read-only) and h (hidden). For more options, type **attrib /?**.

    d.   To change the attributes for text.txt, type the following command:

```
C:\Folder>attrib +r +h text.txt
```

This will add the read-only and hidden attributes to the text file. Verify this by using My Computer/Computer to navigate to the folder and checking its contents. Do any files show up in the folder? _____

e. Now change the attributes for text.txt again so that it's not read-only or hidden anymore. Type the following command:

```
C:\Folder>attrib -r -h text.txt
```

Return again to the folder in My Computer/Computer and verify that the text file has reappeared.

Step 2 One recurring problem you will run into in the field is that one of the services in Windows will stall—in particular the Print Spooler. The Print Spooler is a holding area for print jobs, and it's especially important for network printers. If the print device runs out of paper while printing a document, you may have to stop and start the Print Spooler to enable the print device to receive jobs again. Typically you just open the Computer Management console, select Services, and restart the service. However, there may be times when it is more convenient or just plain necessary to accomplish this task from the command-line interface.

The following steps walk you through stopping and starting the Print Spooler from the command-line interface:

a. Launch the Services console by opening the Control Panel, launching the Administrative Tools applet, and double-clicking Services.

b. Scroll down and highlight the Print Spooler, then select Action | Properties. You should see that the Print Spooler is started and running (see Figure 9-13).

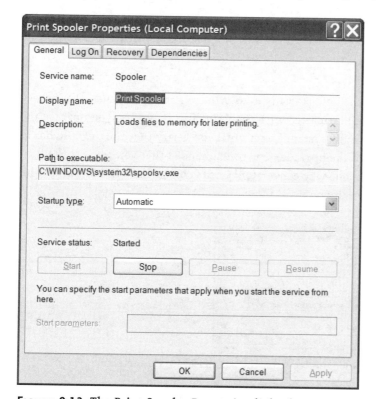

FIGURE 9-13 The Print Spooler Properties dialog box

c. Launch the command-line interface and change the focus to the root directory.

d. Type the following command at the prompt:

`C:\net stop spooler`

The command line should inform you that the Print Spooler service is stopping, and then that the Print Spooler service was stopped successfully (see Figure 9-14).

✔ **Cross-Reference**

You will explore the net command-line utility in the lab exercises for Chapter 12. If you would like to explore the net command while working on this lab, type **net /?**.

---

e. Using ALT-TAB, change your focus to the Print Spooler Properties dialog box you opened earlier. You should be able to confirm that the Print Spooler service has been stopped (see Figure 9-15).

f. Change the focus back to the command-line window, and type the following command at the prompt:

`C:\net start spooler`

The command line should inform you that the Print Spooler service is starting, and then that the Print Spooler service was started successfully (see Figure 9-16).

In the real-world scenario, your Print Spooler service would be restarted, and you should have a healthy, functioning print server once again. Now you just have to figure out where you stored the extra toner!

Step 3 Many of the legacy systems in the field started out as Windows 2000 machines. Often, these systems' hard drives were partitioned and formatted with the FAT32 file system. As you upgrade these systems, you may want to leave the FAT32 file system intact until you verify that the upgrade has been successful. After successful completion of the upgrade, it is recommended that you convert the file system to NTFS. This is a nondestructive, one-way conversion! Once you switch to NTFS, you will have to delete the data and reformat the partition if you want to revert to FAT32.

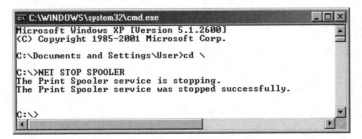

FIGURE 9-14 Stopping the Print Spooler service from the command-line interface

FIGURE 9-15 The Print Spooler Properties dialog box after stopping the service

In this step, you will create a FAT32 partition (unless you already have one from earlier labs) and then use the command-line utility called convert to convert the partition to NTFS.

a. Boot a computer system with at least 1 GB of unallocated hard drive space. If you have access to the system you used to explore RAID 0 (striping), you can use the extra hard drives installed in the system.

b. Launch the Disk Management console. Right-click My Computer/Computer and select Manage.

c. Click Disk Management.

d. Right-click an area of unallocated space and select New Volume from the drop-down menu.

e. Follow the wizard instructions to create a FAT32 partition of at least 1 GB.

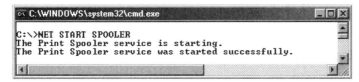

FIGURE 9-16 Starting the Print Spooler service from the command-line interface

---

✔ **Cross-Reference**

To refresh your Disk Management skills, refer to Chapter 4, Lab Exercise 4.03, "Using Windows Tools to Create and Format Partitions."

---

f.   Close the Disk Management console and double-click My Computer/Computer. Create and save a text file to the new drive to verify that the drive is accessible. Right-click the drive and select Properties; notice the tabs and file system (see Figure 9-17).

Now that you have a FAT32 partition, you can launch the command-line window and convert the file system from FAT32 to NTFS. You will then verify that the conversion was indeed nondestructive by opening the text file you created earlier.

g.   Launch the command-line window and change the focus to the root directory using the **cd ** command.

h.   Type the following command at the prompt (substitute the drive letter for your FAT32 partition):

    C:**convert e: /fs:ntfs**

Your results should look similar to Figure 9-18.

i.   Exit the command-line window and double-click My Computer/Computer.

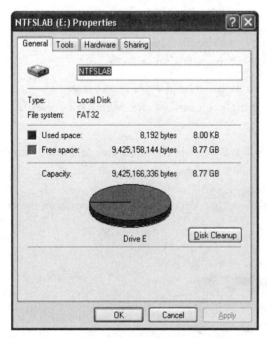

FIGURE 9-17   FAT32 partition properties

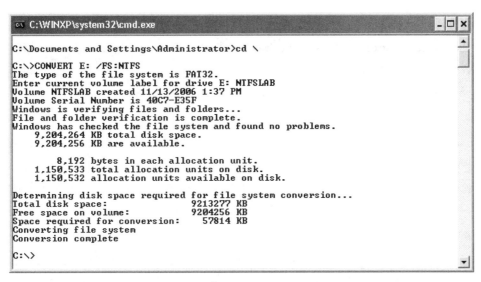

FIGURE 9-18 Converting a partition from FAT32 to NTFS

j.   Right-click the drive that you just converted and select Properties. Your drive should now be formatted with the NTFS file system. Notice the additional tabs for Security and Quota (see Figure 9-19).

k.   Close the Properties dialog box and double-click the drive. The text document you created earlier during the setup should still be there and accessible.

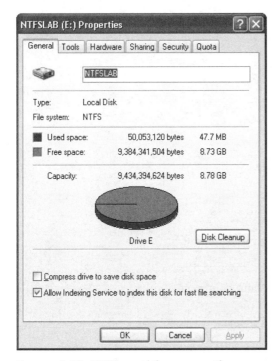

FIGURE 9-19 NTFS partition properties

Lab Analysis Test

1. Nate would like to make backup copies of all of his Word documents in the root directory. He types the following at the command prompt:

    `C:\>copy c:\*.docx`

    Will this command work? Why or why not? What will it do?

2. Which command(s) would you use to make a full copy of a file in the same directory under a different name?

3. The xcopy.exe file is in the System32 directory, which is in the Windows directory that's in the root directory of the primary hard drive. What's the complete command-line path to the file?

4. Explain the 8.3 rule. What does the 8 mean? How about the 3?

5. Thomas was messing around one day and deleted a file named critical.dll from the System32 directory. His friend gave him a copy on a USB thumb drive. What's the exact command he'd use to copy it back to the correct place (assuming the E: drive is his USB thumb drive)?

Key Term Quiz

Use the following terms to complete the following sentences. Not all terms will be used.

/?

/p

/w

cd

copy

del

dir

md

rd

ren

1. The command used to create a new directory is _____.

2. The command used to create a duplicate file is _____.

3. The _____ switch is used to get help about command syntax.

4. When there are too many files to show on the screen while using the dir command, add the _____ switch.

5. For a listing of a directory's contents that displays only the filenames, use the _____ command with the _____ switch.

Chapter 10
Troubleshooting Windows

Lab Exercises

Recall from Chapter 8 that your company has just acquired a small architectural firm. You have patched and updated all of the firm's machines, but users are still managing to find ways to render their PCs unusable. As a technician, you need to use Event Viewer to log what they do to their computers. A few of the computers have contracted malware, corrupting the valuable master boot record (MBR), making the computers nonbootable. You'll need to be more than competent in navigating the Recovery Console to get these systems up and running. Let's take some time in this chapter to discover and use some of the available Windows troubleshooting tools.

 30 MINUTES

Lab Exercise 10.01: Examining and Configuring Log Files in Event Viewer

Windows Event Viewer is a valuable tool to anyone who maintains or troubleshoots systems. It's mostly run as a standalone program, but it can also be added as a snap-in to the MMC (as described in Chapter 2).

Event Viewer monitors various log files and reveals things about the health of the operating system. This utility reports real-time statistics, but normally this data is only used with servers. Desktop computer users are less proactive and usually depend on the after-the-fact log files to help determine the cause of a problem.

Event Viewer displays important events from multiple log files. The log files you see depend on your system. The three most important log files include Application, Security, and System. (More log files are available in the server versions of Windows.) Figure 10-1 shows the contents of the System event log in Event Viewer.

Notice in Figure 10-1 that there are three kinds of log entries: Information, Warning, and Error. The Security event log also shows two other types of entries: Success Audit and Failure Audit. These types of events are logged only when auditing is turned on; again, this is normally done only on servers.

Learning Objectives

You'll become familiar with using Event Viewer to analyze the different logs kept by the system.

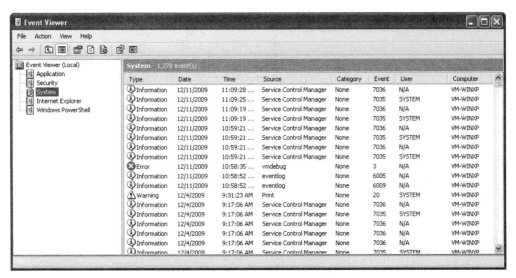

FIGURE 10-1 Viewing the System log in Event Viewer

At the end of this lab, you'll be able to

- Run the Event Viewer program

- Examine an event log entry

- Save the event log

Lab Materials and Setup

The materials you need for this lab are

- A working PC with Windows installed

Getting Down to Business

In Windows XP, you can start Event Viewer from the Control Panel by double-clicking the Administrative Tools applet and then double-clicking Event Viewer. In Windows Vista/7, go to the Start menu Search bar and type **Event Viewer**. Click the program that appears in the search results.

Step 1 Follow these steps to change the size of a log file:

    a. In Event Viewer's left panel, right-click System and select Properties. (In Windows Vista/7, you'll first need to expand the Windows Logs subfolder.)

    b. Change the number in the *Maximum log size* box to **40960** KB (512 is the default in Windows XP, 20480 is the default in Windows Vista/7) and, if it isn't selected already, select *Overwrite events as needed* (see Figure 10-2).

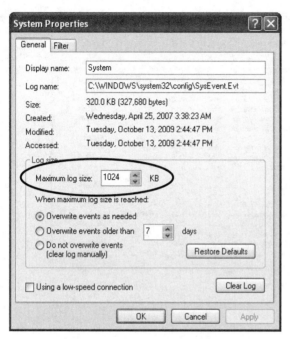

Figure 10-2 Changing the size of a log file

    c.   Do this for the Application, Security, and System logs.

    d.   Sometimes the log can be completely full before you get a chance to look at the entries. Scrolling through all the events can be a little boring and time-consuming, but you can fix that with filter settings. In Windows XP, click on the Filter tab of the log's Properties dialog box (see Figure 10-3). In Windows Vista/7, select the log from the main Event Viewer screen and click on Filter Current Log in the Actions list. The Windows XP and Windows Vista/7 versions differ in appearance, but they accomplish the same task.

You can filter events based on type/level, source, category, ID, user, computer, and more. This only controls what Event Viewer displays; all the events information will still be logged to the file, so you can change your mind about filter settings. Click OK to close the Properties dialog box.

Step 2   To clear, archive, and open a log file, follow these steps:

    a.   Clear the System log by right-clicking System and selecting *Clear all Events* in Windows XP (see Figure 10-4) or *Clear Log* in Windows Vista/7.

    b.   When you're prompted to save the System log, click Yes in Windows XP or Save and Clear in Windows Vista/7.

    c.   You can archive log files using different filenames each time (recommended) and select a location other than the default. Give your file a name you can remember and save it.

    d.   To open a saved file, click the Action menu and select Open Log File in Windows XP or Open Saved Log in Windows Vista/7. Select the file and click Open.

FIGURE 10-3 Viewing Event Viewer's settings

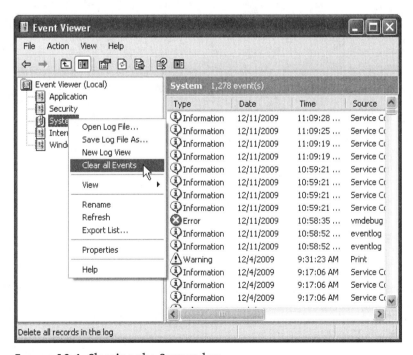

FIGURE 10-4 Clearing the System log

 45 MINUTES

Lab Exercise 10.02: Repairing Windows with Startup Options and Tools

An errant upgrade or a poorly written driver can cause the system to lock up. Some software problems, such as corrupt Registry files, will even prevent the system from booting. This means that you must be ready to use alternative methods to boot the system to make repairs or replace files.

Windows has several ways to boot, and these ways are as different as the operating systems themselves. A Safe Mode boot is available in every version of Windows. There's also a nice recovery tool that comes with Windows XP known as the Recovery Console. Windows Vista/7 use the System Recovery Options menu (also known as the Windows Recovery Environment, or WinRE) on the bootable installation media; available tools include Startup Repair, System Restore, and the Windows Memory Diagnostic (Tool). Another available option is access to the Command Prompt, which works just like the Recovery Console, but with more power.

→ **Note**

From the System Recovery Options menu, you can also use the System Image Recovery (Windows 7) or Windows Complete PC Restore (Windows Vista) option to restore a previously created backup. Return to Chapter 8 to refresh your memory on backing up files.

Learning Objectives

You'll become familiar with alternative methods of booting a faulty system.

At the end of this lab, you'll be able to

- Boot to Windows Advanced Options Menu and enable Safe Mode
- Install the Recovery Console
- Repair the Registry using the Recovery Console/Command Prompt

Lab Materials and Setup

The materials you need for this lab are

- A working PC with Windows XP installed (preferably a non-production system, as you will be corrupting and repairing the Registry)
- A working PC with Windows Vista/7
- The Windows XP installation media

Getting Down to Business

If your system won't boot normally because of some system problem, you need a way to gain access to the hard drive and your files to troubleshoot the problem. There are, happily enough, troubleshooting tools that give you access to these files if the normal boot process won't work. You'll begin this exercise with the first line of defense, the Advanced Options Menu, and boot to Safe Mode. Then, Windows XP users will install and explore the Recovery Console, eventually repairing the Registry manually. Windows Vista/7 users should follow along until they are instructed to skip ahead.

Step 1 Power up a machine with any version of Windows installed. After the POST messages, but before the Windows logo screen appears, press F8. Depending on your system, you will see a number of different boot options. Record the various modes and provide a short description for each:

_____

_____

_____

_____

✔ **Cross-Reference**

For definitions of each of the boot modes, refer to the "Advanced Startup Options" section in Chapter 10 of *Mike Meyers' CompTIA A+ Guide to 802: Managing and Troubleshooting PCs.*

Step 2 Select Safe Mode and press ENTER. The system will proceed to boot into the operating system, but it will inform you many times that it is running in Safe Mode (see Figure 10-5).

Safe Mode is often used when video settings have been changed and the new settings render the display unusable. In Safe Mode, a standard VGA driver is installed, and the minimal settings (16 colors, 640 × 480 resolution) are set. This enables you to revert to previous drivers, and/or correct the settings for the current display or monitor you are using. Complete the following steps to explore the display properties:

    a.   Right-click somewhere in the empty space of the desktop and select Properties from the drop-down menu. This brings up the Display Properties dialog box.

    b.   Click the Settings tab and note the display, color, and screen resolution settings. Record your settings here: _____

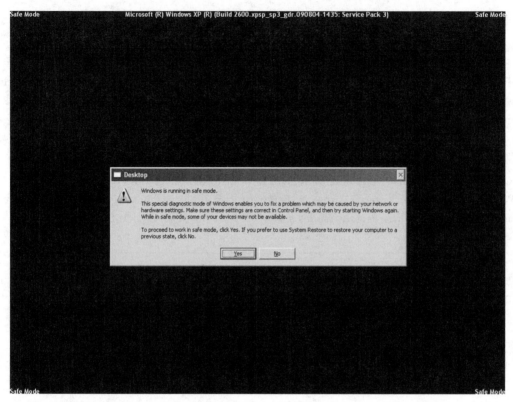

FIGURE 10-5 Windows running in Safe Mode

    c.   Click Cancel to close the Display Properties dialog box.

    d.   Click Start | Shut down.

Step 3   Windows XP users will now use the Repair menu item from the Windows installation media to launch the Recovery Console. If you're using Windows Vista or Windows 7, skip ahead to Step 5.

    a.   Insert the Windows installation disc and then reboot the system, making sure your CMOS is set to boot from your optical drive. The installation program loads a number of files and then displays a screen with the following information:

```
Welcome to Setup
This portion of the Setup program prepares Microsoft
Windows XP™ to run on your computer
        To set up Windows XP now, Press ENTER.
        To repair a Windows XP installation, press R.
        To quit Setup without installing Windows XP, press F3.
```

b. Press R to select the Repair function.

You'll now see a command-line interface asking which installation you want to access. If you have a dual-boot system, you'll have to choose an operating system; type its number from the list and press ENTER. Then type the administrator's password. This is the password for the first account created when you initially installed the operating system. You now have a command-line prompt from which to work.

✖ Warning

Be sure you know what you're doing here. You have access to files that you can add, change, rename, or delete. The old DOS command set is only partially available.

c. To see a list of commands, type **help** and note the results.

d. Type a command followed by **/?** to get an explanation of that command. You'll explore some of these commands later when you install the Windows XP Recovery Console.

→ Note

The Recovery Console operates very similarly to the Windows Command Line that you learned about in Chapter 9.

e. Type **exit** to quit the Recovery Console; the system will reboot.

Step 4 Although you can run the Recovery Console by booting directly to it from the Windows XP installation disc, it's much more convenient to set it up as a startup option on your boot menu (see Figure 10-6). In this step, you'll install the Windows XP Recovery Console as a boot option. (Windows Vista's and Window 7's System Recovery Options menu is located on the installation media or in the Advanced Boot Options menu on boot.)

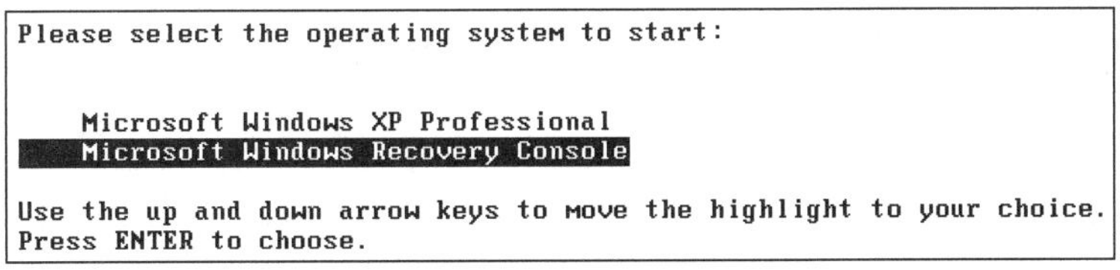

```
Please select the operating system to start:

    Microsoft Windows XP Professional
    Microsoft Windows Recovery Console

Use the up and down arrow keys to move the highlight to your choice.
Press ENTER to choose.
```

FIGURE 10-6 Recovery Console option in Windows XP startup

> ✔ **Hint**
>
> To install the Recovery Console, you must have administrative rights on the computer.

    a.   Put your Windows XP installation CD-ROM into the optical drive; if it autostarts, select Exit. You can also press and hold SHIFT until the disc stops loading.

    b.   Select Start | Run.

    c.   In the Open box, type **D:\I386\Winn32.exe /cmdcons** (where D is the drive letter for your optical drive).

    d.   A Windows Setup dialog box appears, which describes the Recovery Console option. The system prompts you to confirm installation. Click Yes to start the installation procedure.

    e.   When the installation is complete (see Figure 10-7), restart the computer. You will see a Microsoft Windows Recovery Console entry on the boot menu.

> → **Note**
>
> When you're installing the Recovery Console, you must use a Windows installation disc with the same version of Windows that was used for the system's main OS installation. For example, if you used a Windows XP Service Pack 3 installation disc to install Windows on this system, you should not use a pre–Service Pack 3 disc for this procedure. You can, but it may have adverse effects on the system.

It's wise to install the Recovery Console on important servers and on critical workstations.

Step 5   For Windows XP machines, reboot your system, and at the boot menu screen, select the Recovery Console. For Windows Vista/7 users, access the System Recovery options menu either by booting from the installation media and choosing Repair or by opening the Advanced Boot Options menu and choosing Repair Your Computer. Then open the Command Prompt.

FIGURE 10-7 Completing the Recovery Console installation in Windows XP

To see a list of the commands, type **help** at the command prompt. Type a command followed by **/?** to get an explanation of the command's use.

Several commands are worth reviewing; for the CompTIA A+ 220-802 exam, you should know what the following commands do:

- **chkdsk** Checks the clusters and sectors of a disk (fixed or removable) and, if possible, repairs bad clusters or sectors

- **diskpart** A partitioning tool

- **exit** Closes the Recovery Console and restarts your computer

- **expand** Extracts copies of single files from the CAB files

- **fixboot** Writes a new partition table

- **fixmbr** Fixes the master boot record

- **help** Displays a Help screen

✔ **Hint**

Many techs resort to the Recovery Console when a system fails to boot in the normal fashion (from the hard drive). Three of the commands, fixboot, fixmbr, and chkdsk, are particularly important when it seems that the hard disk, the master boot record, or the system partition is missing, corrupt, or damaged. If you come across a system exhibiting these symptoms (and you will), follow good troubleshooting procedures, but remember that you have these tools available to you.

➡ **Note**

Windows Vista/7 replaced fixmbr and fixboot with the bootrec command. The old commands still exist, but are hidden inside bootrec. To access them, you must use bootrec /fixmbr and bootrec /fixboot. Other available options include /scanos, which scans for Windows installations not in the boot configuration store, and /rebuildbcd, which does the same but allows you to add the installation to the boot configuration store.

The files that make up the Windows XP Recovery Console reside on the system partition, making the Recovery Console useless for a system partition crash. In such a situation, you would use the optical drive to access the Windows XP Recovery Console or Windows Vista/7 Command Prompt. The Recovery Console/Command Prompt shines in the business of manually restoring Registry files, stopping problem services, rebuilding partitions (other than the system partition), or using the expand program to extract copies of corrupted files from removable media.

Step 6   As mentioned in the previous step, the Recovery Console/Command Prompt is excellent when you need to restore Registry files. In the following steps, you will crash a system by deleting the System folder, and then repair the folder and recover the system.

✖   Warning

As mentioned in the "Lab Materials and Setup" section for this lab exercise, you are going to purposefully delete/corrupt the System folder of a working Windows system. For this reason, the system you use must be a noncritical, non-production system. Don't risk your family's financial records or your 40-GB photo archive—find another system to use for this exercise!

✔   Cross-Reference

The following steps use many components of Windows and the Recovery Console/Command Prompt. To understand better the files, folders, and Registry components involved, be sure to read the "Registry" section in Chapter 6 of *Mike Meyers' CompTIA A+ Guide to 802: Managing and Troubleshooting PCs*. Microsoft has also gathered invaluable information in their Knowledge Base articles (a component of TechNet). The following lab steps incorporate valuable information from Knowledge Base articles 307545 and 309531. As previously mentioned, Web sites change over time, so if you don't find these exact articles, use your favorite search engine and locate similar articles related to the Recovery Console/Command Prompt and repairing the Registry.

---

a.   Some preparation may be required to complete the steps to corrupt and restore your Registry folders. In Windows XP, open My Computer, then select Tools | Folder Options. In Windows Vista/7, select Start, then type **Folder Options** in the Search bar and press ENTER. Click the View tab. Turn on *Show hidden files and folders* (or *Show hidden files, folders, and drives*), turn off *Hide extensions for known file types*, and turn off *Hide protected operating system files (Recommended)*. Click OK.

b.   Boot to the Recovery Console/Command Prompt, and after logging on as administrator (if needed), type the following commands at the prompt:

```
md C:\%SYSTEMROOT%\Tmp
copy C:\%SYSTEMROOT%\System32\Config\System C:\%SYSTEMROOT%\Tmp\system.b
delete C:\%SYSTEMROOT%\System32\Config\System
exit
```

c.   At this point, the Recovery Console/Command Prompt closes. Restart Windows. Allow Windows to boot normally. Did anything inhibit the normal loading and startup of Windows?

---

d.   Boot to the Recovery Console/Command Prompt once again, log on as administrator (if needed), and type the following commands at the prompt:

```
copy C:\%SYSTEMROOT%\Repair\System c:\%SYSTEMROOT%\System32\Config\System
exit
```

e.   The Recovery Console/Command Prompt again closes. Reboot Windows. Allow Windows to boot normally. Did Windows boot properly this time?

→ **Note**

Windows Vista/7's System Recovery Options menu also includes a handy tool called Startup Repair. It scans your computer for any problems and automatically repairs them. The next time you think you need to delve into Windows Vista/7's Command Prompt to fix any startup-related troubles, try Startup Repair first—it might just save you from having to type all of those backslashes!

 30 MINUTES

Lab Exercise 10.03: Troubleshooting Startup Problems

When it comes to troubleshooting tools, the latest versions of Windows inherited the best of both the Windows NT and 9x OS families. They have vintage tools such as the Last Known Good Configuration startup option for startup failures and the Task Manager for forcing errant programs to close. There is also the Recovery Console/Command Prompt, and Windows Help.

I'll leave the finer details of these tools for you to explore through Windows Help, the main textbook, and other labs. In this lab, you'll explore a simple tool known as the System Configuration utility. The System Configuration utility has been around for some time, having been introduced in Windows 98. It was never incorporated into Windows NT or 2000, but it is included in Windows XP and Windows Vista/7.

Learning Objectives

You'll be reintroduced to some troubleshooting tips using a vintage tool with Windows XP/Vista/7.

At the end of this lab, you'll be able to

- Use the System Configuration utility to perform diagnostic startups

Lab Materials and Setup

The materials you need for this lab are

- A working Windows system

Getting Down to Business

Many systems have way too many startup options enabled. This isn't only a source of boot problems; it can also slow down the boot process and hog RAM from programs that need it. When Windows experiences failures during startup, consider using the System Configuration utility to discover and fix the problem.

Step 1   In Windows XP, select Start | Run, type **msconfig**, and then press ENTER. In Windows Vista/7, select Start, type **msconfig** into the Search bar, and then press ENTER.

The System Configuration utility opens (see Figure 10-8).

Notice that on the General tab, you can select Diagnostic startup. This is useful if you have just added new hardware that's causing intermittent problems, because it enables you to boot with only basic devices.

The Selective startup feature is also nice; it lets you bypass some configuration files to see which one contains the errors that are causing problems.

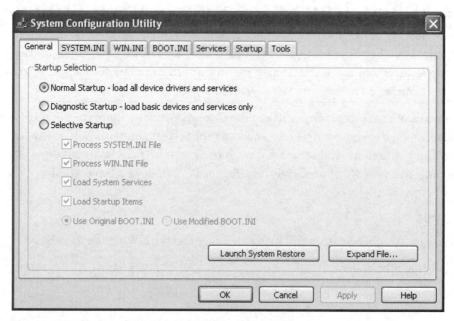

FIGURE 10-8 Using the System Configuration utility

Notice the SYSTEM.INI and WIN.INI tabs, which provide settings that enable you to change the load sequence of your drivers and edit the entries when you find an error.

→ **Note**

The SYSTEM.INI and WIN.INI tabs are not present in Windows Vista/7. Those files still exist, but only for backward compatibility with 16-bit applications.

Step 2 The BOOT.INI tab (labeled Boot in Windows Vista/7) is powerful (see Figure 10-9) and goes well beyond the CompTIA A+ exam requirements, but there are a couple of options you should know about.

One important option for troubleshooting is to create a log of what transpired during the boot process. On the BOOT.INI/Boot tab, you can enable a bootlog to be created each time the system boots.

If you're troubleshooting a problem and you need to start in Safe Mode every time, instead of pressing F8, you can enable the Safe boot (/SAFEBOOT in Windows XP) option.

Step 3 One item that I find useful is under the Services tab. Microsoft has many services that you can disable during bootup if you believe they're causing problems. The Hide All Microsoft Services option, when enabled, only displays those services you've installed—like my VMware Tools Service driver in Figure 10-10.

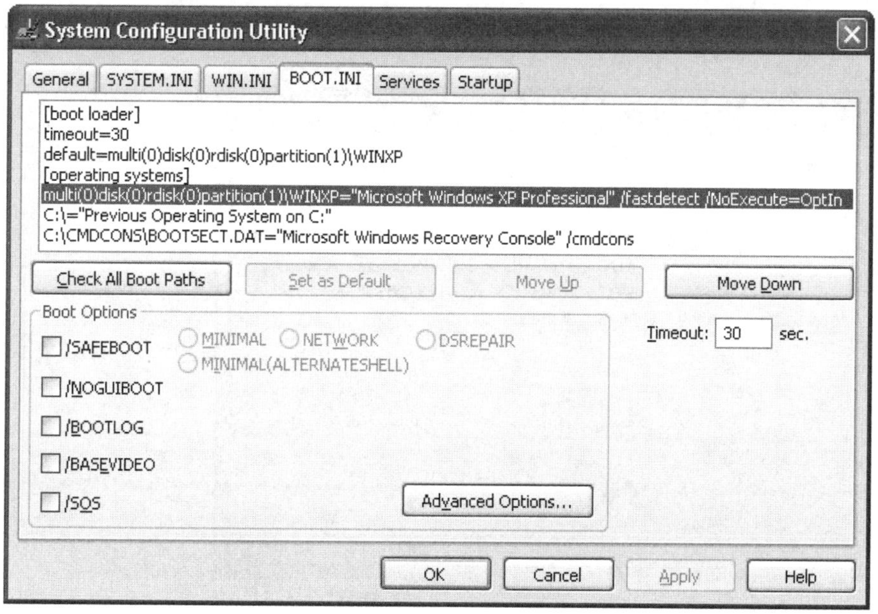

FIGURE 10-9 The BOOT.INI tab

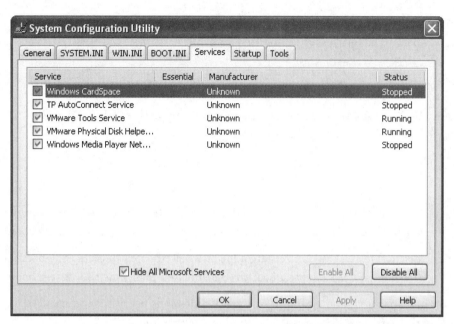

FIGURE 10-10 Using the Services tab with Microsoft Services hidden

Step 4   The Startup tab is perhaps the most useful. You can enable or disable any of the terminate and stay resident (TSR) programs that are installed. This is a good place to look if some unexplained program is trying to load every time you boot, even though you thought you'd uninstalled it.

Notice in Figure 10-11 that one program on the list doesn't have a name. I'm kind of suspicious about what this program might be doing! If you find questionable entries in your Startup tab listing, you should fire up a browser and do some research to see whether or not they're harmful.

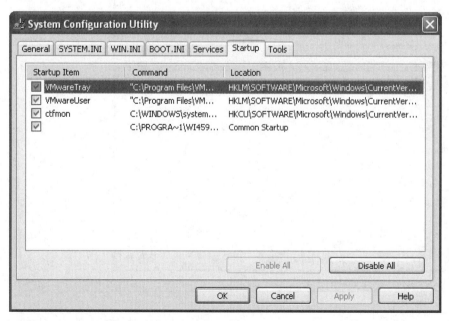

FIGURE 10-11 Checking your startup programs

> ✔ **Hint**
>
> You can also run the System Configuration utility in Safe Mode. If you're having problems, you can boot to Safe Mode and then use this utility to identify the source of the problem.

Lab Analysis Test

1. John has just been infected with malware on his Windows XP computer and his computer now says "NTLDR is Missing" upon bootup. Give John a detailed description of the steps he needs to take to fix the computer.

2. You've installed a new network card and sound card. Every time you boot, the system locks up, and you must boot into Safe Mode to get to a GUI. What tool can you use to locate the source of the problem?

3. Tim is a Windows XP user who feels he's really a programmer at heart—he always seems to be opening the Registry with regedit and changing settings directly in the Registry. Today, it doesn't go so well, and he ends up with the Blue Screen of Death (BSOD). What can Tim use to make his system work again?

4. Laurie suspects that someone is trying to log on to her computer and is failing over and over again. She wants to know when this intrusion attempt is happening, so she has set up auditing for login events on her Windows 7 computer. Where will she go to see the intrusion attempts?

5. William has a computer that has been on the fritz, so he decided to enter Safe Mode. What are the features of Safe Mode that make it so good for troubleshooting?

Key Term Quiz

Use the following terms to complete the following sentences. Not all terms will be used.

Advanced Startup Options menu

Application logs

bootrec

diskpart

Event Viewer

F8

fixboot

fixmbr

msconfig

Recovery Console

Safe Mode

security logs

system logs

System Recovery Options menu

1. You can repair the master boot record on a Windows Vista computer using the _____ command.

2. The _____ can be added as a boot menu option.

3. The _____ in Windows 7 includes Startup Repair, System Restore, Windows Memory Diagnostic, and Command Prompt.

4. The _____ utility is used to troubleshoot startup issues when you can't get into the GUI of Windows.

5. _____ provides three log files to assist with the troubleshooting of a Windows operating system.

Chapter 11

Video

Lab Exercises

Few components affect the PC user like the video system, the primary output for the PC. As you know from the textbook, the video system has two main hardware components—monitor and display adapter—that work together to produce the image on your screen. Both components must be installed and configured properly in Windows or your viewing pleasure will be seriously compromised. Good techs know how to do video right!

In this set of labs, you'll install a display adapter, hook up a monitor, load video drivers, and configure Windows for optimal viewing. You'll then work with the growing practice of using multiple monitors (for example, a projector and a laptop screen) to expand your desktop viewing area. The last lab exercise will run you though some of the typical troubleshooting issues that techs face when dealing with video.

✖ Warning

It is critical to understand that only *trained* monitor technicians should remove the cover of a video monitor (or a television set, for that matter). The inside of a traditional monitor might look similar to the interior of a PC, with printed circuit boards and related components, but there's a big difference: No PC has voltages up to 50,000 volts or more inside, but most CRT monitors *do*. So be sure to get one thing clear—casually opening a monitor and snooping around has the potential to become harmful to you and the monitor—and in cases of extreme carelessness, it can even be deadly! Even when the power is disconnected, certain components (capacitors) still retain substantial levels of voltage for an extended period of time. Capacitors work like batteries. Yes, they can maintain 50,000 volts! If you inadvertently short one of the capacitors, a large discharge will occur into the monitor circuits, destroying them. If you're touching the metal frame, you could fry yourself—to death. Given this risk, certain aspects of monitor repair fall outside the necessary skill set for a standard PC support person, and definitely outside the CompTIA A+ exam domains. Make sure you understand the problems you can fix safely and the ones you need to hand over to a qualified electronics repair shop.

 30 MINUTES

Lab Exercise 11.01: Installing Video

Your office staff's computers need a serious video upgrade. Some of the PCs have tiny 17-inch LCD monitors that simply have to go, while others have decent 19-inch and 20-inch LCDs that have a year or two of life left in them. Your boss has bought new PCIe video cards and some 24-inch-widescreen LCD monitors. You're tasked with installing the cards, loading drivers, and setting up everything in Windows.

Learning Objectives

At the end of this lab, you'll be able to

- Identify the make and model of a video card

- Install a video display adapter card

- Check BIOS for proper video settings

- Adjust the monitor for the proper display

- Optimize the video settings in Windows

Lab Materials and Setup

The materials you need for this lab are

- A working PC with Windows installed

- A working monitor (access to both a CRT and an LCD monitor is recommended)

- A working computer system with access to the Internet

✔ **Hint**

Classrooms that have a variety of different monitor types and video display adapter cards are a plus.

Getting Down to Business

To begin this lab, you'll become familiar with the video components in your system. You'll then step through the proper installation and configuration of a video adapter.

✖ **Warning**

Some versions of Microsoft Windows operating systems have problems when you make changes to the video display adapters, even when you're simply removing and reinstalling the same card into a different slot. If you perform this lab on a test machine, you should have no real problem if things go wrong. If you're using your primary PC to do the lab, however, make certain you have current drivers available for your video card, or a source to get drivers if necessary.

Step 1 Shut down your system properly and unplug the power cable from the system unit and the wall. Remove the cover from the PC to expose the expansion buses.

    a.   Find your video display adapter card (the one to which the monitor is attached). What type of video display adapter is installed: PCIe, AGP, or PCI? _____

✔ **Hint**

Many laptop computers and some low- to mid-level desktop systems include display adapters integrated right into the electronics of the motherboard. On desktop systems with this configuration, the connector will appear in line with the PS/2 and USB ports. If your system uses this type of display adapter, the overall performance of the system may suffer because the display typically "steals" system RAM to serve as video RAM. Laptops are usually designed around this limitation, but if your desktop system is of this type, you can increase the performance (and usually the video quality) by installing a display adapter card and disabling the onboard video in the BIOS.

---

    b.   Detach the monitor's cable from the video card. Using good ESD avoidance procedures, remove the screw that holds the card in place, put it in a secure location, and then remove your video display adapter card (see Figure 11-1). Examine it closely to answer the following questions. Be careful not to touch the expansion slot contacts on the card!

    c.   Look for a name or model number on the adapter's circuit board or chipset. Who is the manufacturer, or what is the model number? Write it down. (Note that for this lab's scenario, you'd actually be looking up the information for the new video cards, not the ones already installed—*those* will most likely be donated to charity!)

FIGURE 11-1 This video card has a large cooling fan for the graphics processing unit (GPU) and its onboard RAM chips

Be sure to write down as much information as you can collect from the display adapter for a later assignment.

   d.   Reinsert the video card into the same slot, and make sure it is properly seated. Reattach the monitor cable and test your system with the case still open to see if it works. This could save you the frustration that results when you close the case, fire up the system, and get a video error. (Not that I've ever done that!)

✔ **Hint**

AGP and PCIe cards can be a little tricky. They must be seated perfectly or they will not work. Many of these types of cards use slots with locking levers—if you were observant when you removed the card initially, you'll know what you have to do now for proper physical installation.

---

   e.   Boot your system and open your favorite browser to search the Web.

Conduct your search using the information you've gathered about the manufacturer and model number of your card.

Can you find the specifications for your display adapter? _____

What is the highest resolution you can achieve with your video adapter according to these specifications? _____

How much memory is available? _____

What type of memory is used? _____

Does the adapter support SLI or CrossFire? _____

Does the adapter have any other features, such as an HDMI connector?

_____

_____

Step 2   Reboot your system and press the proper key sequence to enter the system setup utility. Depending on the BIOS manufacturer and version, there can be as many as five or more video-related settings. My lab system has 10 settings directly related to video or the PCIe slot. Complete each of these questions based on your specific BIOS. Some of the names of the sections will undoubtedly differ from the ones presented here. Search around a bit and you'll find video options in your CMOS.

On the Standard CMOS Setup or similar screen, how many choices are there for video, and how is your video set? _____

On the Chipset Features Setup or similar screen, what is the value for your Video RAM Cacheable setting? _____

Are there any PCIe-specific settings? _____

Are there any settings for the amount of RAM the onboard adapter will use? _____

_____

On the Power Management Setup or similar screen, do you have settings to control how the monitor and video adapter will react when not in use for a period of time? What are your settings?

_____

On the Integrated Peripherals or similar screen, do you have an Init Display First setting? What are the choices?

_____

What does your setting say?

_____

Know that when this setting is wrong, the display might not work.

Step 3   You'll now examine a monitor and see what external controls it has. If you're not in a computer lab, you can go to your local computer store and examine a wide variety of monitors.

Figures 11-2 and 11-3 show the control buttons for adjusting the display attributes for an LCD and a CRT monitor, respectively. Both of these have the controls on the front of the monitor, but some have the controls behind a door under the front of the monitor screen, and others may have them on the back.

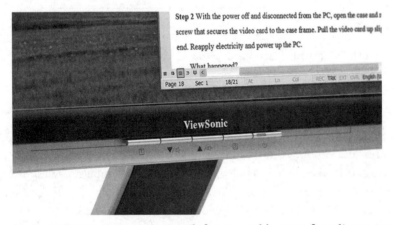

FIGURE 11-2 An LCD monitor with front-panel buttons for adjustments

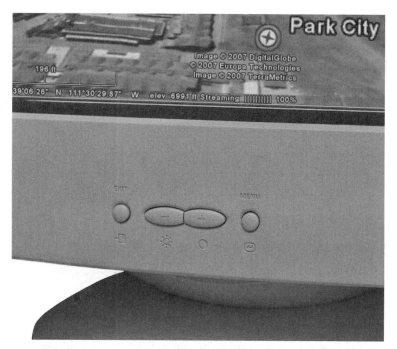

FIGURE 11-3 Front controls on a CRT monitor

A monitor can have quite a few adjustable features. How many of the following can you adjust on your LCD monitor?

Brightness	
Contrast	
Clock	
H-position	
V-position	
Color temperature	
Auto balance	
Sharpness	
Gamma	
Signal select (for LCDs with both VGA and DVI inputs)	
Full screen	
Language	

How many of these can you adjust on your CRT monitor?

Brightness	
Contrast	
Color saturation	
Vertical size	
Vertical position	
Horizontal size	
Horizontal position	
Pincushioning (for adjusting displays that are narrow in the middle but flare out at the top and bottom)	
Keystoning (for adjusting displays that are narrow at the top but flare out at the bottom)	
Degauss (for adjusting displays that have become fuzzy due to electromagnetic interference)	

Play with the controls of your monitor or a test monitor. If the current settings use percentages, write down the settings before doing any adjustments. Then follow these steps:

a.   Change the settings such as color and sizing. Don't be shy!

b.   Put the settings back as close as possible to their original positions.

c.   Optimize the screen for clarity and position.

Step 4   The hardware is set up properly and the BIOS settings should be correct, so now you need to configure and optimize the Windows settings that determine your video display characteristics. To do this, you need to use the Display applet (or Display Settings applet in Windows Vista).

✔ **Hint**

This lab simulates a working PC that you upgrade with new hardware and drivers. All the steps can work just as well for installing a video card into a new system, although the pace of that installation would differ. In a new system, you would physically install the video card, let Windows use generic VGA drivers until you make sure you can boot properly, and only then install the drivers for the video card. Finally, you'd go to the Display/Display Settings applet and optimize the video card settings. Windows is fairly good at finding a suitable driver the first time around, but you should still understand how to locate and update drivers for your video card.

In Windows XP, navigate to the Display applet and click the Settings tab. In Windows Vista, go to Control Panel | Personalization | Display Settings. In Windows 7, go to the Display Control Panel applet and click on *Change display settings*. This displays the monitor settings, such as those shown in Figure 11-4.

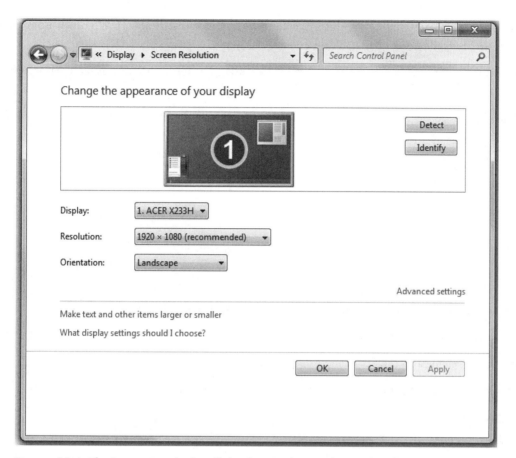

FIGURE 11-4 The Screen Resolution dialog box in the Display applet of Windows 7

✖ **Warning**

You're going to make changes to the look and feel of Windows. Making some of these changes can result in frustrating and time-consuming problems. Use a test machine if you have one available. If you must use your own machine, write down all your display settings before you make any changes.

Each video display adapter manufacturer has different options for its cards. By clicking the Advanced button (Advanced settings in Windows 7), you can access more information about the display adapter. You may see a choice for setting the refresh rate, as well as other features. Look through the settings on the Advanced tab or Properties dialog box, and see what your display adapter manufacturer provides. Remember that the video adapter "pushes" the monitor. If you set the refresh too high, it can cause problems, and in the case of older CRTs may even damage your monitor.

Write down your display's current resolution, color depth, and refresh rate. In Windows 7, you may need to look around to find these. Go ahead and explore!

Close the Advanced/Properties dialog box (if you selected it), but leave the Display Properties/Screen Resolution dialog box open.

Make some changes to the background and colors on your screen. In Windows XP, you'll find these options on the Desktop and Appearance tabs, respectively. In Windows Vista/7, you'll find these options in the Personalization applet. Be sure to note the original settings so you can change things back when you're done.

✔ **Hint**

The setting changes suggested in this step are perfectly safe and easy to undo.

Change the desktop background to something you might like better. Then try the following:

- Experiment with color combinations.

- Make some changes to the displayed fonts and menu bars.

- Experiment with changing the colors and resolution of your display.

  Can your machine run in 16-bit color? _____

  How about 24-bit color? _____

  Can you run 800 × 600 resolution? _____

  Can you run 1024 × 768 resolution? _____

  Can you run 1280 × 960 resolution? _____

  Do you have any other options? _____

In Windows XP, click the Advanced button again. In Windows Vista, click Advanced. In Windows 7, click on the Advanced settings link. Open the Monitor tab. Experiment with changing the refresh rate (see Figure 11-5).

✔ **Hint**

Because of the way that LCD monitors work, the refresh rate setting doesn't really apply to them. As a general rule, LCD monitors display a stable, flicker-free image at 60 hertz (Hz). There are no visible differences between 85 Hz and 60 Hz.

FIGURE 11-5 A typical refresh setting on the Monitor tab

Can you make specific numeric changes? _____

Are the Optimal and Adapter Default settings the only choices you have? _____

✔ Hint

The refresh rate is not an option on all video adapters. This setting may be in a different location, or not on your system at all.

Make sure you return all the settings to their original values, and then close the dialog box.

Check the drivers for your video card and monitor. Are they "standard" drivers, or are they specific to your hardware? Follow these steps:

a. Go to Device Manager, locate your display adapter, right-click, and select Properties.

b. Locate your driver information.

c. Can you identify the version number(s) of your video drivers? Write them down.

_____

d. Go online and find the manufacturer's Web site.

e.   Check to see if newer drivers are available. If so, download and install them. (Do this on a test machine first. Get comfortable with the whole process before you do this on your personal computer.)

How did this affect your machine?

_____

✔ Hint

New drivers will sometimes fail to work properly, thereby crippling your PC. Windows XP and higher have the Roll Back Driver feature that enables you to go back to a driver that worked correctly in case this should happen. Refer to Chapter 8 for a refresher on how to do this.

Step 5   One more place to look for video settings is the Power Options Control Panel applet. Take a look at any power management settings you may have.

a.   Go to the Control Panel and double-click the Power Options applet.

b.   Read through the list of available power management schemes.

Which one do you have running? _____

How long is the period of inactivity before your monitor shuts off? _____

c.   Close the applet and the Control Panel.

 30 MINUTES

Lab Exercise 11.02: Configuring Multiple Displays

Your consulting firm has just been awarded a contract to perform complete upgrades on the 12 digital audio workstations at a local recording studio. Among the various considerations for this type of application—large data storage, backups, fast processors, and loads of memory—the application also requires high-performance display adapters with multiple monitors for each station. It is not unusual for a recording engineer to have three or four critical windows open simultaneously during a session, so the studio design has included three widescreen monitors for each station.

You jump on the project and immediately stage one of the systems in the shop to run it through its paces. You decide to use one of the new ASUS motherboards with three PCIe slots and three high-performance NVIDIA display adapters. You finish the video configuration and attach three 30-inch widescreen monitors—this system looks impressive!

✔ **Cross-Reference**

For additional information on configuring your multiple displays, refer to the "Installing and Configuring Video" section in Chapter 11 of *Mike Meyers' CompTIA A+ Guide to 802: Managing and Troubleshooting PCs*.

Learning Objectives

At the end of this lab, you'll be able to

- Install an additional video display adapter card

- Configure a system to use multiple displays

- Expand the desktop across two or more displays

Lab Materials and Setup

The materials you need for this lab are

- A working PC with Windows installed

- At least one additional display adapter or a display adapter that supports multiple monitors

- At least one additional working monitor (CRT or LCD)

✔ **Hint**

This lab exercise does not require any of the high-end equipment discussed in the scenario. You should be able to complete the steps to configure multiple monitors using a few video cards and the monitors in your classroom lab. You can even use the integrated display adapter on many motherboards and install one additional video card to complete the lab steps. If time permits, hop on a system with Internet access and explore some of the components discussed in the scenario. Manufacturers such as ASUS, NVIDIA, and NEC are always adding new technology to their product lines.

Getting Down to Business

To explore the system configuration presented in the opening scenario, you will install at least one additional display adapter and monitor on a working system. You will then use the Display applet in Windows to configure the multiple monitors for use as an expanded desktop.

Step 1 Shut down your system properly and unplug the power cable from the system unit and the wall. Remove the cover from the PC to expose the expansion bus slots.

a. Verify the type (PCI, AGP, or PCIe) and location of the current video display adapter. Using proper ESD avoidance procedures and one of the available expansion slots (depending on the additional video card available to you), install a second video display adapter in your system. Remember that AGP and PCIe cards can be a little finicky during installation, so make sure they are inserted securely.

→ **Note**

You may have a display adapter that already supports multiple monitors and has two display ports on a single card. If this is the case, you don't need to add a second adapter to set up multiple monitors, but it's good to practice, either way.

b. Attach the second monitor cable to the new display adapter and test your system with the case still open to see if it works.

To verify that the second display adapter and monitor have been installed correctly, are recognized by the system, and have drivers available, open Device Manager and expand the display adapter's icon. View the properties of the newly installed card and select the Drivers tab. Does everything appear to be in order?

c. If the new display adapter is not working properly, you may need to install specific drivers or updated drivers. Access the Internet to download and install the appropriate drivers for your display adapter.

Step 2   Now that the hardware is set up and functioning properly, you will configure Windows to expand your desktop across two or more displays. To do this, you will again open the Display applet.

In Windows XP, navigate to the Display Properties dialog box's Settings tab. In Windows Vista, go to Control Panel | Personalization | Display Settings. In Windows 7, go to the Display applet and click on *Change display settings*. This shows the monitor settings and should now display two monitor icons, as shown in Figure 11-6.

Now complete the following steps to expand your desktop across the displays you have installed.

a. Click the drop-down arrow next to the Display field. Are both of your display adapters available?

_____

b. Select the second monitor icon. In Windows XP, check the *Extend my Windows desktop onto this monitor* box, and click the Apply button. In Windows Vista/7, click on the Multiple displays drop-down box and select *Extend these displays*. Your monitor icons should now look something like Figure 11-7, and the display on your monitors should change accordingly.

c. Click and drag the dialog box or another open window from one monitor to the other. Notice that the standard setup has the second display as the display to the right, so the expansion should allow you to use the second monitor as the rightmost portion of the desktop. Open a few windows and place them in different locations on the two monitors (see Figure 11-8).

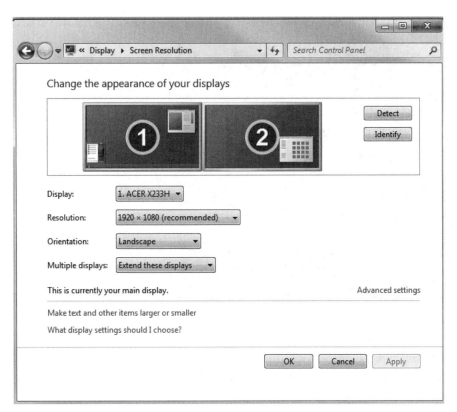

Figure 11-6 The Display applet showing two monitors available

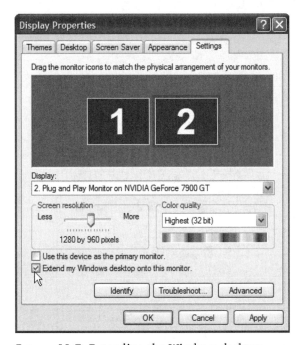

Figure 11-7 Extending the Windows desktop

Figure 11-8 Dual monitors displaying multiple open windows

d. Experiment with the "virtual" placement of the monitors by clicking one of the numbered monitors and dragging it around the other monitor(s). Also click and highlight one of the numbered monitors and select it as the primary display.

Can you place the monitors on top of each other (see Figure 11-9)? _____

Can you set the second display as the primary monitor? _____

· Right-click one of the displays in the Display Properties dialog box and select Identify. What are the results? _____

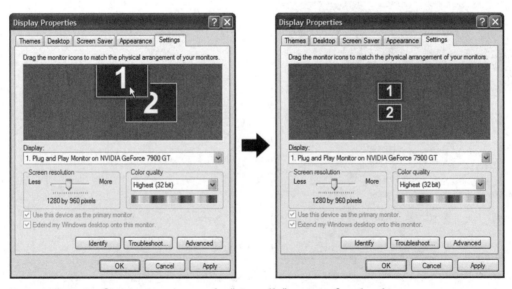

Figure 11-9 Configuring monitors to be "virtually" on top of each other

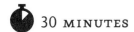 30 MINUTES

Lab Exercise 11.03: Troubleshooting Video

Video troubleshooting really boils down to two distinct questions. First, are the physical video components installed and configured properly, as discussed in Lab Exercise 11.01? Second, do the current video display adapter and CPU support the software technologies you're trying to use? (Or have you loaded that killer game and completely overwhelmed your video subsystem?) In this lab exercise, you'll create connectivity problems to simulate real-world installation problems, and use the DirectX Diagnostic Tool to analyze your system.

Learning Objectives

At the end of this lab, you'll be able to

- Recognize and fix typical video installation and connectivity problems

- Use the Microsoft DirectX Diagnostic Tool to analyze and test the graphic display attributes of a PC system

Lab Materials and Setup

The materials you need for this lab are

- A working PC with Windows installed

- Any version of the Microsoft DirectX Diagnostic Tool installed

Getting Down to Business

If you went through Lab Exercise 11.01 and had typical results—video card not seated properly, forgetting to plug things in all the way, and so on—you can probably skip Steps 1 and 2 of this lab. If you had a perfect reinstall, on the other hand, then definitely do all of the steps!

Step 1 Loosen the screws that hold the monitor data cable securely to the video card. With the system fully powered up and in Windows—and being gentle with your hardware—partially disconnect the monitor cable.

What happened to the screen? _____

With many monitors, a loose cable results in a seriously degraded display. Colors fade out or a single color disappears, or the display may appear grainy or snowy, for example. If you run into these symptoms in the field, check your connectivity!

Connect the monitor cable and tighten the restraining screws to resume normal operation.

Step 2   With the power off and disconnected from the PC, open the case and remove the screw that secures the video card to the case frame. Pull the video card up slightly on one end. Reapply electricity and power up the PC.

What happened? _____

You might have to run through this a couple of times to get the desired effect, which is a seemingly dead PC and some beeping from the system speaker. That long-short-short beep code is pretty universally recognizable as the PC's cry for help: "Hey! My video card isn't seated properly!"

With the power off and disconnected, reseat your video card, reinstall the restraining screw, and power up your PC to resume normal operation.

Step 3   Access the Microsoft DirectX Diagnostic Tool. In Windows XP, select Start | All Programs | Accessories | System Tools | System Information. Select Tools | DirectX Diagnostic Tool. In Windows Vista/7, type **dxdiag** into the Start menu Search bar and press ENTER (see Figure 11-10).

✔ **Hint**

There is a faster way to get to the DirectX Diagnostic Tool in Windows XP too! Just go to Start | Run, type dxdiag, and click OK.

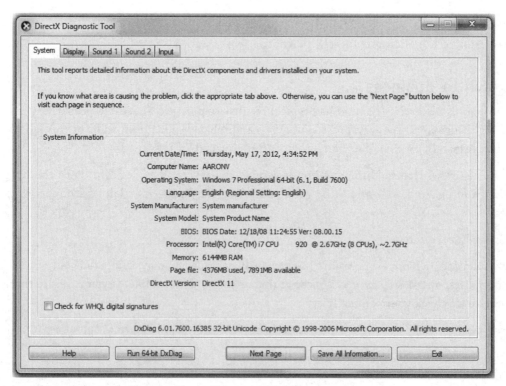

FIGURE 11-10 Using the DirectX Diagnostic Tool

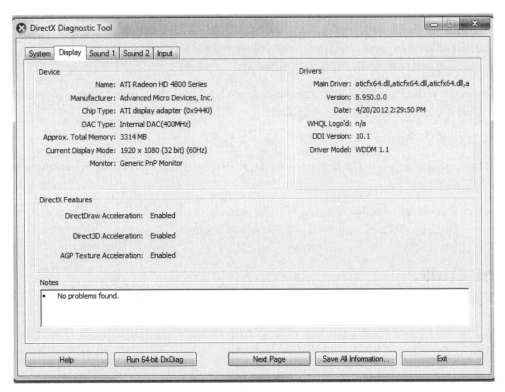

FIGURE 11-11 Viewing the DirectX Diagnostic Tool's Display tab

Step 4 Select the Display tab (see Figure 11-11).

What is the name of your display adapter? _____

How much total memory is on the adapter? _____

What is the current display mode? _____

What is the driver name and version? _____

Does it display a driver version date? _____

Should you look for a more current driver? _____

Step 5 Check out the Notes box at the bottom of the Display tab, and read the information provided. This is where you can find out about any conflicts or problem areas.

Do you see any information about conflicts or problems? If so, what's the conflict or problem?

_____

Lab Analysis Test

1. If you remove an AGP video display adapter and replace it with a PCIe video display adapter, what must you do to be sure the Windows desktop will display properly?

2. Your nephew Brian visited and used your computer last night, and this morning your monitor is dead. What should you do first, second, and third?

3. What can happen if the refresh rate for a CRT is set too high?

4. Teresa installed a new game, but she is frustrated because it responds too slowly. What might she check?

5. Taylor installed a new video display adapter, but the best setting he can adjust it to is 800 × 600 resolution with 256 colors. What must he do to make it go higher?

Key Term Quiz

Use the following terms to complete the following sentences. Not all terms will be used.

application programming interface (API)

degauss

Direct3D

DirectX Diagnostic Tool

Display applet

Display Settings

OpenGL

1. Once software is installed, test your video using Microsoft's _____.

2. The subset of DirectX that handles three-dimensional graphics is called _____.

3. If your CRT monitor is getting strange splotches of color on it, try using its built-in _____ tool.

4. The _____ is the one-stop shop in Windows XP and Windows 7 for changing your video settings. In Windows Vista, many of these same settings can be found in _____.

5. DirectX's main competitor in the field of graphics APIs is _____.

Chapter 12
Ethernet and TCP/IP

Lab Exercises

In this chapter, you'll first learn how to construct an Ethernet patch cable. While you can easily find patch cables at any electronics store, a tech should be able to make his or her own. Next, you'll verify TCP/IP settings such as your IP address and default gateway using both the Control Panel and the command prompt. The third lab exercise in this chapter explains how you can share resources on your computer with the entire network. Finally, you'll return to the command prompt and work with several commands that enable you to test and troubleshoot your network connection.

 30–60 MINUTES

Lab Exercise 12.01: Building an Ethernet Patch Cable

CAT 5e and CAT 6 UTP cabling are now the dominant cabling media for wired networks. This is due to the fact that Ethernet has become the dominant networking technology, and Ethernet uses UTP cabling to electrically transmit the data frames. Ensuring that these data frames are transmitted and received correctly requires that these UTP cables are wired to exacting specifications. The Telecommunications Industry Association/Electronics Industries Alliance (TIA/EIA) defines the industry standards for wiring Ethernet UTP cables.

Typical IT departments will have several lengths of premade patch cables on hand to be used as needed. Nonetheless, a well-versed tech should have a good command of assembling and testing UTP patch cables. Some folks refer to the building of UTP patch cables, which requires stripping the insulation, arranging the wires to meet the TIA/EIA standards, and crimping the RJ-45 connectors onto the ends of the wire, as an "art." You will now practice the art of building UTP patch cables.

Learning Objectives

In this lab, you'll assemble a TIA/EIA 568B patch cable.

At the end of this lab, you will be able to

- Identify proper orientation of RJ-45 connectors

- Identify the wire pairs of a UTP patch cable according to the specifications of the TIA/EIA 568A and 568B standards

- Successfully crimp an RJ-45 connector to the end of a UTP cable

- Verify proper wiring of a completed patch cable using a commercial cable tester

Lab Materials and Setup

The materials you need for this lab are

- A working computer with Internet access

- A length of CAT 5, CAT 5e, or CAT 6 UTP cable

- RJ-45 connectors

- Wire strippers

- Wire snips

- A crimping tool

- TIA/EIA 568B color codes

- A cable tester

→ **Note**

Though CAT 6 UTP cable is the current choice for high performance, it can prove much more difficult to use when making cables. CAT 6 cable has a plastic spine that must be trimmed before inserting it into the RJ-45 connectors. There are many variations on the RJ-45 connectors for CAT 6 cable, and special crimping tools may be required.

Getting Down to Business

The TIA/EIA 568A and 568B standards define the arrangement of four-pair UTP cabling into RJ-45 connectors. When purchasing commercial, premade cables, the emerging default standard to follow is TIA/EIA 568B. For the purposes of this lab, you will adhere to the default industry standard of TIA/EIA 568B.

You'll find that once you develop some technique, you will enjoy making patch cables. As mentioned earlier, in the eyes of some, this is an "art." I want to caution you against spending too much time making cables, however, or spending too much time completing this lab exercise. The skill you develop will not be tested on the CompTIA A+ 220-802 exam, and even in the field, making cables will not be the prime example of your skills as a tech.

That said, you will want to spend enough time to know the basics so that you will not look like a novice when it comes to whipping up a few patch cables.

Step 1   You'll begin with a cut length of UTP cable. Your instructor may define the lengths based on actual implementation. Shorter, 2- to 5-foot cables may be made to patch in a new switch or router, and medium lengths of 15 to 25 feet may be used to connect computers and printers to wall jacks. What lengths of cable will you be using?

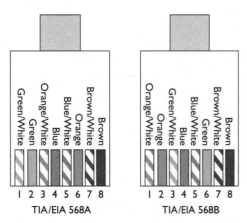

FIGURE 12-1 The TIA/EIA 568A and 568B standards

Step 2 Using the Internet, conduct a search for TIA/EIA 568A and 568B wiring diagrams. There are many sites that offer color-coded diagrams of the standards for wiring both straight-through and crossover patch cables. I found a nice diagram on the Web site of the Internet Centre, an Alberta, Canada Internet provider, at www.incentre.net/content/view/75/2/. I have also included the wiring diagram from the *Mike Meyers' CompTIA Network+ Guide to Managing and Troubleshooting Networks* textbook (see Figure 12-1).

Using either the diagram shown in Figure 12-1 or a diagram you've found on the Web, record the proper color wire for each of the pins of the RJ-45 modular connector when assembled using the TIA/EIA 568B standard:

Pin 1: _____

Pin 2: _____

Pin 3: _____

Pin 4: _____

Pin 5: _____

Pin 6: _____

Pin 7: _____

Pin 8: _____

Step 3 Using wire strippers (often the crimping tool has wire strippers and snips built in), carefully remove approximately 0.5 inch of the outer insulating jacket of each end of the UTP cable.

→ **Note**

After removing the outer insulating sheathing, look for any damaged or cut wires. This is a very delicate procedure, so finesse is required. If any of the eight wires have been damaged, use the wire snips to cut off the entire end (all eight wires and insulation) and repeat Step 3.

Figure 12-2 Aligning the wires and evening the ends

Step 4 Separate each pair of wires and align them in the correct sequence according to the TIA/EIA 568B standards defined in Step 2. The next step, where you insert the wires into the RJ-45 connector, will go more smoothly if you take your time during this procedure. Once the sequence is correct, grasp the wires firmly between your thumb and forefinger, and carefully snip the edges of the wires to make them even, as shown in Figure 12-2.

Step 5 With the pins of the RJ-45 connector facing up and away from you, slide the wires all the way into the connector. The outer insulating sheath should be just past the first crimping point in the connector, and you should be able to see the copper of all eight wires if you look at the head of the RJ-45 connector, as shown in Figure 12-3.

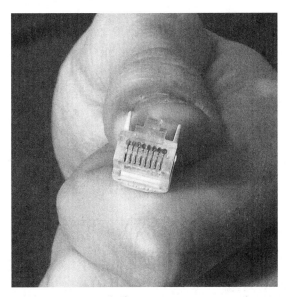

Figure 12-3 Head of an RJ-45 connector showing all eight wires firmly inserted

Step 6   Place the RJ-45 connector into the crimping tool. Firmly squeeze the handle of the tool until the wires are crimped into place. The crimp should bind each of the wires tightly, and the connector should bind the outer jacket. If any of the wires can be pulled from the connector with a gentle tug, the connection is incorrect. Snip the RJ-45 connector off and return to Step 3.

Step 7   To complete the assembly of the patch cable, repeat Steps 3–6 to add a connector to the other end of the cable.

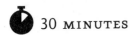 30 MINUTES

Lab Exercise 12.02: Verifying TCP/IP Settings

As you are probably aware, TCP/IP has emerged as the standard transport protocol for network communication. Microsoft operating systems normally use the Dynamic Host Configuration Protocol (DHCP), which automatically retrieves and assigns client TCP/IP settings from a DHCP server. This makes it easy to set up a small home or business network of PCs. All systems in the network will communicate with each other using these settings. The problem is that most businesses have their own set of TCP/IP settings (either automatically configured through DHCP or manually configured) that must be used for all new or repaired systems introduced into the network. Your responsibility as a PC technician is to verify the TCP/IP settings.

✔ **Cross-Reference**

To review additional details of TCP/IP, re-read the "Configuring TCP/IP" section in Chapter 12 of *Mike Meyers' CompTIA A+ Guide to 802: Managing and Troubleshooting PCs.*

Learning Objectives

In this exercise, you'll access and verify the TCP/IP settings for a given PC system.

At the end of this lab, you'll be able to

- Define Automatic Private IP Addressing (APIPA)

- Use the ipconfig command-line utility

- Manually configure the TCP/IP settings on a PC

Lab Materials and Setup

The materials you need for this lab are

- A PC system that's properly configured for LAN access using Windows

- A list of TCP/IP settings provided by the instructor

Getting Down to Business

Typically, in corporate environments, the network protocol configuration scheme has been defined by the senior systems administrators. Unless you've had some experience with the configuration, you would not automatically know all of the TCP/IP settings for a network. For instance, even when you're setting up a small network (one that connects to the Internet), you'll need to contact your Internet service provider (ISP) to set up your router's TCP/IP settings. So don't worry if you have no idea what settings to use. The trick is to learn how to get them.

TCP/IP requires each system to have two basic settings for accessing a LAN and two additional settings for accessing other LANs or the Internet. You can configure your system to automatically obtain the following settings when you log on (Microsoft's default settings), or you can specify them, depending on the requirements of your network:

- IP address (unique to the PC)

- Subnet mask (identifies network information)

- Default gateway (address of the router to the external realm)

- Domain name service (DNS)

Step 1 First, you'll locate and verify your current TCP/IP settings.

a. You can accomplish this by going to the Control Panel. If you have a Windows Vista/7 system, open the Network and Sharing Center applet. In Windows Vista, click on *Manage network connections*, and in Windows 7, click *Change adapter settings*. Go to the Properties dialog box of the appropriate adapter. If you are on Windows XP, open the Network Connections applet, then open the Properties dialog box of the appropriate adapter. Highlight the Internet Protocol (TCP/IP) entry and click the Properties button. When the Internet Protocol (TCP/IP) Properties dialog box appears, one of the setting options shown in Figure 12-4 will be selected.

b. If the settings are manually configured, you will be able to verify them in the TCP/IP Properties dialog box. Write the settings down and verify them with the settings given to you by the instructor.

IP address _____

Subnet mask _____

Default gateway _____

Preferred DNS server _____

c. If the system is configured to use the Microsoft Automatic Private IP Addressing (APIPA) settings or if the network has a DHCP server (ask the instructor), the *Obtain an IP address automatically* and *Obtain DNS server address automatically* radio buttons will be selected. You will not be able to verify the values of the TCP/IP settings from this window. Close this window by clicking OK. To verify the settings, launch a Command Prompt window and, at the prompt, type the following command:

```
C:\Documents and Settings\%USERNAME%\>ipconfig /all
```

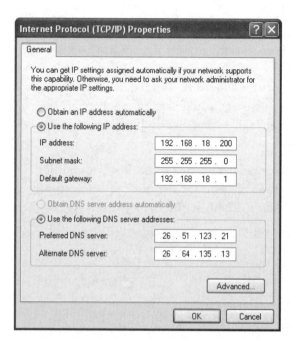

Figure 12-4 Viewing manually configured TCP/IP Properties in a Windows XP system

This produces a listing similar to the one shown in Figure 12-5. Use these values to fill in the following settings and then verify them with your instructor.

IP Address _____

Subnet Mask _____

Default Gateway _____

DNS Servers _____

Step 2 You should be familiar with one final configuration: Automatic Private IP Addressing, or APIPA. If Windows is configured to obtain an IP address automatically and no DHCP server is available, Microsoft will automatically configure an address in the 169.254.0.0 network. Follow these steps to explore APIPA:

a. In a classroom lab environment, have the instructor disable the DHCP server if applicable. Alternatively, you can disconnect the DHCP server's UTP cable from the hub or switch.

b. Verify that your TCP/IP Properties settings are set to *Obtain an IP address automatically* and *Obtain DNS server address automatically*. Close all windows and reboot the system.

c. Launch a Command Prompt window and, at the prompt, type the following command:

```
C:\Documents and Settings\%USERNAME%\>ipconfig /all
```

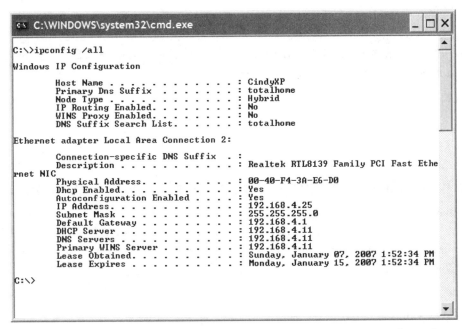

Figure 12-5 Windows ipconfig /all command results on a system configured to use DHCP

This produces a listing similar to the one shown in Figure 12-6. Use these values to fill in the following settings and then verify them with your instructor.

IP Address _____

Subnet Mask _____

Default Gateway _____

DNS Server _____

```
C:\WINDOWS\System32\cmd.exe                              _ □ ×

C:\>ipconfig /all

Windows IP Configuration

        Host Name . . . . . . . . . . . : test-v93yi93158
        Primary Dns Suffix  . . . . . . :
        Node Type . . . . . . . . . . . : Unknown
        IP Routing Enabled. . . . . . . : No
        WINS Proxy Enabled. . . . . . . : No

Ethernet adapter Local Area Connection:

        Connection-specific DNS Suffix  . :
        Description . . . . . . . . . . : VMware Accelerated AMD PCNet Adapter

        Physical Address. . . . . . . . : 00-0C-29-CC-40-76
        Dhcp Enabled. . . . . . . . . . : Yes
        Autoconfiguration Enabled . . . : Yes
        Autoconfiguration IP Address. . . : 169.254.81.77
        Subnet Mask . . . . . . . . . . : 255.255.0.0
        Default Gateway . . . . . . . . :

C:\>_
```

Figure 12-6 Windows ipconfig /all command results on a system using APIPA

    d.   Exit the Command Prompt window and launch the TCP/IP Properties dialog box again. Return all settings to the normal classroom configuration. Click OK to finish and close all the windows. Reboot the system, verify that it's working properly, and verify that you have reestablished network communication to its prior state.

 30 MINUTES

Lab Exercise 12.03: Testing Your LAN Connections

Various tools are available that will help you test and troubleshoot your new network. The textbook covers using these tools in detail. Some of these tools will be beneficial to you as a CompTIA A+ certified technician and are covered on the CompTIA A+ 220-802 exam. This lab exercise lets you practice using several key network troubleshooting tools.

Learning Objectives

In this exercise, you'll be introduced to troubleshooting tools for determining proper installation of network components. These tools are covered in order of importance. First, you'll verify local settings. Next, you'll try to access other systems on the same LAN. Finally, you'll test Internet connectivity.

At the end of this lab, you'll be able to

- Use the ipconfig command to determine local network settings
- Use the net config command to check the local system name and who is logged on as a user
- Use the ping command to test the local TCP/IP software and adapter
- Use the net view command to check for other computers on the network
- Use the ping command with switches to test connectivity to other computers
- Use the nslookup command to translate IP addresses and domain names
- Use the tracert command to check the path to other computers

Lab Materials and Setup

The materials you need for this lab are

- A PC system that's properly configured for network access using Windows
- Access to the Internet

✔ **Hint**

The commands vary slightly depending on the operating system you use. You should practice with each operating system if possible. Test the LAN first by accessing another computer on the network using My Network Places/Network.

Getting Down to Business

As a PC technician, you should be familiar with several networking tools, both for your own good and because they're covered on the CompTIA A+ 220-802 exam. You'll begin by looking at ipconfig.

✔ Hint

Since you have already used the ipconfig /all command, run through the steps again, either on your own system or on a different lab machine. Ask the instructor if any different networks or system configurations are available to explore.

Step 1   You have already examined ipconfig in Lab Exercise 12.02. You'll now use the ipconfig command again to determine local network settings. As you have already learned, checking the automatic TCP/IP settings given to you by a DHCP server and verifying your manual settings is easy: just open a Command Prompt window, type **ipconfig /all**, and press ENTER. The details of your local network connection appear on the screen.

Does the display contain the settings that were automatically assigned by the DHCP server or the ones you entered manually?

_____

Record your settings here:

IP Address _____

Subnet Mask _____

Default Gateway _____

DNS Servers _____

Leave the Command Prompt window open; you'll use it throughout the rest of this exercise.

Step 2   You'll now use the net config command to check the local system name and to see who is logged on as a user. To confirm the computer name and discover who is currently logged on, you'll again use the command line.

Type **net config workstation** at the command prompt and press ENTER. You'll see how the identification is set up for your local PC. There's a lot of information listed, but you're only interested in a couple of items (see Figure 12-7).

How are these listed?

Computer name _____

User name _____

Workstation domain (workgroup) _____

Software version _____

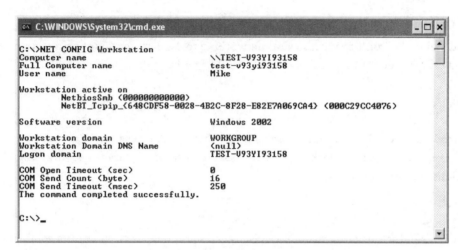

Figure 12-7 Using the net config workstation command in Windows XP

Step 3   You'll now use the ping command to test the local TCP/IP software and adapter.

At the command prompt, type **ping 127.0.0.1** (including the periods) and press ENTER. This is known as the IPv4 loopback or localhost address and will test the TCP/IP software and the internal part of the local network card. Look at Figure 12-8 to see a successful test. If you don't see the test results, there are serious problems with the software. Reinstall your network drivers, and reconfigure the TCP/IP settings.

→ **Note**

Want to see some IPv6 action? At the command prompt, type **ping ::1**. The IPv6 loopback address is ::1. When you ping it, it's just like running ping using 127.0.0.1, but it uses IPv6 instead.

Step 4   You'll now use the net view command to check for other computers on the network.

```
C:\WINDOWS\system32\cmd.exe

C:\>ping 127.0.0.1

Pinging 127.0.0.1 with 32 bytes of data:

Reply from 127.0.0.1: bytes=32 time=8ms TTL=128
Reply from 127.0.0.1: bytes=32 time<1ms TTL=128
Reply from 127.0.0.1: bytes=32 time<1ms TTL=128
Reply from 127.0.0.1: bytes=32 time<1ms TTL=128

Ping statistics for 127.0.0.1:
    Packets: Sent = 4, Received = 4, Lost = 0 (0% loss),
Approximate round trip times in milli-seconds:
    Minimum = 0ms, Maximum = 8ms, Average = 2ms

C:\>
```

Figure 12-8 A successful ping test

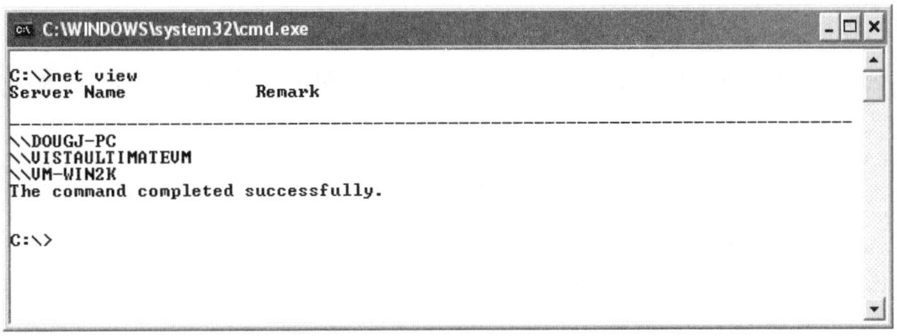

FIGURE 12-9 Using the net view command

You want to establish that other computers are available on the network so that you can test that your network card can transmit and receive data in Step 5.

At the command prompt, type **net view** and press ENTER. You'll see which other computers are on the network by a listing of their computer names (see Figure 12-9).

Step 5 Now you'll use the ping command to test your ability to connect to other computers on the network.

In Step 4 you obtained the names of other systems on the LAN, so now you want to check whether you can actually communicate with them.

At the command prompt, type **ping** *computer name*, where *computer name* is another PC's host name on the network you found in Step 4, and press ENTER. The results will look the same as when you used ping to see your own computer, but with the other computer's IP address (see Figure 12-10). Be sure to put a space between the ping command and the computer name. If you get errors, use the net view command again to be certain of the computer name's spelling. If the DNS is down, you can adjust by pinging the other computer's IP address instead of its name.

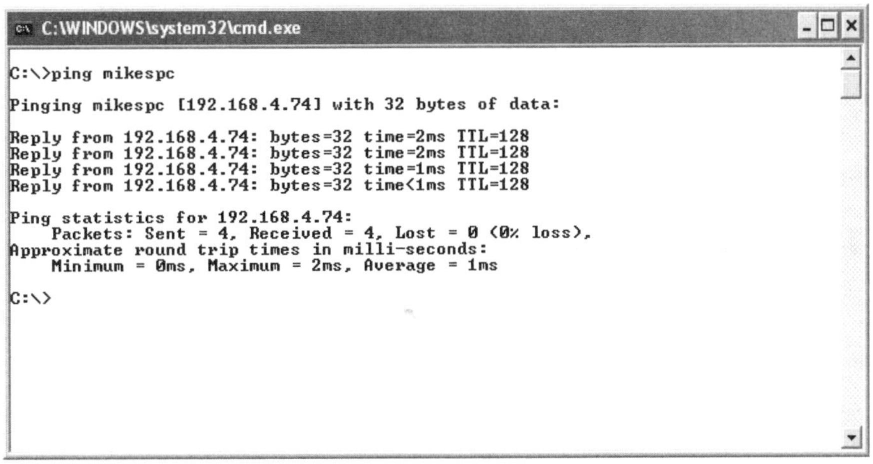

FIGURE 12-10 Pinging a computer by its name

→   **Try This: Ping Switches**

The humble ping command is one of the most frequently used troubleshooting tools for TCP/IP. As you saw in Step 5, you can actually use ping to test whether DNS is working. If you do not receive a response from the computer using its host name, but you do receive a response when using the IP address, this points to a problem with DNS.

Ping also has a number of switches that add to the functionality of the command. If you need to explore the switches, type the following at the command prompt:

```
C:\>ping /?
```

This will list all of the available switches and their functions. The following combination is typically used for a connection that seems to drop packets intermittently. You would run the command indefinitely and increase the packet size to overload the connection. Type the following command:

```
C:\>ping -t -l 65000 computername
```

To stop the continuous ping, press CTRL-c to break the program.

Step 6   You'll now use the nslookup command to translate an Internet domain name to an IP address or an IP address to an Internet domain name.

This is a good command for finding out the IP addresses of Web sites. Why do I want this, you ask? Well, when you use a URL in your browser, it has to be translated somewhere to an IP address. This slows down your access time. If you know the IP address and type that into the address of your Internet browser, the site will pop up faster. Follow these steps:

  a.   Type **nslookup microsoft.com**, and then press ENTER.

   What's the IP address(es) of http://www.microsoft.com? _____

   Try **nslookup totalsem.com**.

   What's the IP address(es) of http://www.totalsem.com? _____

  b.   Now enter the IP address you got when you did a lookup for http://www.microsoft.com. If you get a different result, it could be that a Web site is being hosted by someone other than the original domain you looked up.

Step 7   You'll now use the tracert command to check the path to other computers or Web sites on the Internet.

This command will show you where the bottlenecks are in the Internet. The tracert command will list the time it takes to get from your PC to the Web site or other system you're accessing. Follow these steps:

a. Type **tracert google.com**, and then press ENTER.

Was it successful? _____

How many hops did it take? _____

What's the IP address of the first hop? _____

b. Use the nslookup command with the IP address of the first hop to see where your first server is located.

Go ahead—have fun with this! Part of the learning process with PCs is to dive in and tackle a subject that you're not completely familiar with. As long as you remember to write down any information you want to change before you change it, you can enjoy exploring the amazing world of computers and still have a recovery point.

Lab Analysis Test

1. A user complains that after you installed the new NIC in her system, she can see everyone on the network but can't access the Internet. What did you forget to do? Are there any other configuration problems that could cause this to happen?

2. What command would you use to test the NIC's internal TCP/IP capabilities? What would the "human readable" address be?

3. Jerry is attempting to make a crossover cable for a customer. Jerry has forgotten the wire pattern to create the cable. Remind Jerry of what the TIA/EIA standards are along with the color arrangement of the wires from left to right.

4. How do you access the Local Area Connection Properties dialog box in Windows 7?

5. Tanner has replaced his old 100BaseT NIC with a new 1000BaseT NIC. The office network is set up and works fine for everyone else. Now he can't see anyone on the network or access the Internet. Where should he start checking and in what order?

Key Term Quiz

Use the following terms to complete the following sentences. Not all terms will be used.

568A

568B

Automatic Private IP Addressing (APIPA)

crimpers

crossover cable

default gateway

Dynamic Host Configuration Protocol (DHCP)

domain name service (DNS)

dynamic

IP address

ipconfig

net view

Network and Sharing Center

Network Connections

nslookup

ping

RJ-45

snips

static

straight-through cable

subnet mask

tracert

1. The _____ and _____ are the minimum addressing requirements for setting up a network card using the TCP/IP protocol.

2. A(n) _____ address is an address that is self-assigned by the computer to make local communication in the event that a DHCP server can't be reached.

3. A user should go to the _____ in Windows 7 to view and manage all of their network settings.

4. A(n) _____ is used to connect two similar devices together for communication, such as connecting two switches together.

5. The _____ command is used to query the state of DNS servers.

Chapter 13

Implementing and Troubleshooting Wireless Networks

Lab Exercises

Wireless networks are so common today that most people don't take the time to understand the differences between a hard wired network and a wireless one. With mobile computing on the rise, it's important for CompTIA A+ certified technicians to know as much about wireless networks as possible so that they are prepared to provide quality service in any situation to the users they support. New technicians may be asked questions like, "When should you set up a network with a server," and, "How do you set up a wireless network?" You need to know not only how to set up a wireless network, but also how to configure and secure that network. In the lab exercises in this chapter, you'll set up, configure, and secure a couple of wireless networks so that you are prepared to do the same in a real-world setting.

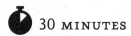 30 MINUTES

Lab Exercise 13.01: Setting Up a Wireless Network

Your neighbor is interested in starting a home business and has asked you to help him set up a wireless network. The only equipment he currently has is a desktop computer, a laptop computer, a mobile phone, and a USB printer, all of which he is considering using with his business. He wants to be able to communicate with his clients wirelessly from any room in his house. He's asked you to help him decide what additional equipment he needs to purchase.

Learning Objectives

This lab tests basic wireless network setup skills and helps you to think about scenarios you might encounter.

At the end of this lab, you'll be able to

- Recommend proper wireless equipment (for example, wireless cards and routers)
- Identify solutions for proper placement of equipment
- Set up and configure a wireless router

Lab Materials and Setup

The materials you need for this lab are

- A working desktop computer running Windows, with some form of broadband Internet connection

- A laptop with wireless connectivity

- Two Ethernet cables

- A wireless router

Getting Down to Business

First, you will need to tell your friend that he needs to buy a wireless router. He'll also need a Wi-Fi adapter (if he doesn't have one already). Once he's purchased the necessary equipment, he needs to connect it. It may seem strange, but you have to plug in several cables ("wires") when you set up a wireless network.

Step 1 Figure out how your neighbor's computer is physically connected to the Internet. If you are at his home, chances are that he has either a DSL or cable modem that connects to his computer via an Ethernet cable. In order to set up the wireless network, disconnect the Ethernet cable from your computer.

Step 2 Plug the Ethernet cable running from the wall jack or modem into the back of the wireless router. There is often a specific jack labeled "Internet" for you to use. Plug in the router and turn it on, if it doesn't turn on automatically. The router is ready when all the lights remain on and steady. There may be one or two blinking lights—it's okay.

Step 3 Now plug one end of the second Ethernet cable into the wireless router and the other end into the desktop computer's RJ-45 Ethernet port. You may be thinking that this wireless network isn't looking very wireless so far, but think of it this way: how often do you pick up your entire desktop setup and move it into another room? Not very often, I'd wager.

Step 4 Now that all the cables are in place, go to the laptop and see if you can find the wireless network. Windows alerts you with a pop-up once it locates a new wireless network (see Figure 13-1). Clicking on the message bubble will then present you with a list of all the found networks.

When you have finished the exercise, have your instructor initial here: _____

Figure 13-1 Windows has detected wireless networks

 30 MINUTES

Lab Exercise 13.02: Configuring and Securing a Wireless Network

Now that you've installed a wireless router, you must configure it properly so that it is secure from pesky invaders. Be sure to follow these step-by-step instructions so you can reduce the chances of your data being exposed, stolen, or attacked by hackers.

Learning Objectives

This lab enables you to configure and secure your network.

At the end of this lab, you'll be able to

- Properly configure a wireless router

- Set up security options to keep intruders out

Lab Materials and Setup

The materials you need for this lab are

- A working desktop computer running Windows with some form of Internet connection

- A laptop with wireless connectivity

- A wireless router

Getting Down to Business

Failing to configure and secure a wireless network is like leaving your debit card on the sidewalk outside your house with the PIN written on it—chances are that someone will take advantage of the situation and do something unscrupulous. Configuring and securing your wireless network is a fairly easy task. Just be sure to do it. Many people will simply hook up a wireless router, turn it on, and go about their business, not realizing what they've opened themselves up to. For the sake of your private data, follow the steps in this lab exercise.

Keep in mind that configuring a wireless network depends heavily on the router/wireless access point being used. The following steps lead you through the basics, but for more details, check the manual that came with your device.

Step 1 To secure your wireless network, you will use the configuration tool included with your router/wireless access point. To access it, open a Web browser and type **192.168.1.1** (or sometimes **192.168.0.1**) into the address bar. This is the most common address used for the setup utility. You may get a pop-up dialog box or other screen asking for a user name and password. Again, the defaults for these are often **admin** and **password**. This is true across multiple brands, which is all the more reason to change them as soon as possible!

Step 2   You should now be in the setup utility. Different devices use different names, but look for the Wireless Settings page (see Figure 13-2). If it's not called that, look for a screen with options for network name, security options, or MAC address options. Once you've found it, find the box used to enter a network name, or SSID. Delete the one that is there already and create a new one that is unique but memorable. When you try to connect to your wireless router, you'll want to know which one is yours, and changing the SSID will help your router stand out.

Step 3   Usually on the same page as the network name are wireless network security options. These include choices such as WEP, WPA, WPA2, and None. (You'll also see terms like Personal or PSK and RADIUS.) If it's available, select WPA2-PSK; otherwise, select WPA-PSK. WEP is an older encryption technology that is far less secure. There should also be an empty box labeled "password" or "passphrase" or "pre-shared key." Enter a unique and memorable password to be used whenever you want to connect to the wireless network. Save these settings.

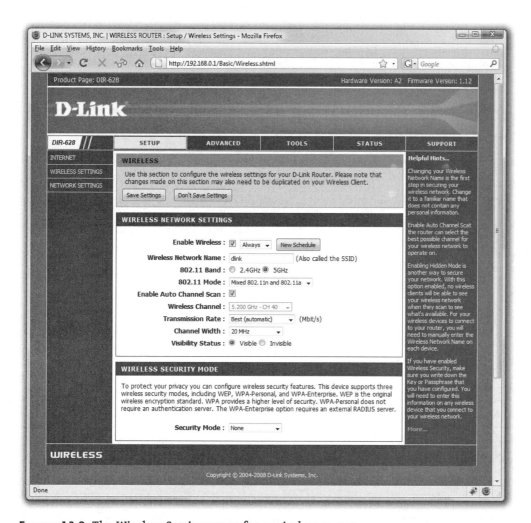

Figure 13-2 The Wireless Settings page for a wireless router

Step 4 Finally, now that you've secured the wireless connection by enabling WPA2 or another encryption option, you need to secure the router itself. Remember that 99 percent of routers use "admin" and "password" as the user name and password to access the router's setup utility. Failing to change these is an invitation to intruders. Find the setup utility's administration options, or something similar, and change the user name and password to something unique and memorable.

When you have finished the exercise, have your instructor initial here: _____

→ **Note**

You may hear that turning off the SSID broadcast will help secure your wireless Internet. This is actually a bit of a mixed bag. Users will still need to learn the SSID of your network to join it, but modern versions of Windows display available wireless networks even if the SSID isn't broadcast. Disabling the SSID broadcast makes it more difficult to join a wireless network, but it doesn't entirely hide your network.

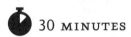 30 MINUTES

Lab Exercise 13.03: Setting Up an Ad Hoc Wireless Network

Okay, so you've set up a traditional wireless network and learned how to secure it. But what if all you really want to do is play a game with someone, share some files, or search the Internet without a bunch of wires and a router? In CompTIA A+ terminology, we would call this an ad hoc peer-to-peer network.

Learning Objectives

This lab gives you another option for setting up a network.

At the end of this lab, you'll be able to

• Connect two or more computers together wirelessly

Lab Materials and Setup

The materials you need for this lab are

• Two computers with wireless connectivity and Windows XP, Windows Vista, or Windows 7 installed

Getting Down to Business

The process for setting up an ad hoc wireless network is even simpler than the process for setting up a normal wireless network. However, due in part to their temporary nature, ad hoc wireless networks are not nearly as common. Still, the next time you've got two laptops but no network, and you desperately need to share some files, you'll be glad you know how to set up an ad hoc wireless network.

Step 1 (Windows XP)   In Windows XP, open the Control Panel and double-click Network Connections. Right-click Wireless Network Connection and click Properties. In the Wireless Network Connection Properties dialog box, select the Wireless Networks tab. Verify that the *Use Windows to configure my wireless network settings* box is selected. If it is not, select it. Click Add.

Step 2 (Windows XP)   The Wireless network properties dialog box opens (see Figure 13-3). In the Network name (SSID) text box, enter the name of the network you want to add. I suggest calling it something simple, like "temp." Create a password and confirm it. Uncheck the *The key is provided for me automatically* checkbox and check the *This is a computer-to-computer (ad hoc) network; wireless access points are not used* checkbox. Click OK. You are returned to the Wireless Networks tab, and the new network name appears in the Preferred networks list.

Step 1 (Windows Vista/7)   In Windows Vista/7, go to the Control Panel and open the Network and Sharing Center. Select *Manage wireless networks* and click Add.

→ **Note**

The *Manage wireless networks* option appears only if you have a wireless network card.

Step 2 (Windows Vista/7)   In the *Manually connect to a wireless network* dialog box, choose *Create an ad hoc network*. Click Next, and then create a simple network name. Select a security type from the menu

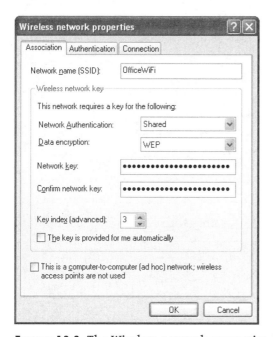

Figure 13-3 The Wireless network properties dialog box

provided (WPA2 is preferred) and enter a password. Check the *Save this network* checkbox and click Next. You've now set up the ad hoc wireless network.

When you have finished the exercise, have your instructor initial here: _____

Lab Analysis Test

1. What are the primary differences between WEP, WPA, and WPA2?

2. What are two common IP addresses for wireless routers?

3. In what situations would you recommend an ad hoc network to a user?

4. What is the path used to get to TCP/IP properties for a network adapter in Windows XP?

5. How does a wireless router communicate signals?

Key Term Quiz

Use the following terms to complete the following sentences. Not all terms will be used.

49

54

802.11n

ad hoc

cell phone

WEP

wireless access point

WPA

WPA2

wireless router

1. Network adapters wirelessly connect your computer to your _____.

2. A(n) _____ router is ideal for multimedia (gaming) applications because of its significant range and speed.

3. An 802.11g router can communicate up to _____ Mbps with a throughput of up to 22 Mbps.

4. You create a(n) _____ network when you connect two computers directly via a wireless connection.

5. When securing your wireless network, use _____ encryption because it is the most secure.

Chapter 14

Implementing and Troubleshooting Networks

Lab Exercises

Computer networks and kindergarten have one big thing in common: the importance of sharing. Sharing files and other resources among computers is the primary reason that computer networks were invented in the first place. Without the ability to share, networked computers would just sit there, linked together, with nothing to do. This chapter will cover the process of sharing files and other resources in a Windows network. Not only that, but you'll learn how to test that your LAN connections are all working properly so that you can share files (legal ones!) to your heart's content.

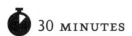 30 MINUTES

Lab Exercise 14.01: Sharing Resources

The entire concept of networking is based around sharing resources. You can share any folder or other resource. Optical drives, hard drives, and printers can all be shared.

Learning Objectives

In this lab exercise, you'll set up file sharing for others to access information from their system.

At the end of this lab, you'll be able to

- Enable and configure shared directories and other resources

Lab Materials and Setup

The materials you need for this lab are

- A PC system properly configured for LAN access using Windows

Getting Down to Business

Whew! That last exercise was interesting, but the job is only half done. Now you'll find where to set up sharing for a particular resource.

Step 1   Open My Computer/Computer, double-click the C: drive, and create a new folder on the C: drive. Name it **Shared**. Right-click the Shared folder icon to see the folder options, and select Sharing and Security in Windows XP or Share in Windows Vista/7. This will open the Properties dialog box with the Sharing tab selected (see Figure 14-1).

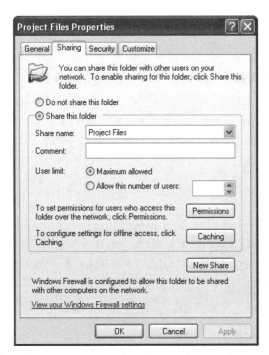

FIGURE 14-1 The Properties dialog box's Sharing tab in Windows XP

✔ **Hint**

If the Sharing tab isn't there, you probably forgot to enable the File and Printer Sharing option in the Networking applet. Go back and do that.

✔ **Hint**

If you're running Windows XP Home Edition or Windows XP Professional Edition in a workgroup environment, the Sharing tab is much simpler. It contains *Do not share this folder* and *Share this folder* buttons and a space to provide a share name.

Step 2   Try sharing and unsharing the folder. Note that the share name and permissions are grayed out when you select *Do not share this folder*. Share the folder again, change the share name, and look at the various levels of permissions: Full Control, Change, and Read.

Step 3   When you're done, click OK to close the dialog box.

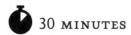 30 MINUTES

Lab Exercise 14.02: Testing Your LAN Connections

Various tools are available that will help you test and troubleshoot your new network. The textbook covers using these tools in detail. Some of these tools will be beneficial to you as a CompTIA A+ certified technician and are covered on the CompTIA A+ 220-802 exam. This lab exercise lets you practice using several key network troubleshooting tools.

Learning Objectives

In this lab exercise, you'll be introduced to troubleshooting tools for determining proper installation of the network components. These tools are covered in order of importance. First, you'll verify the local settings. Next, you'll try to access other systems on the same LAN. Finally, you'll test the Internet connectivity.

At the end of this lab, you'll be able to

- Use the ipconfig command to determine local network settings
- Use the net config command to check the local system name and who is logged on as a user
- Use the ping command to test the local TCP/IP software and adapter
- Use the net view command to check for other computers on the network
- Use the ping command with switches to test connectivity to other computers
- Use the nslookup command to translate IP addresses and domain names
- Use the tracert command to check the path to other computers

Lab Materials and Setup

The materials you need for this lab are

- A PC system properly configured for network access using Windows
- Access to the Internet

✔ **Hint**

The commands vary slightly depending on the operating system you use. You should practice with each operating system if possible. Test the LAN first by accessing another computer on the network using My Network Places / Network.

Getting Down to Business

As a PC technician, you should be familiar with several networking tools, both for your own good and because they're covered on the CompTIA A+ 220-802 exam. You'll begin by looking at ipconfig.

✔ **Hint**

Since you have already used the ipconfig /all command, run through the steps again, either on your own system or on a different lab machine. Ask the instructor if any different networks or system configurations are available to explore.

Step 1 You have already examined ipconfig in Lab Exercise 12.02. You'll now use the ipconfig command again to determine local network settings. As you have already learned, checking the automatic TCP/IP settings given to you by a DHCP server and verifying your manual settings is easy: just open a command-line window, type **ipconfig /all**, and press ENTER. The details of your local network connection appear on the screen.

Does the display contain the settings that were automatically assigned by the DHCP server or the ones you entered manually? _____

Record your settings here:

IP Address: _____

Subnet Mask: _____

Default Gateway: _____

DNS Servers: _____

Leave the command-prompt window open; you'll use it throughout the rest of this exercise.

Step 2 You'll now use the net config command to check the local system name and to see who is logged on as a user. To confirm the computer name and discover who is currently logged on, you'll again use the command line.

Type **net config workstation** at the command prompt and press ENTER. You'll see how the identification is set up for your local PC. There's a lot of information listed, but you're only interested in a couple of items (see Figure 14-2).

How are these listed?

Computer name: _____

User name: _____

Workstation domain (workgroup): _____

Software version: _____

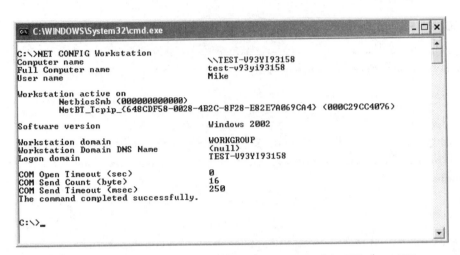

FIGURE 14-2 Using the net config workstation command in Windows XP

Step 3   You'll now use the ping command to test the local TCP/IP software and adapter. At the command-line prompt, type **ping 127.0.0.1** (including the periods) and press ENTER. This is known as the IPv4 LOOPBACK or LOCALHOST address and will test the TCP/IP software and the internal part of the local network card. Look at Figure 14-3 to see a successful test. If you don't see the test results, there are serious problems with the software. Reinstall your network drivers and reconfigure the TCP/IP settings.

Step 4   You'll now use the net view command to check for other computers on the network. You want to establish that other computers are available on the network so that you can test that your network card can transmit and receive data in Step 5.

At the command-line prompt, type **net view** and press ENTER. You'll see what other computers are on the network by a listing of their computer names (see Figure 14-4).

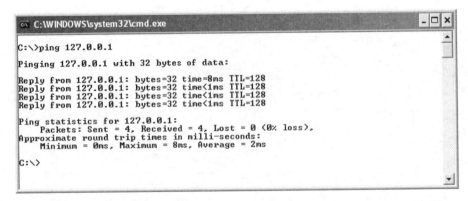

FIGURE 14-3 A successful ping test

```
C:\WINDOWS\system32\cmd.exe                                          _ □ ×

C:\>net view
Server Name              Remark
-----------------------------------------------------------------------
\\DOUGJ-PC
\\VISTAULTIMATEVM
\\VM-WIN2K
The command completed successfully.

C:\>
```

Figure 14-4 Using the net view command

Step 5 Now you'll use the ping command to test your ability to connect to other computers on the network.

In Step 4 you obtained the names of other systems on the LAN, so now you want to check whether you can actually communicate with them.

At the command-line prompt, type **ping** *computer name*, where *computer name* is another PC's host name on the network you found in Step 4, and press ENTER. The results will look the same as when you used ping to see your own computer, but with the other computer's IP address (see Figure 14-5). Be sure to put a space between the ping command and the computer name. If you get errors, use the net view command again to be certain of the computer name's spelling. If the DNS is down, you can adjust by pinging the other computer's IP address instead of its name.

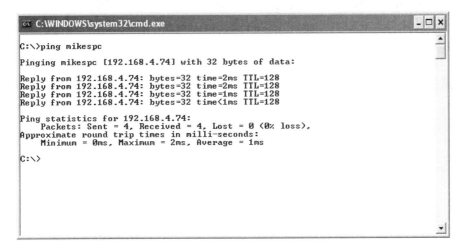

Figure 14-5 Using ping to view a computer by its name

→ **Try This: Ping Switches**

The humble ping command is one of the most frequently used troubleshooting tools for TCP/IP. As you saw in Step 5, you can actually use ping to test whether DNS is working. If you do not receive a response from the computer using its host name, but you do receive a response when using the IP address, this points to a problem with DNS.

Ping also has a number of switches that add to the functionality of the command. If you need to explore the switches, type the following at the command prompt:

```
C:\>ping /?
```

This will list all of the available switches and their functions. The following combination is typically used for a connection that seems to drop packets intermittently. You would run the command indefinitely and increase the packet size to overload the connection. Type the following command:

```
C:\>ping -t -l 65000 computername
```

To stop the continuous ping, press CTRL-C to break the program.

Step 6   You'll now use the nslookup command to translate an Internet domain name to an IP address or an IP address to an Internet domain name.

This is a good command for finding out the IP addresses of Web sites. Why do I want this, you ask? Well, when you use a URL in your browser, it has to be translated somewhere to an IP address. This slows down your access time. If you know the IP address and type that into the address of your Internet browser, the site will pop up faster. Follow these steps:

a. Type **nslookup microsoft.com**, and then press ENTER.

What's the IP address(s) of http://www.microsoft.com? _____

Try **nslookup totalsem.com**.

What's the IP address(s) of http://www.totalsem.com? _____

b. Now enter the IP address you got when you did a lookup for http://www.microsoft.com. If you get a different result, it could be that a Web site is being hosted by someone other than the original domain you looked up.

Step 7   You'll now use the tracert command to check the path to other computers or Web sites on the Internet.

This command will show you where the bottlenecks are in the Internet. The tracert command will list the time it takes to get from your PC to the Web site or another system you're accessing. Follow these steps:

a.   Type **tracert google.com**, and then press ENTER.

Was it successful? _____

How many hops did it take? _____

What's the IP address of the first hop? _____

b.   Use the nslookup command with the IP address of the first hop to see where your first server is located.

Go ahead—have fun with this! Part of the learning process with PCs is to dive in and tackle a subject that you're not completely familiar with. As long as you remember to write down any information you want to change before you change it, you can enjoy exploring the amazing world of computers and still have a recovery point.

Lab Analysis Test

1.   Write a paragraph about the three types of network organizations for Windows computers.

2.   Anne is starting a small business with eight employees. The employees will need to use several different PCs in the office. Write a short paragraph describing what kind of network Anne should set up.

3.   Jerry is having trouble connecting to the Internet. He can access his local network, but can't connect to any Web sites. Describe how you would troubleshoot that problem.

4.   How do you test a network interface card (NIC) to make sure it's working properly?

5.   Ron needs to share some files within the government department he runs. Tell Ron how he can do this.

Key Term Quiz

Use the following terms to complete the following sentences. Not all terms will be used.

activity light

link lights

loopback plug

loopback test

toner

tone generator

tone probe

1. _____ tell you if a NIC is physically connected to a network.

2. You can run a(n) _____ to make sure your NIC is working.

3. A(n) _____ shows you when there's traffic on the network.

4. A(n) _____ is a small device that links a NIC back on itself.

5. You can use a(n) _____ to trace wires within your network.

Chapter 15
Portable Computing

Lab Exercises

The world has gone mobile, and accomplished technicians travel right along with it. General technicians have always worked on the software side of portables, tweaking power management options to optimize battery life for the users. Working on the hardware side of portable computing devices of all stripes, however, used to be the realm of only highly specialized technicians. As portable computing devices become increasingly common and the technology inside becomes more modular, however, frontline general technicians (think CompTIA A+ certified technicians here) increasingly get the call to upgrade and repair these devices.

Most laptops and netbooks have parts that a user can easily replace. You can swap out a fading battery for a newer one, for example, or add a second battery in place of an optical drive for long airplane trips. Lurking beneath access panels on the underside or below the keyboard on some models are hardware components such as RAM, a hard drive, a network card, and a modem—just like laptop batteries, these units can be easily accessed and replaced by a technician. Some laptops even have panels for replacing the video card and CPU.

In this series of labs, you'll do four things. First, you'll use the Internet to research the upgrades available for portable computing devices so you can provide proper recommendations to employers and clients. Second, you'll open a laptop and gut it like a rainbow trout—removing and replacing RAM, the most common of all hardware upgrades. Third, you'll perform the traditional task of a portable PC technician, tweaking the power management options to optimize battery life on particular models. Finally, you'll tour a computer store to familiarize yourself with the latest and greatest portable offerings.

 30 MINUTES

Lab Exercise 15.01: Researching Laptop Upgrade Paths

Your boss just sent word that one of your most important clients wants to extend the life of their sales force's laptop computers by upgrading rather than replacing. You've been asked to provide an upgrade track for your client. This requires you to research the laptops used by the company to determine which upgrades you can make, and to verify that the laptops themselves are not so old that the cost to upgrade them outweighs the cost of new laptops with new technology. You have to determine whether you can add RAM, replace the hard drives, or replace the aging batteries. Get to work!

Learning Objectives

Given the manufacturer and model number of a notebook computer, you'll figure out how to upgrade your client's computers.

At the end of this lab, you'll be able to

- Determine the replacement price of a battery

- Determine memory upgrades, including the quantity and type of RAM

- Determine hard drive upgrades, including the capacity and price of a hard drive

Lab Materials and Setup

The materials you need for this lab are

- A working PC with Internet access

Getting Down to Business

Limber up your surfing fingers because you're about to spend some time on the Web. Researching information about hardware and software is something technicians do all the time. The better you are at it, the better you are at your job!

When you're searching for replacement and upgrade parts and information, always take a look at the device manufacturer's Web site. Most major PC manufacturers, such as Dell and Lenovo, have comprehensive product specification sheets available to the public on their sites. You can even order replacement parts directly from them! A popular tactic for researching upgrades is to grab the upgrade specs from the manufacturer's site and then search the Internet for the best prices. Not only are you doing your job well, but you'll be saving your company money too!

In the following steps, you'll navigate the tumultuous seas of the Internet in a quest to find the Golden Fleece of laptop battery, memory, and hard drive upgrades.

Step 1 Fire up your Web browser, and surf over to the device manufacturer's Web site. Try www.dell.com, or do a Google search for **laptop battery**. Many sites sell every laptop battery imaginable. The goal of this exercise is to become familiar with using the Internet to identify parts, confirm the specifications, and purchase replacement batteries. Once you reach a suitable Web site, answer the following questions:

You need replacement batteries for several Dell Precision M4400 laptops. What's the vendor's part number and price for this battery?

_____

What's the voltage and power capacity of the battery?

_____

✔ Hint

Just like any other electrical power source, batteries are rated according to voltage (9.6 V, for instance), current capacity (2600 milliamps per hour, or mAh), and sometimes power capacity (72 watts per hour, or WHr). When purchasing laptop batteries from third-party vendors (that is, vendors other than the laptop manufacturer), make sure to buy a battery that matches the voltage recommended by the manufacturer. Depending on the type of battery (Ni-Cd, Ni-MH, or Li-Ion), the current or power capacity of replacement batteries may be greater than that of the original battery. This is not a problem—increased current/power capacity means longer run times for your portable PC.

Step 2   Search the manufacturer's Web site for information on memory. If that isn't available, flip your browser over to www.kahlon.com to check RAM prices and availability. If the site isn't available, perform a Google search to find other Web sites that sell **laptop memory**. Then answer the following questions.

Your client has a Dell Precision M4400 with 1 GB of RAM. How much RAM can you install? How many sticks of RAM will it take to upgrade this machine to a respectable 4 GB of memory, and how much will it cost?

_____

_____

Step 3   Stay where you landed in your search for memory upgrades. Does the vendor have replacement or additional hard drives available as well? If not, try www.kahlon.com, but now research possible hard drive upgrades for the Dell Precision M4400 the client owns. Answer this question:

The client's Dell Precision M4400 laptops have 160-GB hard drives plus a currently unused modular media bay that could be used to house a second hard drive. How much would it cost to add a second 320-GB hard drive to the Dell?

_____

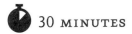 30 MINUTES

Lab Exercise 15.02: Replacing and Upgrading RAM

Your client settled on the RAM upgrades as the first step for making their laptops more usable, and you get tagged as the person to remove the old RAM and install the new. Upgrading RAM is the most common technician-performed upgrade on portable PCs and something you're likely to run into in the real world.

Learning Objectives

In this lab, you'll learn essential skills for upgrading portable PCs.

At the end of this lab, you'll be able to

- Access the RAM panel in a laptop
- Remove RAM in a laptop
- Install RAM properly in a laptop

Lab Materials and Setup

The materials you need for this lab are

- A working portable computer
- A very tiny Philips-head screwdriver
- An anti-static mat

✖ Warning

Opening a portable computer can result in a nonfunctional portable computer. Don't use the instructor's primary work laptop for this exercise!

Getting Down to Business

You're about to open the sensitive inner portions of a portable computer, but before you do, it's a great idea to refresh your memory about avoiding electrostatic discharge (ESD). The inside of a laptop looks different from the inside of a desktop or tower case, but the contents are just as sensitive to static electricity. Watch out!

Step 1 Using your handy screwdriver or other handy tool, open the access panel for the RAM. Every portable PC offers a different way to access the RAM, so I can't give you explicit directions here. Most often, you'll find a removable plate on the bottom of the laptop secured with a tiny Philips-head screw. Some laptops require you to remove the keyboard, unscrew a heat spreader, and then access the RAM. Figure 15-1 shows a typical panel, accessible from the underside of the laptop.

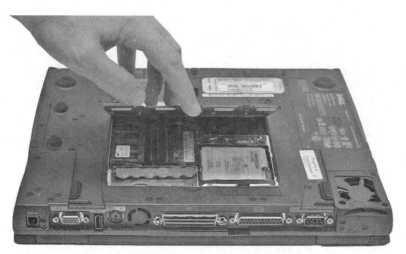

FIGURE 15-1 Opening the access panel to find RAM

Step 2   Once you have the panel open, push outward on the restraining clips on the RAM stick(s). This will cause the RAM to pop up partially (see Figure 15-2).

Step 3   Remove the RAM gently, gripping only at the noncontact edges. Place the stick(s) on an anti-static pad or in an anti-static bag.

FIGURE 15-2 Releasing the RAM

Step 4   Install the replacement RAM into the laptop, reversing the process of removal. Place the stick(s) at an angle into the RAM slots and push firmly. Once the contacts have disappeared, press the body of the RAM into the restraining clips.

✔ **Hint**

If you don't have new RAM to install, simply install the RAM you removed in Step 3. This gives you the opportunity to practice!

Step 5   Replace the access panel.

Step 6   Power on the laptop to confirm that the new RAM is recognized and functioning properly.

 30 MINUTES

Lab Exercise 15.03: Adjusting Power Management to Optimize Battery Life

Several of your sales staff members have to attend a conference on the other side of the country. The conference came up on short notice, so everyone needs time to prepare, even while on the flight to the conference. You've been tasked with configuring power management on their laptops to optimize battery life so they can work as long as possible while on the plane.

Learning Objectives

In this lab, you'll adjust the power management features for a PC, a task that's vital to proper support of portable PCs.

At the end of this lab, you'll be able to

- Enable and disable power management in the CMOS

- Change power management settings in Windows

Lab Materials and Setup

The materials you need for this lab are

- A working computer with Windows installed

- A BIOS that supports power management

✔ **Hint**

> Having a notebook computer available is a plus. Performing these steps on a notebook computer will allow you to configure the settings for the Portable/Laptop power scheme and then remove the power cord, running on battery power to experience the actual results. If you're practicing on a regular desktop PC, keep in mind that a notebook will have two options for each adjustment: one for when the notebook is using battery power, and one for when it's connected to the alternating current (AC) source.

Getting Down to Business

Windows PCs have two separate areas for power management: the CMOS setup program and the Control Panel. You'll start with CMOS and then go to the Control Panel.

Step 1   Boot your system, and enter the CMOS setup program.

✔ **Cross-Reference**

> Refer to the "Power Management" section in Chapter 15 of *Mike Meyers' CompTIA A+ Guide to 802: Managing and Troubleshooting PCs* for more information on power management on portable PCs.

Now follow these steps:

a.   Go to the Power Management Setup screen.

b.   Enable power management if it's currently disabled.

c.   Look at each option for common-sense settings. For example, when operating on battery power, the portable should be configured for maximum energy efficiency, thus increasing run time.

d.   Make sure the ACPI setting is enabled if the BIOS supports it.

e.   Save your settings, and boot the system to the Windows desktop.

✔ **Hint**

> ACPI is short for Advanced Configuration and Power Interface, a power management specification developed by Intel, Microsoft, and Toshiba. ACPI enables the operating system to control the amount of power given to each device attached to the computer. With ACPI, the operating system can turn off peripheral devices, such as optical drives, when they're not in use.

Step 2   Access the Power Options applet in the Control Panel, and make a note of your current power management settings.

Check out the different power schemes available (this will depend on your specific system) and change the settings to see how they affect when the monitor and hard drives turn off. Each of these schemes has adjustable times. The tabs and settings will differ depending on which version of Windows you're running. Be sure to look at them all. To see more detailed power scheme settings in Windows Vista/7, be sure to click *Change power/plan settings* and then *Change advanced power settings*.

✔ Hint

The Windows XP Power Options Properties dialog box (on a notebook) has five tabs: Power Schemes, Alarms, Power Meter, Advanced, and Hibernate (see Figure 15-3). You can use the Alarms tab to set the time when the battery alarm is activated. The Power Meter tab shows the percent of charge remaining in the battery.

✖ Warning

Some PCs and some components don't like standby and suspend modes. They can cause your computer to lock up. Be aware of that, and if your computer locks up, turn those settings off.

Step 3 Once you've finished experimenting, enable or disable power management as you prefer.

Figure 15-3 Accessing the Windows XP power options on a portable computer

OPEN

Lab Exercise 15.04: Field Trip to Play with the Latest Portable PCs

The best way to understand portable PCs (laptops, netbooks, tablet PCs, and smartphones) is to play with one. If there isn't one available in the classroom, then this exercise is for you.

Learning Objectives

This lab will take you into the field for a little computer browsing—for educational purposes, of course!

At the end of this lab, you'll be able to

- Recognize the variations in key features among different portable PCs

Lab Materials and Setup

The materials you need for this lab are

- A local computer store or other retailer with a good selection of portable PCs you can examine

✔ **Hint**

If you don't have a store nearby, use the Web to browse a computer store such as CompUSA (www.compusa.com), or go to a manufacturer's Web site such as Dell's (www.dell.com) and customize a laptop to your heart's content. Be sure to explore all the options and customizations you can add to it. Just make sure you don't click Buy!

Getting Down to Business

Portable PCs are manufactured by a wide variety of companies, and no two notebooks are created equal. Some notebooks feature a slim and lightweight profile and are designed for the busy traveler; others feature a full complement of ports and rival desktop PCs in their power and features. Netbooks are smaller, compact versions of laptops that are ideal as long-term traveling companions. They can fit in a purse or backpack and thus are handy for browsing or doing e-mail on the road. Tablet PCs have pen-based interfaces that allow you to use them like a paper notepad. Smartphones are great for staying connected everywhere you go—we'll take a closer look at smartphones and their tablet relatives in Chapter 16. Take a look at all the available models and compare their features.

Step 1   Go to your local computer store or office supply store and check out the portable PCs on display. Try to find a store with a variety of brands. Bring this lab manual (or a copy of the following chart) with you to record the different specs you find.

Step 2 Pick out three portables, preferably from different manufacturers. For each portable, record the following information.

Feature	Portable 1	Portable 2	Portable 3
Size/weight			
Screen type/size			
CPU			
RAM			
Pointing device(s)			
I/O ports			
ExpressCard(s)			
Hard disk drive/solid-state drive			
Floppy/optical drive(s)			

Lab Analysis Test

1. Bill wants to upgrade his memory from 2 GB to the maximum amount of RAM his notebook can take. He has a Lenovo ThinkPad T500 notebook. How much RAM does he need to buy?

2. Teresa complains that her Windows XP notebook turns itself off without any warning. What should she adjust?

3. Maanit will be traveling from the United States to India. He'll use his laptop to watch DVDs on the way, usually on battery power. Lately, the battery seems to run out of juice well before the battery specifications indicate. What could possibly cause this recent development? Are there any recommendations you would make to Maanit to improve his laptop's performance?

4. During your research earlier in these exercises, which did you discover to be the most expensive—hard drives, memory, or batteries? Which component was the most inexpensive to replace?

5. Would the LCD screen or hard drives turn off, for energy conservation, if you set your power scheme to Always On and you walked away for a long period of time? Why or why not?

Key Term Quiz

Use the following terms to complete the following sentences. Not all terms will be used.

Advanced Configuration and Power Interface (ACPI)

battery

hard drive

hibernate

memory

netbook

notebook

Power Meter

Power Options

Power Scheme

standby

1. The amount of time the hard drive will continue to spin once it's no longer being accessed is determined by the _____ setting in Windows XP and the advanced power settings in Windows Vista/7.

2. You can use the _____ applet in the Control Panel to set the power conservation options for the notebook computer.

3. The battery, _____, and _____ are all upgradeable laptop components.

4. The amount of power remaining in a battery can be determined by looking at the _____.

5. Software can control power consumption if _____ is turned on in the CMOS setup program.

Chapter 16
Mobile Devices

Lab Exercises

The Internet-connected experience has jumped off of our desks and into our hands. Smartphones and tablets, grouped into a category called "mobile devices," enable you to consume, communicate, and create all sorts of digital goodies on the go. You don't even need to sync them with your desktop if you don't want to; they can function independently of any other device. In fact, most of today's smartphones and tablets are more powerful than the PC you had five years ago. These devices are everywhere, so you need to know something about them. As a PC tech, people will assume you know how to fix anything technical, including smartphones and tablets. The following lab exercises are meant to familiarize you with the most basic features of Apple iOS and Google Android smartphones and tablets.

 30 MINUTES

Lab Exercise 16.01: Comparing Apple iOS and Google Android

Several companies compete for mobile device dominance, but two of the biggest (and most important for the CompTIA A+ 220-802 exam) companies are Apple and Google. As much as some might hate to admit it, Apple practically invented the modern touchscreen smartphone with the first iPhone. On the other hand, there are a lot more Android devices available (in multiple form factors and prices, unlike Apple's single smartphone and tablet offerings). While other mobile device ecosystems exist (like Windows Phone 7 and BlackBerry), you'll encounter Apple iOS and Google Android devices so much more often in the field that it makes sense to focus on these two mobile OSs when doing research in this lab exercise.

Learning Objectives

In this exercise, you'll research the differences between Apple iOS and Google Android.

At the end of this lab, you'll be able to

- Differentiate between Apple iOS and Google Android

Lab Materials and Setup

The materials you need for this lab are

- An Internet-capable PC for research

- Optional: An iOS device and an Android device for comparison

Getting Down to Business

At first glance, Apple iOS and Google Android devices have a lot in common: big touchscreens, icons you can tap, Web pages you can swipe, and so on. Peek under the surface, however, and you'll see how different the two mobile operating systems really are. You need to understand how both Apple iOS and Google Android operate, what they have in common, and how they differ.

Step 1   First take a look at Apple's mobile operating system, iOS. A mobile operating system is a lot different from a desktop OS, so make sure you know all the details. Open your Web browser and search for the following topics.

a.   What is the latest version of Apple iOS?

_____

b.   What devices use iOS?

_____

c.   List five features of the latest version of Apple iOS.

_____

_____

_____

_____

_____

Step 2   Next, take a look at Google's mobile operating system, Android. Android devices don't all use the latest OS, and most device manufacturers customize the OS with a special user interface. Keep this in mind when searching for information about Google Android.

a.   What is the latest version of Google Android?

_____

b.   List a few smartphone and/or tablet manufacturers that use Android.

_____

c. List five features of the latest version of Android.

_____

_____

_____

_____

_____

Step 3 For each feature, fill in the following table with a **Yes** or **No** response to indicate whether or not it applies to each OS. Some features are present in both Android and iOS devices.

	Android	iOS
A closed source operating system	_____	_____
An open source operating system	_____	_____
Can sync with iTunes	_____	_____
Can be used with smartphones and tablets	_____	_____
Can install apps	_____	_____
Devices use a capacitive screen	_____	_____
Devices use a resistive screen	_____	_____
Can connect to Bluetooth devices	_____	_____
Devices can expand storage through external flash memory	_____	_____
Has mouse support	_____	_____

 30 MINUTES

Lab Exercise 16.02: Installing Apps in iOS

Installing an app (a short and hip way of saying "application") is probably one of the more important skills to have when using any mobile device. In this exercise, you'll connect to a wireless access point and download an app using an Apple iOS device like the iPad, iPhone, or iPod. Remember that you can do this on Android devices as well, but with multiple app stores and sources available, the Android app ecosystem can seem a lot more confusing. Apple's closed app ecosystem means that the process is centralized and straightforward.

→ **Note**

Installing an app on an Android device can be quite different, but I encourage you to try both!

Learning Objectives

In this lab, you'll connect to a WAP, then download and install an app.

At the end of this lab, you'll be able to

- Configure an iOS device for wireless access and install a new app

Lab Materials and Setup

The materials you need for this lab are

- An iOS-compatible device with access to the Internet

- An Apple ID

Getting Down to Business

I'm sure we've all heard the line, "There's an app for that," but you're about to test that theory. Finding and installing the right app is what makes a modern smartphone smart.

Step 1   First, you will connect to a Wi-Fi network so that you can get on the Internet. If you don't have an available Wi-Fi connection, skip to Step 2.

    a.   Go to the home screen by pressing the home button on your device (the big physical button beneath the screen). Tap on the Settings icon (see Figure 16-1); you might need to swipe to another screen if you've moved the Settings icon. Tap on Wi-Fi. Make sure the Wi-Fi is set to ON. Tap on the appropriate SSID to connect.

    b.   If the Wi-Fi network is encrypted, provide the password on the next screen. Tap Join.

FIGURE 16-1 iOS Settings button

c. You should now see a checkmark next to the network you chose. Tap the small arrow button on the Wi-Fi network you joined to view the network settings. You should see all of your DHCP information (see Figure 16-2). You can also tap Forget this Network, which removes any profile information you have for that particular SSID. (Don't do that right now, though.)

d. Press the home screen button to return to the home screen. When connected to a wireless network, you should see your Wi-Fi signal strength in the status bar at the top of the screen, near the time.

Step 2 Now that you are connected to the Internet, you will download an app from the App Store.

a. Tap on the App Store icon, then tap Top 25. List the current Top 5 Free apps.

_____

_____

_____

_____

_____

b. Tap Search, then type **mactracker** in the search box. Tap the Search button.

Figure 16-2 Wi-Fi network settings screen

c. Tap Mactracker. (It should be the top search result.)

d. Give a short description of this app.

_____

_____

e. What is the app's version number and how big is it?

_____

f. Tap INSTALL and enter your Apple ID password.

g. The Mactracker app will download and install onto your device. Depending on your Internet connection speed, this might take a while.

Step 3   Once Mactracker has successfully downloaded, you should see the app on one of your home screens.

a. Tap the app to open it (see Figure 16-3). What you are seeing is a historical listing of every Apple product ever made.

FIGURE 16-3 Mactracker app running

b. Swipe (scroll) down and tap on iPhone. Tap iPhone 4S. Fill in the following specifications.

Initial price for the 16-GB model: _____

Display resolution: _____

Capacities: _____

Processor type: _____

Processor speed: _____

Number of cores on processor: _____

What version of iOS was released with this device? _____

How long will the battery last while talking over a 3G network? _____

c. Exit the app by pressing the home button. Once you are at the home screen, you might think the app has been closed because you can't see it anymore. But guess what? That app is still loaded in your device's RAM.

d. Double-tap the home button quickly. The home screen slides up to reveal a row of apps on the bottom. This bar works a lot like the taskbar in Windows.

e. Tap the Mactracker app and hold your finger on the screen. All of the icons should start jiggling. This is referred to, in all seriousness, as "jiggle" mode.

f. Tap the white minus sign in the red circle on the Mactracker app. It has now been officially released from RAM! Tap on the faded top half of the screen to exit the task switcher and return to the home screen.

Step 4 Now that you've used the Mactracker app, you will uninstall it from your phone.

a. To uninstall the Mactracker app, find it on one of the home screens. Tap and hold the Mactracker icon. The entire screen will enter jiggle mode. Tap the white × on the black circle. It will ask for a confirmation. Tap Delete.

b. Press the home button to exit jiggle mode.

 30 MINUTES

Lab Exercise 16.03: Setting Up the Lock Screen

Just like your computer, your smartphone or tablet can contain a lot of private information. Your smartphone might have access to an e-mail account with messages that you don't want prying eyes to see, or maybe you're 16 years old and don't want your parents snooping around your text messages. In either case, it may be necessary to implement security on your mobile device.

Learning Objectives

In this exercise, you'll be setting up screen locking on an iOS device.

At the end of this lab, you'll be able to

- Lock a screen with any iOS device

- Navigate the available security settings in iOS

Lab Materials and Setup

The materials you need for this lab are

- An iOS-capable device such as an iPhone, iPad, or iPod

Getting Down to Business

You will enable the lock screen on your iOS device. Note that this lock screen only protects your iOS device when it falls asleep. Also keep in mind that touchscreens have a bad habit of revealing lock screen passcodes through the smudges left on the screen by your fingers. Clean your screen!

Step 1 First, you will enable the passcode on your iOS device.

    a.   Turn on your iOS device and go to the home screen.

    b.   Tap the Settings icon, then tap General. Tap on Passcode Lock (see Figure 16-4).

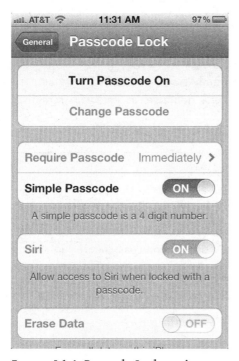

FIGURE 16-4 Passcode Lock settings

c. Tap Turn Passcode On.

d. Enter a four-digit passcode that you can remember. Re-enter your passcode.

e. Congratulations! You have just set up the passcode. Now take a look at how the security works and all the different configuration settings you can enable.

f. What will happen if you turn on Erase Data?

_____

g. Look at the Require Passcode option. How long can you delay requiring a passcode to unlock the iOS device?

_____

h. What happens when you turn off Simple Passcode?

_____

Step 2 Now that you've enabled the passcode, test that it works and locks your iOS device.

a. Tap the home button to return to the home screen.

b. Tap the power button (lock button) to make your screen go dark. Tap it again to wake up your device. Swipe to unlock it, and then enter your passcode. (If you changed the Require Passcode time, you will need to wait longer to wake up your iOS device.) You should be prompted to enter the passcode. Enter it now.

c. Tap the power button to make the screen go dark. Tap it again to wake up your device. Swipe to unlock it. Type your passcode *incorrectly*. Do it again…and again…and again! How many times can you enter your passcode incorrectly before the device no longer accepts your attempts? How long are you prevented from entering it again?

_____

Step 3 You can keep the passcode feature turned on if you like it, but if you don't like it, you can follow these steps to turn it off.

a. Return to Settings. Tap on General, then Passcode Lock. Tap in your passcode.

b. Tap Turn Passcode Off. Enter your passcode. The passcode is now disabled.

Lab Analysis Test

1. Piotr wants to get a new tablet so he can play games, check his e-mail, and watch his favorite TV shows. He can only afford a 16-GB model, but is concerned that he'll run out of space. Give him a good recommendation for a tablet and explain your reasoning.

2. Kitty wants to back up all of the data and apps on her iPhone to her PC. What software does she need and how would she make the backup?

3. Explain the difference between capacitive and resistive touchscreen devices.

4. Xavier wants to purchase a mobile device, but he isn't sure of the difference between a smartphone and a tablet. Explain the differences and similarities between the two device types.

5. What are the different ways you can get data (documents, music, and movies) onto your smartphone?

Key Term Quiz

Use the following terms to complete the following sentences. Not all terms will be used.

Android

Android Market

app

App Store

Apple

Bluetooth

capacitive

closed source

Google

Google Play

home screen

iOS

iPad

iPhone

iPod

jiggle

open source

passcode

resistive

smartphone

swipe

sync

tablet

tap

1. All Apple smartphones and tablets use a(n) _____ screen.

2. To download an app on an Android device, you must go to what is currently called the Android _____. This used to be called the Android _____.

3. A(n) _____ is a mobile device that is the perfect "couch surfer." It is great for checking e-mail, reading a book, or even watching a TV show on a 10-inch screen.

4. The three Apple devices, _____, _____, and _____, all use a(n) _____ platform.

5. When you use an iOS device and want to delete an app, you must first enter _____ mode.

Chapter 17

Troubleshooting Printers

Lab Exercises

Printers continue to be a major part of the day-to-day working environment, both at home and in the office, despite attempts to create a "paperless office." What this means is that the PC technician will have to understand the operation of several types of printers and be able to keep them in good working order. Many companies have service contracts for their more expensive printers (they're usually leased property anyway!), but there will always be printers that need a good technician's love and care.

This chapter's lab exercises will take you through a scenario in which your boss walks into your office and tells you five printers are being delivered to you—two impact printers using legacy parallel ports, two USB inkjet printers, and an HP LaserJet laser printer using a network interface. You need to install them and make sure they work properly so that they're accessible by anyone in the company who needs them. You'll learn about some of the key differences between the two most popular types of printers (inkjet and laser printers), and you'll load printer drivers. Finally, you'll look at some of the maintenance issues that are required to keep the printers up and running and some of the techniques to follow when they stop.

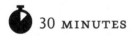 30 MINUTES

Lab Exercise 17.01: Installing a Printer

The key to a successful printer installation is having the correct software drivers and understanding how the printer will interface with the computer. You'll most likely need the drivers when you install those five printers your boss is having delivered to you, and you'll also have to configure the printers you are installing to use parallel, USB, and network interfaces. A common practice in multiple-user environments—companies considered to be small office/home office (SOHO)—is to use a printer with its own network interface card (NIC), so that computers from anywhere in the network can print directly to the printer through the network interface.

Learning Objectives

In this lab, you'll install a printer, first as a directly connected device, and then as a network device. You will then explore and change its settings.

At the end of this lab, you'll be able to

- Recognize the variations in key features of laser printers

- Install a laser printer in Windows

- Change laser printer settings in Windows

- Configure a TCP/IP port for a network printer

Lab Materials and Setup

The materials you need for this lab are

- A working computer with Windows installed

- An inkjet or laser printer for installation (or you can skip Step 1)

- Optional: A print device with a network interface card

Getting Down to Business

These days, installing a printer is a fairly straightforward task. This is good news, because you'll probably do your fair share of it as a computer technician.

Step 1 To install a plug-and-play printer:

a. Connect the printer to your system via a parallel or USB port.

b. Turn on the printer, and then turn on the PC.

c. As the boot sequence progresses, the plug-and-play feature will locate the printer and install it for you. Follow the instructions on the screen.

✔ Hint

Here's the twist. If your printer is older than your operating system, the OS should install the printer drivers with little interaction on your part. If the printer is newer than your OS, then you'll need to have the driver disc handy because the system will stop and ask you for it. Some printer manufacturers actually require you to start their own printer installation programs even before connecting the printer to a system. As always, consult the manufacturer's instructions first.

Step 2 To install a printer that is not plug and play:

a. Access the Printer applet. In Windows XP, select Start | Printers and Faxes. For Windows Vista, select Start | Control Panel | Printers. In Windows 7, go to Start | Devices and Printers.

b.   Click the Add a Printer button or link. A wizard should pop up on the screen. Click Next to proceed (Windows XP only).

c.   You want to install a printer attached to your PC, so select the local printer option (see Figure 17-1). In Windows Vista/7, clicking on the option will advance the wizard automatically. In Windows XP, select the local printer option and click Next.

d.   Follow the steps through the Add Printer Wizard by selecting LPT1 and then a printer from the list of printers or your driver disc. Finish the installation by printing a test page.

✱ Warning

If you weren't able to install an actual print device for this exercise, don't print a test page when it asks. You'll receive some interesting messages if you do.

Step 3   In the following steps, you will set up a TCP/IP printer interface port for a Hewlett-Packard LaserJet printer with a built-in NIC (a technology Hewlett-Packard calls JetDirect). If you have access to a printer with a network interface, or your classroom is equipped with one, use the IP address or printer name of the printer when configuring the port. This will allow you to actually test the installation.

a.   In Windows XP, open the Printer & Faxes folder by way of Start | Control Panel | Printers & Faxes and launch the Add Printer Wizard by clicking *Add a printer* under Printer Tasks. On the welcome screen, click Next. In Windows Vista, go to Start | Control Panel | Printers. Right-click in the window and select Add Printer. In Windows 7, go to Start | Devices and Printers and click on *Add a printer*.

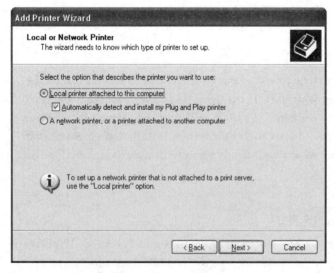

FIGURE 17-1 Installing a local printer

b. While it may seem counterintuitive, select the local printer installation option again. Windows considers installing a printer via IP address as installing a "local" printer because it uses a "local" port.

c. Click the *Create a new port* radio button and select Standard TCP/IP Port from the drop-down menu.

d. In Windows XP, this launches the Add Standard TCP/IP Printer Port Wizard (see Figure 17-2). You'll see the same options in Windows Vista/7, but without the extra wizard. Click Next.

e. In the Add Port dialog box, enter the IP address of the network printer. The Add Standard TCP/IP Printer Port Wizard (XP)/Add Printer Wizard (Vista/7) automatically creates the port name (see Figure 17-3). Click Next.

f. If the IP address is fictitious, for the purpose of completing the lab steps, the Add Standard TCP/IP Printer Port Wizard (XP)/Add Printer Wizard (Vista/7) will be unable to identify the printing device. In the Additional Port Information Required dialog box, click the drop-down menu for Standard and select (in this case) Hewlett Packard JetDirect (see Figure 17-4). Click Next.

g. Review the port characteristics and click Finish (see Figure 17-5).

h. You will now follow the steps through the Add Printer Wizard by selecting a printer from the list of printers or your driver disc as you did when directly connecting to the printer in Step 2.

Figure 17-2 The Add Standard TCP/IP Printer Port Wizard

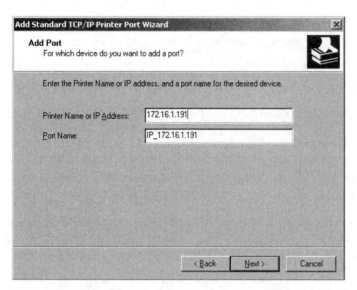

FIGURE 17-3 The TCP/IP address and port name of a network printer

✖ Warning

Again, if you are unable to install an actual print device for this exercise, don't print a test page. You'll receive some interesting messages if you try.

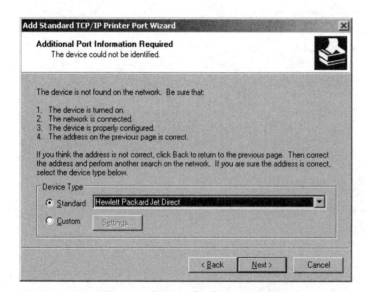

FIGURE 17-4 Selecting the Standard HP JetDirect device type

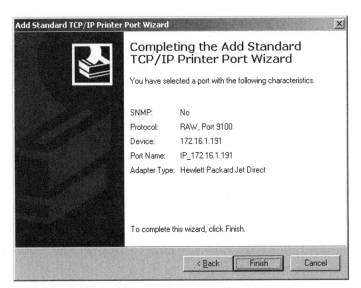

FIGURE 17-5 Port characteristics

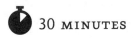 30 MINUTES

Lab Exercise 17.02: Maintaining and Troubleshooting Printers

It is estimated that technicians, especially those working for the help desk or desktop support group for a small- to medium-sized organization, spend approximately 30 percent of their time on printer issues. If you think about it, of all the components used in computing technology, printers have the highest percentage of moving parts. Moving parts are more likely to need maintenance than are static components.

Printers also like to be finicky and stop printing, usually resulting in a phone call from the client to the help desk for quick resolution. The following exercises will help you develop some understanding of laser printer and inkjet printer maintenance, and what steps to take when they stop printing.

Learning Objectives

In this lab, you'll research laser printer maintenance kits, clean dirty inkjet nozzles, and troubleshoot a failed print job.

At the end of this lab, you'll be able to

- Select a proper maintenance kit for various laser printers

- Clean and verify operation of inkjet nozzles

- Manage print jobs in Windows

- Restart a stalled print spooler

Lab Materials and Setup

The materials you need for this lab are

- A working computer with Windows installed

- A connection to the Internet

- Access to an inkjet printer

Getting Down to Business

The following exercises will round out your activities as you finish with the rollout of the five new printers in your office. You will want to get your Internet connection fired up again and research the maintenance kit available for your laser printer. Then you'll check the print-head nozzles of the inkjet printers and run the cleaning routine if necessary. Finally, you should prepare for any print errors so that you can correct them quickly and efficiently.

Step 1 Laser printers are, by design, highly precise machines. They typically move thousands of sheets of paper per month through the printing mechanism, placing 1200–1600 dots per inch (DPI) of toner on each page. As such, toner cartridges need to be replaced from time to time and parts that wear out need to be refurbished. Most manufacturers offer a maintenance kit for the printer to assist in the upkeep of the printer when these common parts age or fail. It would be a good idea to have a maintenance kit on hand for each model of laser printer in your organization.

✔ **Hint**

Most of the current manufacturers of laser printers—HP, Lexmark, Kyocera, Canon, and so forth—offer some form of maintenance kit for their printers. You should be able to find via an Internet search the available kits, their contents, and competitive pricing. Don't be surprised to find the maintenance kits somewhat costly, though they should still be only a fraction of the cost of replacing the printer.

Select a laser printer make and model, and perform an Internet search to identify the appropriate maintenance kit, its contents, and the average cost of the kit. Use this information to fill in the following items:

Printer model: _____

Maintenance kit: _____

Contents: _____

_____

Price: _____

Step 2 Though you have just installed new inkjet printers, if the printer sits idle for an extended period of time (a few weeks or months), or the ink cartridges have been replaced, you may need to check the print quality and clean the nozzles. The following steps were performed on an Epson Stylus PHOTO 890 in Windows XP, but are similar to the steps required on HP and Lexmark inkjet printers. Consult the manual for specific instructions. Note that available maintenance options vary widely from printer to printer, so you will need to read the documentation that came with your printer.

✖ Warning

The nozzle cleaning process uses a fair amount of the expensive ink. If you are working on a personal inkjet printer, or one in the classroom, after printing the nozzle check page, run the nozzle cleaning process only if required.

a. Open the printer applet (whatever your version of Windows happens to call it) and select your inkjet printer.

b. In Windows XP, right-click the printer and select Properties. In Windows Vista/7, right-click the printer and select Printing Preferences.

c. In Windows XP, click the Printing Preferences button (see Figure 17-6).

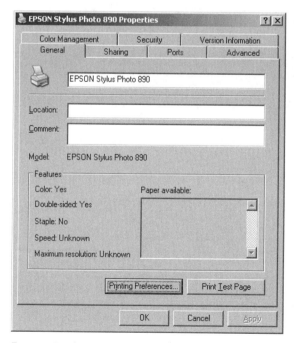

FIGURE 17-6 Properties window showing Printing Preferences button

d.   Select the Utility tab (see Figure 17-7) and click Nozzle Check. This will print a test pattern using the cyan, yellow, magenta, and black ink nozzles.

e.   If the printout is not clear or there are dropouts, click Head Cleaning to clear the nozzles and then return to the Nozzle Check to verify performance.

Step 3   When you are called upon to troubleshoot a failed print job, you should follow a logical step-by-step process to make sure that no obvious, possibly simple failure has occurred. If the power cord has been kicked out or the paper tray is open, troubleshooting the network connectivity or the printer driver would waste valuable time. Once you know the print device is online and ready and there are no paper jams or mechanical errors, it might be time to open the Print Manager and attempt to restart the document.

The following steps are meant to be a rough guideline to troubleshoot and diagnose a failed print job:

a.   First, check the physical print device:

- Is the printer plugged in, and is the power turned on?

- Is the printer out of paper or is there a paper jam?

- Is the toner low or in need of replacement?

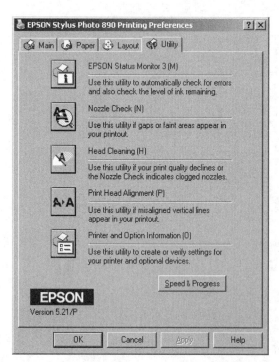

Figure 17-7 Utility tab under Printing Preferences

- Are there any error messages on the printer's LCD readout or any error indicator lights flashing?

- Is the printer online and ready to print?

    If you examine all of these areas and find everything appears to be in working condition, then you may have a problem with the connectivity between the computer and the printer, or there may be problems with the document or drivers.

b. Make sure that the connections between the computer and the printer are in good condition and securely fastened. These may be USB, Firewire, parallel, or UTP using RJ-45 connectors.

✔ **Hint**

To create a failed print job, disconnect the printer cable, shut the power off on the printer, or open the printer paper tray. If you do not have a physical printer, create a printer, following the steps in Lab Exercise 17.01. Send a print job to the printer; the printer icon should appear in the system tray and indicate that the print job has failed. Then continue with Step 3.

---

c. After checking all of the physical components, try to resend the document. Open the Print Manager by clicking the icon in the system tray/notification area.

    In the Print Manager, select the failed print job by highlighting the job with *Error* in the Status column (see Figure 17-8).

    Select Document | Restart. If you are creating the printer problem, the printer icon in the system tray/notification area indicates that the print job has failed once again.

d. Highlight the document once again, and then select Document | Cancel to delete the document.

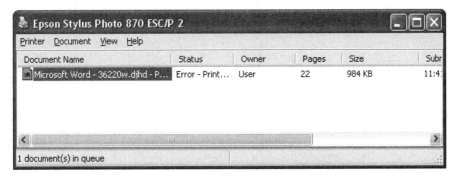

FIGURE 17-8 Print Manager showing error status on a Word file

If this were a real scenario, you would verify that the print drivers were installed and are the correct drivers for the operating system. You would then perform Step 4 to see if the problem is related to the print spooler.

Step 4 If the print device is online and ready, there are no paper jams or mechanical errors, and restarting the document is of no help, you can check to see if the print spooler is stalled. The print spooler is a holding area for print jobs and is especially important for network printers. If the print device runs out of paper while printing a document, you may have to stop and start the print spooler before the print device will receive jobs again.

In Chapter 9, you accomplished this task using the command line. Now you will use the Services snap-in for the Microsoft Management Console (MMC) to do the same thing, only more quickly and in a GUI.

a. Launch the Services console by opening Administrative Tools in the Control Panel and then double-clicking Services.

b. Scroll down and highlight Print Spooler. Select Action | Properties. You should see that the print spooler is started and running (see Figure 17-9).

c. Click the Stop button. The print spooler indicates that it has stopped.

FIGURE 17-9 Print Spooler Properties dialog box

d.   Click the Start button. The print spooler indicates that it has started.

e.   Alternatively, you can highlight Print Spooler in the Services console and select Action | Restart. You'll see a message stating that the print spooler is stopping, and then another message indicating that the print spooler is starting.

In the real-world scenario, your print spooler service would be restarted, and you should have a healthy, functioning print server once again.

Lab Analysis Test

1.   Theresa is using Windows and just purchased a printer from a friend. When she installs it using the original driver disc that came with the printer, it won't install properly. Why?

2.   Danyelle has just joined a large organization as a level II tech and is tasked with the evaluation of all the laser printers in use. The business managers are concerned that all of the units will need to be replaced because of frequent paper jams and poor print quality. Danyelle makes her recommendations, and is actually awarded a bonus for saving the company money. What is her recommendation?

3.   Brandon has sent a document to the printer, but the document never actually prints. Where can Brandon check to see the status of the document?

Key Term Quiz

Use the following terms to complete the following sentences. Not all terms will be used.

calibration

denatured alcohol

error codes

maintenance kit

material safety data sheet (MSDS)

multimeter

paper dander

1.   _____ can build up around a laser printer's rollers, letting you know the printer needs to be cleaned.

2.   You can use a _____ to repair and replace basic parts of a laser printer.

3.   You can use _____ as a general-purpose cleaning solution for all types of printers.

4.   You can use a _____ to test for electrical problems.

5.   _____ let you know what's wrong with your printer, but you often have to consult the printer's manual to interpret them.

Chapter 18

Securing Computers

Lab Exercises

Obviously, keeping your computer secure is important. Several chapters have already been devoted to securing Windows and networks. But there are still a few more helpful tools you should know about to keep things running smoothly. Local Security Settings (also labeled Local Security Policy, sometimes in the same version of Windows) enables you to set a variety of rules about using the system; Event Viewer shows you information about events you didn't even know were happening; and Microsoft Security Essentials is a free tool that enables you to clean your system of, and protect your system against, viruses and other malicious software. Each of these tools increases the power you have over your own security and the security of your computer. You'll also learn how to handle a computer that has illegal materials on it or is part of a criminal investigation.

 15 MINUTES

Lab Exercise 18.01: Configuring Local Policies

NTFS permissions are powerful tools to control with great detail what users and groups can do to folders and files. However, NTFS does not cover a number of important security issues that don't directly involve the file system. For example, what if you don't want a particular user group to shut down the computer? What if you want to make sure all accounts use a password of at least eight characters? What if you want to prevent certain users from reformatting the hard drive? These types of security settings are all controlled under the umbrella term of *local policies*.

✔ **Hint**

There are hundreds of different policies that you may configure for a system. This lab only covers a few of the most basic policies!

Learning Objectives

At the end of this lab, you'll be able to

- Locate and open the Local Security Policy/Settings utility

- Create, modify, and delete local policies with Windows

Lab Materials and Setup

The materials you need for this lab are

- A Windows PC with the C: drive formatted as NTFS

- Access to the local administrator password

Getting Down to Business

Local Security Settings is a very powerful applet that enables you to adjust all sorts of settings for and details about your system. Simply put, it is a series of rules you define, ranging from how many log on attempts to log on a user is allowed to who can change the time on the clock!

Step 1 Log on using an account with administrator rights. From the Control Panel, open Administrative Tools. Double-click Local Security Policy. When opened, it should look something like Figure 18-1.

Double-click (or single-click in Windows Vista/7) the Account Policies icon to expand its contents: Password Policy and Account Lockout Policy. Click Password Policy in the left column, right-click *Password must meet complexity requirements* in the right column, and select Properties. Enable this policy, as shown in Figure 18-2, and click OK.

Create a normal user account and call it **Janet**. Try making a simple password like **janet** and see what happens. Keep trying to make a password until you get one that is accepted. What do you need to do to make an acceptable password? Hint: Use the help in the User Accounts Control Panel applet to get some ideas as to what you need to do.

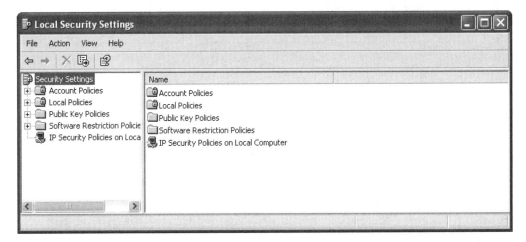

Figure 18-1 Local Security Settings in Windows XP

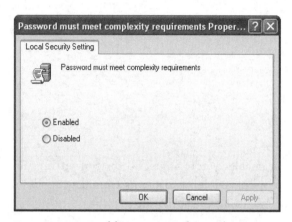

FIGURE 18-2 Enabling password complexity

Step 2   Head back to the Password Policy in Local Security Settings and enable Enforce Password History. Open the User Accounts applet from the Control Panel and try to change a password to the same password you already have. What happens?

_____

Step 3   In Local Security Settings, click Account Lockout Policy under Account Policies in the left column. An account lockout is when the operating system no longer allows a certain account the right even to *try* to log on. Try to change the properties on the *Account lockout duration* setting—it is disabled until you set the *Account lockout threshold* to something other than the default of 0. Try changing the *Account lockout threshold* to 3 attempts. Note that Windows now automatically sets the *Account lockout duration* and the *Reset account lockout counter after* settings to 30 minutes.

Log off the computer. Use the Janet account and intentionally attempt to log on using incorrect passwords. What happens after the third try?

_____

 20 MINUTES

Lab Exercise 18.02: Reviewing Security Events

With all the pop-ups, dialog boxes, and little message bubbles that Windows throws at you all day long, you would think it's telling you everything that happens every minute of every day—Windows Vista, doubly so. But it isn't. Of course, there are many processes that go on in the background, but even when Windows alerts you of an event, there may be more to the story. Perhaps an application crashes unexpectedly and Windows provides little or no feedback. It's possible that one tool in Administrative Tools took notice and can help—Event Viewer.

→ **Note**

> You learned about Event Viewer in Chapter 10 as a troubleshooting tool. This lab shows you how it can also be used as a security awareness tool.

Learning Objectives

In this lab, you'll practice using Event Viewer.

At the end of this lab, you'll be able to

- Work with Event Viewer to track events on your system

Lab Materials and Setup

The materials you will need for this lab are

- A PC with Windows

Getting Down to Business

Think about your actions on a computer as a series of events: you log on, you open an application, you close it, you log off, and so forth. This is how Event Viewer sees things, but in a lot more detail. If something goes wrong, Event Viewer usually records it. It also records a lot of things that are perfectly normal—the trick is being able to sort through all the information, which Windows makes fairly simple.

Step 1 Access Event Viewer by going to the Control Panel and opening Administrative Tools. Double-click Event Viewer to open it (see Figure 18-3).

Step 2 Windows Vista/7 adds the extra step of expanding the Windows Logs folder in the left column and adding an Actions panel on the right side, but otherwise Event Viewer is very similar in each version of Windows. Four or five logs should be listed. The important one for now is Application; the events in this log all concern the operation of applications on your system. Click it in the left column and a long list of events should appear on the right.

Step 3 Scroll through the list and look at the different levels used by Windows to describe events (the Type column in Windows XP; the Level column in Windows Vista/7). Click the column label at the top of the list to sort the events by level. You should see a lot of events labeled Information. These are your everyday events—any successful operation, such as proper use of a driver, is marked as Information.

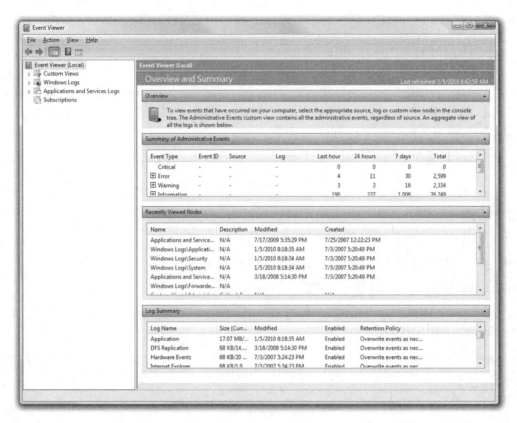

FIGURE 18-3 Event Viewer

Step 4   There might also be a few events labeled Warning or Error. Warnings do not indicate that something bad *is* happening but rather that something bad *will* happen. An example of a Warning event is when Windows is low on resources, such as disk space. Errors are more serious. These events occur when there is a failure or loss of functionality, such as when an application crashes.

Go through the list and see if you can find any Warnings or Errors. Double-click one and look at the Event Properties dialog box that pops up for more information on what happened. A lot of Event Viewer's reports can be very cryptic, which is why Windows Vista/7 now has a handy Event Log Online Help link built into Event Viewer. Clicking the link opens a dialog box asking for permission to send information about the event over the Internet. Your browser will open and take you to the Microsoft TechNet database. There isn't information available on every single event, but it can be very useful in tracking down problems.

If you don't have Windows Vista or Windows 7, you can always record the Event ID number that is listed with the event and search for it on the Internet. For example, if it is Event ID 1002, simply search for **"Event Viewer ID 1002"** and see what comes up. You're likely to find out at least a little more than you knew before.

Step 5   Search through the Security and System logs to see what sorts of events they record. In the Security logs, use the Task Category detail to see what each event records. Write down three Task Categories recorded by the Security log.

_____

_____

_____

 30 MINUTES

Lab Exercise 18.03: Cleaning and Protecting a Client's Computer

Geek Squad, the popular PC repair arm of Best Buy, reports that over 75 percent of their service calls involve cleaning malware off of a computer and then showing customers how to protect their PCs from malware and other attacks.

Windows comes with many programs and features to protect your computer, but these tools are useless if they are not used properly. In this lab exercise, you will check the computer for malware, clean the malware from the computer, and then go through the steps to reduce the likelihood of another attack.

Learning Objectives

At the end of this lab, you'll be able to

- Remove malware from a Windows system

- Configure Internet security software (antivirus/antimalware)

Lab Materials and Setup

The materials you need for this lab are

- A Windows XP (SP2 or later), Windows Vista, or Windows 7 PC

- Microsoft Security Essentials (or another Internet security suite)

✔ **Hint**

This is a great lab for students who want to bring a PC from home—or one that belongs to a friend—for testing and cleaning.

Getting Down to Business

A new system brings with it new problems. You've set up user accounts with passwords and activated firewalls, but there is still one more important piece of protection required. Antivirus and antimalware software can actively and passively protect you from unwanted malicious activity. Actively, you can usually scan entire computers for any issues. Passively, many tools are available that will constantly monitor your PC as you use it and watch out for viruses and other problems you may encounter on the Internet.

This lab will walk you through setting up Microsoft Security Essentials software, compatible with Windows XP (SP2 or later), Windows Vista, and Windows 7, available at www.microsoft.com/Security_Essentials. There are, of course, other software solutions available, some of them free, but Microsoft's tool is fairly complete and multifunctional (and yes, free).

Step 1 The first step is to download the software (if you haven't already done so). When you open the executable, it will extract itself and begin the installation. Follow the instructions. Then it will run itself, update itself, and scan itself—it's all quite impressive to watch (see Figure 18-4).

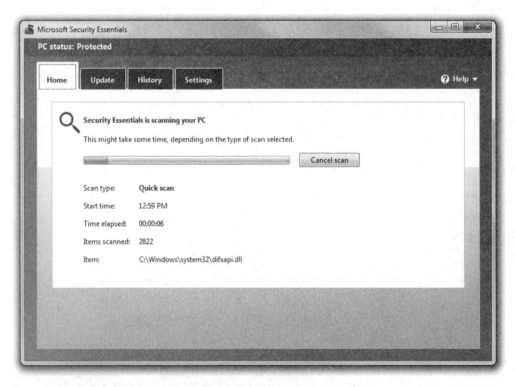

FIGURE 18-4 Microsoft Security Essentials performing a scan

Step 2   Microsoft Security Essentials will finish the scan and report its findings. It will give you the option to clean your computer or perform another action, but the defaults are usually correct. If a malicious file is found, the file can be quarantined or destroyed, and Microsoft Security Essentials will alert you when it has finished.

Step 3   Now that you've completed your initial scan, there are other options available to you. You can pick between running a Quick scan or a Full scan. A Full scan performs the same actions as the Quick scan, but also goes through the Registry. You can also set up a Custom scan to scan only certain directories.

The Update tab allows you to update virus and spyware definitions, although Microsoft Security Essentials also does this automatically. The History tab keeps track of all the potentially harmful items the software finds and what actions it performed. The Settings tab allows you to set up the program as you wish, including scheduling regular scans, setting what files and locations to exclude from scans, and adding removable drives to the scan (see Figure 18-5).

To add removable drives to the scan, under the Settings tab, click Advanced in the left column. Check the box for *Scan removable drives*. Microsoft Security Essentials will now scan the contents of each removable drive, such as USB thumb drives.

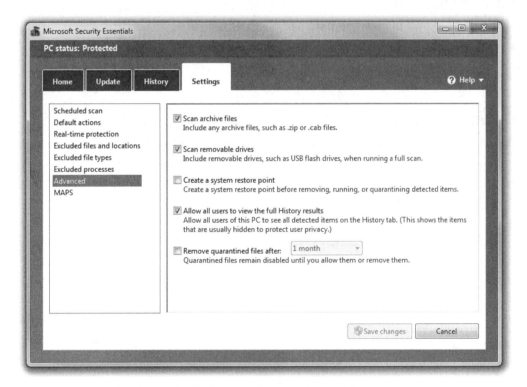

FIGURE 18-5 The Settings tab of Microsoft Security Essentials

 30 MINUTES

Lab Exercise 18.04: Protecting the Chain of Custody

When dealing with computers and electronics, any device you work on could have illegal or prohibited content on it. As a technician, you need to be able to identify any such material and then report it to the proper channels. One method of dealing with this sort of content is by following the chain of custody (CoC).

Learning Objectives

In this lab, you will identify the fundamentals of dealing with prohibited content and/or activity.

At the end of this lab, you will be able to

- Define the chain of custody

- Explain why you use the chain of custody

Lab Materials and Setup

The materials you need for this lab are

- A PC with Internet access

- A notepad and pen

Getting Down to Business

In Chapter 18 of *Mike Meyers' CompTIA A+ Guide to 802: Managing and Troubleshooting PCs*, you read that dealing with prohibited content can be a very important part of your job as a technician, especially when your equipment becomes evidence in an investigation. This lab exercise will give you a better understanding of the procedures that they use to get their job done.

Step 1 The Environmental Protection Agency (EPA), as part of their training materials, has an easy-to-understand chain of custody tutorial on their Web site (www.epa.gov/apti/coc/) that I'll reference for this lab exercise. Under the section titled "Introduction to the Chain of Custody," click on the Overview link. This should bring up a smaller window, titled Introduction to Chain of Custody. Time for some reading! Follow the navigation arrows in the bottom-right corner to click through the presentation.

   a.   After reading page 2, run the animation. Write down how ignoring the chain of custody has affected the court case.

   _____

   _____

b. Using your own words, define chain of custody.

_____

_____

c. In what four situations are samples and data legally considered to be in your custody?

_____

_____

_____

_____

d. The presentation lists quite a few guidelines for how to conduct chain-of-custody procedures. List the three you feel are the most important from the guidelines given.

_____

_____

_____

Step 2 After going through the presentation on chain-of-custody procedures, answer the following questions.

a. When should you follow chain-of-custody procedures?

_____

b. Why should you follow chain-of-custody procedures?

_____

Lab Analysis Test

1. While browsing the Internet, Maxel has been getting a lot more pop-ups lately. He assumes he has some kind of adware on his system. What should he do to fix this?

2. Jason is working on a document when Word crashes. Which log in Event Viewer will give him more information? Which level would it be most likely identified as?

3. In the Local Security Policy/Settings applet, what does *Account lockout threshold* control?

4. What is the path used in Windows 7 to access the Security log in Event Viewer?

5. What are two methods of learning more about a particular event in Event Viewer?

Key Term Quiz

Use the following terms to complete the following sentences. Not all terms will be used.

    adware

    antivirus program

    chain of custody

    definition file

    event auditing

    Event Viewer

    incidence reporting

    Local Security Policy/Settings

    object access auditing

    phishing

    polymorph virus

    pop-up

    spam

    spyware

    Trojan

    virus

    worm

1. _____ is a type of unsolicited e-mail that usually contains hoaxes and get-rich-quick schemes.

2. A(n) _____ appears as a new window in front of whatever application you are using.

3. It is necessary to have a(n) _____ to protect your computer from malicious programs and other malware.

4. _____ keeps track of every event that occurs on your system and assigns it a level, such as Information or Warning.

5. A piece of malicious software that gets passed from computer to computer is known most generically as a(n) _____.

Chapter 19
Virtualization

Lab Exercises

Virtualization is the latest big trend in computing. Using virtual machines, you can run an entire virtual operating system on top of your existing OS. If you have Windows 7 installed, for example, you can download a virtualization application like VMware Player or Oracle VM VirtualBox, install Ubuntu Linux on it, and run Ubuntu inside Windows! The difference between software and hardware gets confusing when you realize that the virtual OS uses virtual hardware to re-create virtually everything in the system case beneath your desk.

Virtualization promotes efficient use of hardware and energy resources, and also enables you to easily create images of the virtual machine, providing excellent fault tolerance and disaster recovery options.

In this chapter, you'll explore some of the features of common virtual machine technologies, install a virtual machine on your PC, and then use Windows Virtual PC to set up a special virtual machine called Windows XP Mode.

In Lab Exercises 19.02 and 19.03, you will be using virtualization software to create virtual machines. Virtual machines are exactly like physical computers in that they need operating systems to work. Prior to beginning the lab exercises, you will want to prepare the operating system installation media. Lab Exercise 19.02 requires a copy of Ubuntu Linux and Lab Exercise 19.03 uses Windows XP Mode, which requires Windows 7 Professional, Ultimate, or Enterprise. Ubuntu 10.04 LTS (Long-Term Support) will be supported for five years, from April 2010 to April 2015, and is a free Linux distribution. It can be downloaded at www.ubuntu.com. Create an installation disc or copy the installation disc image (.iso) to a flash drive for use in the lab exercises. You can find instructions for this procedure on the Ubuntu Web site.

 20 MINUTES

Lab Exercise 19.01: Identifying Virtualization Technologies

As discussed in the introduction to this chapter, virtualization takes on many aspects of the physical devices used every day in the computing environment. Organizations may choose to install multiple virtual servers on one physical machine to handle Web services, e-mail services, file sharing, and print services, to name a few. Before you work with the actual virtualization programs and before you take the CompTIA A+ 220-802 exam, you will want to explore all of the technologies associated with virtualization.

Time to explore!

Learning Objectives

At the end of this lab, you'll be able to

- Define virtual desktop technologies

- Define virtual server technologies

Lab Materials and Setup

The materials you need for this lab are

- A PC with Internet access

Getting Down to Business

You will actually install and configure a number of virtualization technologies and operating systems in the next few lab exercises. Before you do, it is important that you understand the underlying solutions that virtualization technology provides. In this lab, you will use your textbook and the Internet to develop a brief description and summary of the characteristics of the virtualization technologies.

Step 1   Start by researching virtual desktop technology. There's plenty of information to be found using Google. Use keywords like "virtualization" or "VMware" (a popular brand) to locate good information. What are they key features of most virtual desktops?

_____

_____

_____

_____

Step 2   Virtual servers are similar to virtual desktops but provide some advanced features and support for applications not found in the virtual desktop offerings. Describe the differences between a virtual desktop and a virtual server.

_____

_____

_____

_____

 45 MINUTES

Lab Exercise 19.02: Installing and Configuring VMware Player

VMware is arguably one of the leading developers of virtualization applications. To introduce you to VMware, you will download VMware Player and install it on a Windows 7 machine, and then you will run Ubuntu Linux in the virtual machine. You'll see what it's like running a second OS inside your native OS.

Learning Objectives

In this lab exercise, you will use VMware Player virtualization software to install a virtual Ubuntu machine on a Windows 7 PC. You will then navigate a few of the Ubuntu programs and commands.

At the end of this lab, you'll be able to

- Install and configure VMware Player on a Windows 7 host system

- Install and run Ubuntu 10.04 LTS as a virtual operating system in VMware Player

Lab Materials and Setup

The materials you need for this lab are

- A system connected to the Internet or access to VMware Player

- Ubuntu installation media

- A Windows 7 system

Getting Down to Business

You will be working with the VMware Player application to install a virtual operating system.

Step 1 Launch your browser and navigate to www.vmware.com, the home of VMware. Move your pointer over the Support & Downloads tab at the top of the page. Go to the Product Downloads menu and select All Downloads. Click on VMware Player, listed under the Desktop & End-User Computing category. On the VMware Player page, click the Download button as shown in Figure 19-1. To download VMware Player, you will have to register using your e-mail address. Complete the registration and download the latest version of VMware Player for Windows. Once downloaded, proceed to launch the setup file to install the application.

FIGURE 19-1 The VMware Player download page on the VMware Web site

Step 2 At the Welcome to the installation wizard for VMware Player screen, click Next (see Figure 19-2).

The next screen is the Destination Folder screen, where you may choose the default location or select Change to install in a different folder. Choose the default location or change the folder where the VMware Player program will be installed.

Click Next once again, choose the checkbox to *Check for product updates on startup*, and click Next. Now uncheck the checkbox to *Help improve VMware Player* and click Next. Select where you would like to create shortcuts for VMware Player, and click Next.

Now you will see a window labeled to Perform the Requested Operations. Click Continue to begin the process. VMware Player setup will perform the installation. This may take several minutes.

You will now be instructed that the setup wizard needs to restart your system. Click Restart Now to reboot the Windows machine.

FIGURE 19-2 VMware Player 4 welcome screen

Step 3 Now you will launch the VMware Player, create a new virtual machine, and use Easy Install to automatically install Ubuntu on the new virtual machine. Perform the tasks in the following instructions to create a new virtual machine.

    a.   Double-click the VMware Player icon and accept the VMware End User License Agreement.

    b.   At the Welcome to VMware Player screen, click the Create a New Virtual Machine icon to create a new virtual machine. This will launch the New Virtual Machine Wizard (see Figure 19-3).

    c.   At this screen, you will choose where to install the operating system from. You are going to use the Easy Install method, installing the operating system as you build the virtual machine. Using your Ubuntu installation media, either insert the optical disc into the system, choose the *Installer*

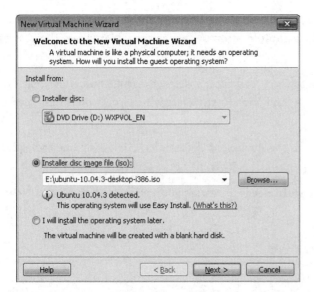

FIGURE 19-3 The VMware Player New Virtual Machine Wizard

disc radio button, and select the optical drive from the drop-down menu, or choose the *Installer disc image file (iso:)* option and browse to the disc image. Click Next.

d. Now you will set up a user name and password for the Ubuntu virtual operating system. Enter the full name **Student** in the dialog box. Then enter the user name **student** in lowercase and enter a password of your choosing. Click Next.

e. You will now name the virtual machine and choose the location for the virtual machine folder. You may use the defaults or change the name and location. Click Next.

f. Specify the disk capacity. The recommended size for Ubuntu is 20 GB. Leave the default setting for *Split virtual disk into multiple files* and click Next, splitting the virtual disk (vmdk) into multiple, smaller files. This helps facilitate copying the virtual machine to other media such as a flash drive.

g. Now you are ready to create the virtual machine. Review the virtual machine settings as shown in Figure 19-4, check the box *Power on this virtual machine after creation*, and then click Finish to begin building the virtual machine.

h. Depending on your physical hardware, you will receive several hints:

  • VMware Player requires a 64-bit processor to run a 64-bit virtual operating system. Click OK.

  • Removable media, such as flash drives, cannot be mounted to both the host operating system and the guest operating system simultaneously. You may mount the removable media at a later time. Click OK to accept the default.

i. If your machine is connected to the Internet, you may choose to install VMware Tools for Ubuntu. VMware Tools is a suite of utilities that enhances the performance of the virtual machine's operating system and improves management of the virtual machine.

  If you choose to install the tools at a later time, you will receive an error message at the bottom of the VMware Player window when the system boots. You may ignore this for the lab exercise.

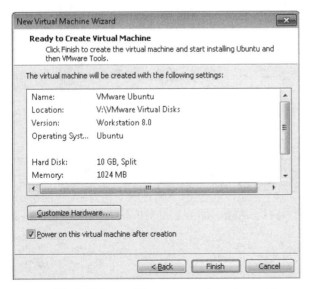

FIGURE 19-4 VMware Player new virtual machine summary page

Step 4 When the VMware Ubuntu virtual machine reboots, you will be prompted for your user name and password. After entering your information, you will now have a fully functioning installation of Ubuntu as a virtual operating system on top of the host operating system. To explore some of the features of VMware Player, complete the following steps:

a. Insert a flash drive into the physical host machine.

b. At the top of the VMware Ubuntu virtual machine window, click on the Virtual Machine tab item to open a drop-down menu.

c. Click on Removable Devices and, from the expanded menu, choose the flash drive (it may identify the manufacturer, such as SanDisk Cruzer) and select Connect (Disconnect from host). You will receive the message "A USB device is about to be unplugged from the host and connected to this virtual machine." Click OK.

d. Now in the Ubuntu system, click Places and navigate down to the Computer icon. Click Computer to open the window. Do you see the icon for the flash drive? (See Figure 19-5.)

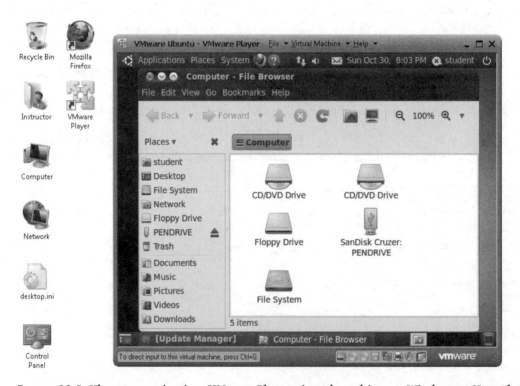

FIGURE 19-5 Ubuntu running in a VMware Player virtual machine on Windows 7. Note the flash drive icon.

 30 MINUTES

Lab Exercise 19.03: Installing and Configuring Windows XP Mode and Windows Virtual PC

As is fairly typical with Microsoft, if there is a technology related to computer applications or operating systems, they have probably designed a product to compete in the market. This is the case with virtualization. To this end, Microsoft offers Windows Virtual PC.

Microsoft has continued to offer their Virtual PC virtualization software with the inclusion of Windows XP Mode in Windows 7 to facilitate running legacy programs on a virtual machine running Windows XP, rather than in a "compatibility mode."

✔ Tech Tip

Microsoft is very particular with the distribution of Windows XP Mode and Windows Virtual PC. These products will only install on the following systems: Windows 7 Professional, Windows 7 Ultimate, or Windows 7 Enterprise. In addition, you will have to download and install a Windows Activation Update, which is automatically launched when you begin the steps to download Windows XP Mode and Windows Virtual PC.

Learning Objectives

In this lab exercise, you will install Windows Virtual PC and then install Windows XP Mode (a preconfigured Windows XP Professional virtual machine).

At the end of this lab, you'll be able to

- Install Windows Virtual PC
- Install and configure Windows XP Mode on a Windows 7 system

Lab Materials and Setup

The materials you need for this lab are

- Windows 7 Professional, Enterprise, or Ultimate
- Internet connectivity

Getting Down to Business

To facilitate legacy applications in Windows 7, Microsoft introduced the Windows XP Mode virtual machine. Windows XP Mode (XPM) is a virtual machine package for Windows Virtual PC containing a preinstalled, licensed copy of Windows XP Professional with Service Pack 3 as its virtual operating system.

The Windows XP Mode virtual machine is seamlessly integrated into Windows 7 and offers "one-click launch of Windows XP Mode applications."

In this lab, you will install Windows XP Mode and Windows Virtual PC and evaluate their functionality.

Step 1 Boot a Windows 7 Professional, Ultimate, or Enterprise system, launch your browser, and navigate to www.microsoft.com/windows/virtual-pc/default.aspx. Click on *Get Windows XP Mode and Windows Virtual PC now*, then select your system and language as shown in Figure 19-6. After you have entered your operating system and language information, a list of four steps will be displayed.

Use the following instructions to complete the four steps:

a. In Step 1, it is recommended that you either e-mail or print the instructions before restarting your computer.

b. In Step 2, click the Windows XP Mode Download button to begin the download. Microsoft will install an Activation Update and run a Windows validation process. Once the validation process completes successfully, click Continue and save the file WindowsXPMode_en-us.exe.

c. In Step 3, click the Windows Virtual PC Download button and save the file Windows6.1KB958559-x86-RefreshPkg.msu.

d. You will only need to perform Step 4 if you are running Windows 7 without Service Pack 1 (SP1) installed. If you are not running SP1, click on the Windows XP Mode Update button. Verify that all of the required files are in the Download folder and close the browser window.

✔ **Hint**

Earlier versions of Windows 7 and Windows Virtual PC required Hardware Assisted Virtualization Technology. Step 4 enables Windows XP Mode for PCs without Hardware Assisted Virtualization Technology. If you are running Windows 7 with Service Pack 1 (SP1), you will not be required to run Step 4.

Step 2 Click Start | Computer | Downloads and launch the Windows6.1-KB958559-x86-RefreshPkg.msu installation file located in the Downloads folder, as shown in Figure 19-7.

Depending on the version of Windows 7, you will either install the x86 (32-bit) or the x64 (64-bit) Windows Virtual PC Update installation file. Some versions of Windows 7 also ship with Windows Virtual PC preinstalled. If your system displays the message "The update is not applicable to your computer," as shown in Figure 19-8, then check your Start | All Programs menu to see if Windows Virtual PC is already installed. What are your results?

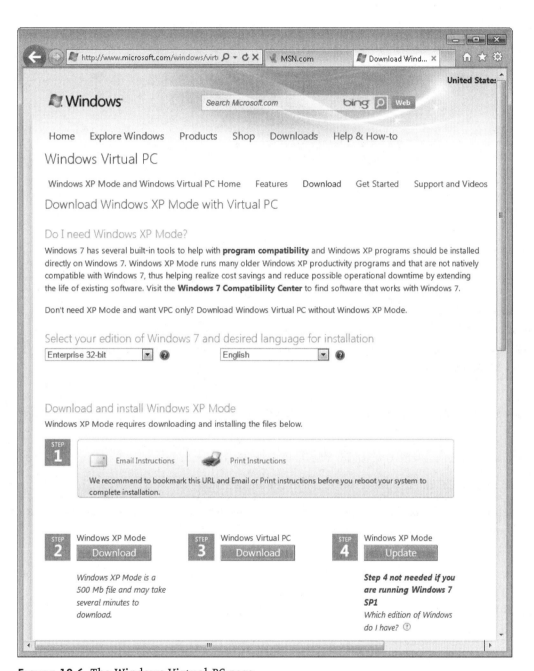

FIGURE 19-6 The Windows Virtual PC page

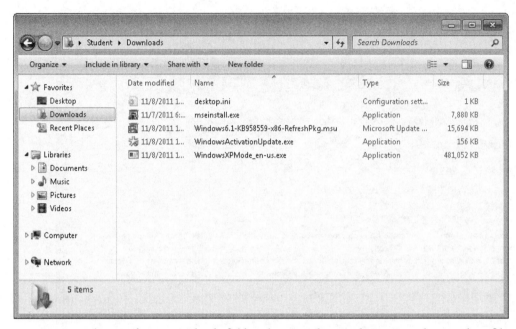

Figure 19-7 The Windows Downloads folder showing the Windows Virtual PC Update file and the Windows XP Mode file

If Windows Update KB958559 (Windows Virtual PC) was not previously installed, follow these directions to install it:

   a.   Select Yes to install the Update for Windows (KB958559).

   b.   Read and accept the license terms to begin the installation.

   c.   When the installation has completed, you will be instructed to restart your computer for the updates to take effect. Click Restart Now.

Step 3   After your computer reboots, you will install the Windows XP Mode virtual machine. Open Start | Computer | Downloads and double-click the WindowsXPMode_en-us.exe file located in the Downloads folder, as shown earlier in Figure 19-7. Perform the installation directions as follows:

   a.   Select Run when you receive the Open File – Security Warning.

   b.   In the Welcome to Setup for Windows XP Mode screen, click Next.

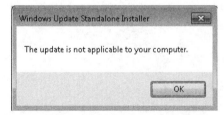

Figure 19-8 Windows Update Standalone Installer message

c. Select the default location of C:\Program Files\Windows XP Mode\ and click Next.

d. When the setup completes, uncheck Launch Windows XP Mode and click Finish.

Step 4 You will now install and configure Windows XP in the Windows XP Mode virtual machine.

a. Click Start | All Programs | Windows Virtual PC | Windows XP Mode to begin the Windows XP Mode Setup wizard.

b. Accept the license terms and click Next.

c. Select the installation folder and enter a password for the XPMUser, as shown in Figure 19-9, and click Next.

d. Next, you can choose to activate Automatic Updates, which will help protect your computer. Choose either *Help protect my computer by turning on Automatic Updates now (recommended)* or *Not right now* and then click Next.

e. Click Start Setup to start the Windows XP Mode setup. This will take a few minutes, and while setting up, the wizard will display some features of Window XP Mode and the steps that are being performed.

f. When the setup completes, check the box to launch the Windows XP Mode virtual machine, and then click Finish. The Windows XP Mode virtual machine will launch, as shown in Figure 19-10.

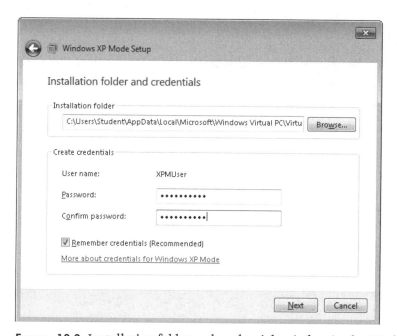

FIGURE 19-9 Installation folder and credentials window in the Windows XP Mode Setup

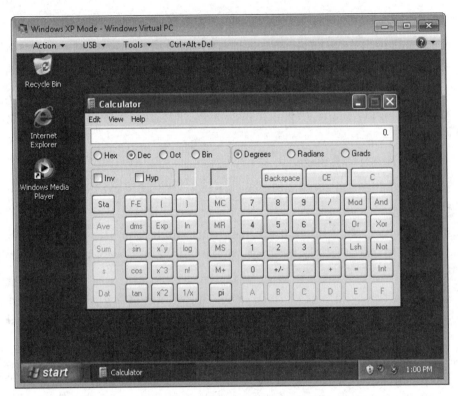

FIGURE 19-10 Windows XP Mode – Windows Virtual PC

Lab Analysis Test

1. Matthew has worked through the lab exercises in this chapter, but he is still unclear about the exact differences between a virtual desktop and a virtual server. Detail some of the characteristics of each to help Matthew with his studies.

2. Create three short examples that help to explain why someone might use virtualization in the workplace.

3. While downloading VMware Player, Jonathan notices some of the other free products that VMware offers. He asks if you know the differences between the various offerings. Using the Web site www.vmware.com, write a short description of each of the free products that VMware offers.

4. What are some of the hardware requirements for running virtual machines on a PC?

5. What are the primary differences between VMware's products and Microsoft's Windows Virtual PC/ Windows XP Mode packages?

Key Term Quiz

Use the following terms to complete the following sentences. Not all terms will be used.

bare-metal virtual machine

hosted virtual machine

hypervisor

snapshot

virtual desktop

virtual machine manager (VMM)

virtual server

VMware Player

Windows Virtual PC

1. The two terms typically used to describe virtualization software are _____ and _____.

2. VMware has established itself as one of the leaders in the virtualization software market. It currently offers two free products. One of these is called _____.

3. When working with virtual machines, one of the convenience features is to be able to take a(n) _____ to capture the current configuration of the machine.

4. Typically, when building a virtual server, the virtualization software is going to be of the _____ variety. This is also known as a "native" virtual machine.

5. Windows XP Mode uses _____ to run a virtual version of Windows XP.

Chapter 20
The Complete PC Tech

Lab Exercises

At this point, you're well on your path to becoming a CompTIA A+ certified technician. You have an excellent understanding of the major technical aspects of computer systems: hardware, software, networking, and the Internet.

When a client launches an application, that person isn't thinking about what happens behind the scenes: "Hey, look at me! I'm using the keyboard and mouse to input data! The processor is calculating all of the information to produce the desired results and present the output on the screen or in hard copy form on a printer. This is only possible because the operating system, applications, and data were successfully stored on the hard drive." You, as the tech, *do* have to think about all of this, but you also need the user's perspective. When you look at the computer system as a whole—that is, as a practical tool that can create and process everything from your résumé to the latest Hollywood thriller—you'll have a better understanding of how your clients envision the computer.

In the real world of PC tech, you also have to work with people: customers, clients, supervisors, coworkers, family members, maybe even spouses. You have to develop the skills for calmly gathering information about the state the computer is in and how it arrived there. Usually, your clients won't use the most technical language to explain the situation, and they may be frustrated or even a little on the defensive, so you need to be understanding and patient. You want them to see you as an ally, and to ensure that they do, you'll need to treat them with respect and kindness. You also need to develop the skills that will enable you to get a job—you might be the best tech in the world, but you need to know how to communicate that to a potential employer.

Bear in mind that someone who doesn't understand computers can still be quite intelligent and capable in other areas; talking down to a client is a bad idea! The client also trusts in your integrity to solve the problem in the most efficient and cost-effective manner possible, and to return their machine and data uncompromised.

Finally, and most importantly, you should cultivate a good troubleshooting methodology. It's difficult to give you a specific checklist, but the following guidelines should help:

- Identify the problem.

    - Question the user and identify user changes to the computer and perform backups before making changes.

- Establish a theory of probable cause (question the obvious).

- Test the theory to determine the cause.

    - Once the theory is confirmed, determine the next steps to resolve the problem.

    - If the theory is not confirmed, reestablish a new theory or escalate the problem.

- Establish a plan of action to resolve the problem and implement the solution.

- Verify full system functionality and, if applicable, implement preventative measures.

- Document findings, actions, and outcomes.

→ **Note**

You should be familiar with the six steps of the troubleshooting theory for both real-world application and the CompTIA A+ 220-802 exam.

Don't forget that often the client will be there with you, hanging on your every word. Explain the steps you are taking to configure a new system, or to repair damage and recover data from hardware failure or malicious software. When backing up data prior to working on a system, err on the side of caution; make your best effort to determine which data is vital to your client and to their business, even if they are vague about what data needs to be protected. Try to give them realistic expectations of what you likely can or cannot do so that the outcome is a pleasant surprise rather than a bitter disappointment.

The scenarios presented in this chapter will make you think about how to act as a gainfully employed PC technician and show you some of the situations you'll encounter out in the field. You can also think about the scenarios from a job seeker's perspective—chances are good that a prospective employer will ask you how to deal with situations like the ones described in this chapter. First, however, let's look at how to handle the interview itself.

✔ **Hint**

Ideally, for the lab exercises in this chapter, you should have a partner play the role of the client while you play the role of the PC tech (or the interviewer and job seeker for the first lab exercise). Work through the scenarios in a live, person-to-person role-playing of each situation, just as if it were real. If you are working in a classroom setting, try to work with different classmates through each of the different scenarios.

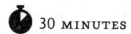 30 MINUTES

Lab Exercise 20.01: Preparing for the Technical Interview

Sitting for an interview and selling yourself to complete strangers is the stuff of many a PC tech's nightmares. Trust me! You might think it sounds easy, but once you're in the hot seat and actually doing it, everything changes. So buckle down and pay attention during this lab because it could make or break your chance of landing that job!

Before we get started in earnest, here are some tips to keep in mind when interviewing for a job:

- No chewing gum.

- Turn your cell phone off and keep it out of sight. No texting!

- Comb your hair and keep it out of your eyes (if you have to swing your hair to the side every minute, get a haircut). Messy hair looks very unprofessional and reflects poor self-image.

- Brush your teeth.

- Males—Tuck in your shirt, pull up your pants, and wear a belt.

- Females—No miniskirts or low tops, and keep your stomach covered.

- Shake hands firmly.

- Maintain good eye contact at all times.

- No sneakers allowed!

- Do not offer information that is not pertinent to the interview. Think before speaking and always tell the truth.

For more tips on job interviewing, see "10 Killer Job Interview Questions and Answers," by Carole Martin, available at www.bspcn.com/2007/08/24/10-killer-job-interview-questions-and-answers.

Learning Objectives

In this lab exercise, you will practice role-playing as an interviewee (if no interviewers are present, you may also have to role-play as an interviewer). You will be critiqued as you are probed to say and do the right thing at all times. So get ready for some fun in preparing for the interview process.

At the end of this lab, you'll be able to

- Speak clearly, professionally, and technically

- Describe how IT affects the workplace

- Effectively communicate what you know

- Know what to bring and wear to the interview

Lab Materials and Setup

The materials you need for this lab are

- An updated résumé that lists all your skills; technology courses that you're currently taking or have completed; and reliable references, other than family—preferably customers or people who know your skill level and character, and have worked with you for a period of a minimum of six months.

- A digital portfolio (a CD) that includes an updated copy of your résumé; pictures or short video clips of you working on computers, possibly building a computer; any presentations or technology-related projects you've been involved in implementing; a log of customers you've supported; and any Web sites you've created that demonstrate your skills—not MySpace or Facebook! By the way, you will leave this CD with your interviewer, so make it good.

Instructors: For the setup, enlist or bring in at least four volunteers from the technology industry, such as local PC repair shop managers, Geek Squad reps, and so forth, to help you interview your students. Use people from the business world as much as possible, but if you're under tight timelines, just ask your school's principal, guidance personnel, media specialists, or other teachers to assist you. They make great interviewers because your students most likely do not know them as well as they know you and thus will take this exercise more seriously.

Getting Down to Business

This is a work-in-progress lab that will be beneficial to you for life. Once you've started the process of learning to present yourself effectively, you will be surprised at how many opportunities you'll get to use these skills.

Step 1 Type your résumé and save it to multiple places. Have your instructor guide you as to what to include and what not to include. Run a spell check! Print and proof it yourself first and then allow your instructor to critique it.

✔ Hint

The Web offers many places for the serious job seeker to post a completed résumé electronically, such as www.monster.com, but it is wise to have properly formatted paper copies as well to turn in with your application.

Step 2 Type a list of personal and professional references on a separate document. Contact each reference and ask him or her if they will be a reference for you. Make your references aware they may get a call about your potential interview.

Step 3   On the day of the interview, "dress for success;" evaluation of your appearance comprises 50 percent of your grade. As a class, set up a room with at least four tables/stations, one for each volunteer interviewer, with at least three chairs at each station.

Step 4   Enter the interview area quietly. Make sure to have your printed résumé, references, and digital portfolio ready to turn in. Interviews should last no more than 10 minutes. Ideally, the interviewers will ask everyone the same questions, but you never know what you'll be asked.

Step 5   Once you have been interviewed, the interviewers will compare their thoughts and choose two or three top students to be interviewed by the entire group of interviewers. This is called a panel interview and is the type of interview students will most likely encounter when being interviewed for various jobs.

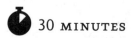 30 MINUTES

Lab Exercise 20.02: Scenario #1: Computer Obsolescence and Expense of Replacement

An independent salesperson for a multiline musical instrument dealer walks into your shop carrying a weathered laptop case. He lays the case on the counter and asks simply, "Is there anything you can do?" You open the case to find an early-2000s model IBM ThinkPad. You open the lid on the ThinkPad and see a semicircle indentation and spider-web cracks all across the screen. The LCD panel has been completely smashed!

As the expert in this situation, you have to make some decisions about what would ultimately be the most timely and cost-effective solution. You then have to explain your recommendations to the client carefully and respectfully because either solution will most likely be costly and therefore stressful for him.

✔ **Cross-Reference**

Before you work through the role-playing scenarios, go back and reread Chapter 20 in *Mike Meyers' CompTIA A+ Guide to 802: Managing and Troubleshooting PCs.*

Learning Objectives

This exercise will test your ability to stay cool in the face of a concerned client, even as you may have to deliver news that the client doesn't want to hear.

At the end of this lab, you'll be able to

- Assess the damage and back up the client's data

- Convey the options available to the client

- Provide a recommended solution to the client

Lab Materials and Setup

The materials you need for this lab are

- A partner or classmate to play the role of the client (if you don't have a partner, you can still work through the scenario and complete the Lab Analysis Test at the end of the chapter)

- A notepad or computer-generated "trouble ticket" to simulate the practice followed in many computer support organizations

- Optional: A demo machine and/or Internet access, to re-create the scenario and research options on vendor Web sites and tech forums

Getting Down to Business

To begin, have your partner read the Client section that follows. You will then read the PC Tech section and use the specifics to analyze the situation and recommend the best course of action. Sit down and work through the scenario with your partner. If possible, use the Internet or demo machines to make the role-playing scenario more valid.

CLIENT:

You are an independent salesperson for a multiline musical instrument dealer and spend about 20 days a month on the road. You use the laptop to keep all of your customer data and product information up to date. You were finishing up a particularly busy week when you fell asleep with the laptop on your lap. You placed the laptop next to your bed in the hotel only to step on it in the middle of the evening. Your entire business relies on the information contained in the computer, and having it down, even for a short time, is going to create problems.

Along with the time-critical issues, you are also an independent salesperson and self-employed— you pay your own travel and lodging expenses, health benefits, and life insurance. A costly repair or replacement was not in your planned budget.

PC TECH:

As the technician, you are going to analyze the laptop and quickly recommend that the hard drive be backed up immediately. Using a laptop IDE harness and duplicating the hard drive to a volume on the shop data server, you can alleviate the customer's concern that all his data will be lost.

You know that the machine is over 10 years old, and that the replacement screen and labor to install it are probably going to cost a fair amount. You use the Internet to research replacement LCD screens and try to estimate the overall cost of the repair. Not only is it expensive, the availability of the screen is backlogged over three weeks. It is also a good bet that other components in the machine will begin to age and fail even if the screen repair is warranted.

Your job is laid out before you. You need to discuss the options of repairing the current machine, warts and all, or having the client upgrade to a more modern laptop.

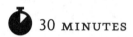 30 MINUTES

Lab Exercise 20.03: Scenario #2: Hardware Failure, or I Can't See Anything!

One of the marketing analysts in your company calls the help desk and complains that he's unable to get his monitor to work. He arrived this morning and the computer just never booted. There's a mission-critical presentation on this system that is due to be presented today at 2:00 P.M. It's now 1:00 P.M. and nobody has returned his call, even to say that his initial request was received! The analyst storms into the IT department and demands some assistance. You look up from your screen just in time to see your supervisor and the analyst barreling toward your cubicle. Your supervisor asks if you will accompany the analyst to his department and see if you can figure this out.

In cases such as this, the tech's job is not only to troubleshoot the problem and provide a solution, but also to provide customer service and present a good image of the IT department to other employees. As the expert in this situation, you not only have to solve the issue—you must also make your best effort to diffuse the agitation of the anxious analyst.

Learning Objectives

The plan is to have a classmate play the role of the client, and you to play the role of the PC tech. This exercise will give you a great opportunity to display not only your tech skills, but also your professionalism in a tough, time-crunch situation.

At the end of this lab, you'll be able to

- Analyze the problem with input from the client

- Diffuse the frustration of the client

- Provide a complete solution

Lab Materials and Setup

The materials you need for this lab are

- A partner or classmate to play the role of the client (optionally, if you do not have a partner, work through the scenario and complete the Lab Analysis Test at the end of the chapter)

- A notepad or computer-generated "trouble ticket" to simulate the practice followed in many computer support organizations

- Optional: A demo machine or Internet access to re-create the scenario and research options on vendor Web sites and tech forums

Getting Down to Business

To begin, have your partner read the Client section that follows. You will then read the PC Tech section and use the specifics to analyze the situation and recommend the best course of action. Now sit down and work through the scenario with your partner. If possible, use the Internet or demo machines to make the role-playing scenario more valid.

CLIENT:

You arrived this morning and started your normal routine: You dropped your briefcase in the corner of your cube, carefully placed your coffee on the file cabinet (away from the computer), and pressed the power button on the computer. You exchanged a few pleasantries with your fellow workers and sat down to make the finishing touches on the presentation you will be delivering at 2:00 P.M. today, only to find a completely blank screen. You attempted to reboot the computer, and verified that the power light was lit on the monitor (you do know *that* much about computers). But it was still a no-go!

You placed a call with the help desk and tried not to panic. Some friends invited you to lunch, and you joined them with the hope that the IT department would visit while you were gone so that you could return to a working machine. When you returned, nothing had been done!

You are a little tense, but you know that you are at the mercy of the IT group. You head on down to the IT department and visit directly with the support supervisor. He introduces you to one of the techs, who is now traveling to your desk with you. The only thing you can remember doing differently was authorizing an Automatic Windows Update last night as you were leaving.

PC TECH:

Well, you've certainly been here before—a critical situation with severe time constraints, but now it's 1:20 P.M. and the analyst is very tense. You arrive at the analyst's desk and have him run through the routine that he followed when he arrived this morning. You ask if anything has changed since yesterday when the machine worked. You then run a check of the obvious diagnoses and troubleshooting steps.

✔ **Hint**

It is imperative that you keep detailed records of the diagnosing and troubleshooting steps. If you have set items that you check first (remember: simple to complex), then you will perform a quick check of the power lights, power cord connections, monitor connections, and whether the monitor settings menu is accessible, enabling you to rule out simple items that may have been overlooked in a time of stress.

If none of the simple solutions appears to work, you have two issues on your hands. One is that you need to get the system back up and running, and the other is that your client has a big presentation due in 30 minutes (yes, it took 10 minutes to check the simple items, so it's now 1:30 P.M.). You know that your organization has all of the employees save their documents to Documents, which is mapped to the server to facilitate backups. You have the analyst log on to a coworker's machine, access his Documents folder, and fine-tune his presentation with 10 minutes to spare.

You send a calmer analyst to the meeting, complete the analysis of the system, and perform the required repairs. Record the additional steps you would take to complete this trouble ticket. How would you communicate your findings with the analyst? Share the results with your instructor.

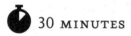 30 MINUTES

Lab Exercise 20.04: Scenario #3: What Do You Mean, a Virus?

You're just finishing up lunch when one of your neighbors walks into your shop with her family computer under her arm. She knows you from the neighborhood, and has heard that you know a fair amount about computer systems (I hope so, since you are working in a computer shop!). She asks if you can take a look at her system.

You ask what seems to be the problem, to which she responds, "It seems to be running really slow. We can't find some of the documents and pictures we used to have, and every time we try to access the Internet, it kicks us off!"

You recommend that she return to whatever she was doing and leave the machine with you; it just so happens that your schedule is open this afternoon, so you should be able to take a quick look at the system. You ask if there are any passwords you'll need, and the client responds, "No, we don't worry about passwords." You fill out a trouble ticket with the contact information and let her know you'll be in touch with her shortly.

Learning Objectives

Viruses are a simple fact of life in today's computing landscape, and any tech should be able to both remediate existing virus infections and take preventative measures against future infections. It's sometimes tempting to treat customers as though their virus infection serves them right, but you have to maintain your professional demeanor in these situations, as you'll come across a lot of them.

At the end of this lab, you'll be able to

- Analyze the machine to determine if it exhibits the symptoms the customer has indicated

- Perform routine maintenance and optimization

- Make recommendations to the client for the upkeep of her machine

Lab Materials and Setup

The materials you need for this lab are

- A partner or classmate to play the role of the client (optionally, if you do not have a partner, work through the scenario and complete the Lab Analysis Test at the end of the chapter)

- A notepad or computer-generated "trouble ticket" to simulate the practice followed in many computer support organizations

- Optional: A demo machine or Internet access to re-create the scenario and research options on vendor Web sites and tech forums

Getting Down to Business

To begin, have your partner read the Client section that follows. You will then read the PC Tech section and use the specifics to analyze the situation and recommend the best course of action. Now sit down and work through the scenario with your partner. If possible, use the Internet or demo machines to make the role-playing scenario more valid.

Client:

The computer you are dropping off to the shop is the family computer and is used by all the family members—two teenagers, you, and your spouse. The machine is constantly online, using a high-speed cable Internet connection, and there are tons of music files, pictures, and games stored on the hard drive.

You are not completely computer-savvy, so if asked by the tech, you respond that you do not know if there is any antispyware or antivirus software installed, although it's possible that the kids have installed something. All you know is that the machine is running slowly, you have lost some documents and pictures that you wanted, and the machine will no longer connect to the Internet.

When you drop the machine off at the repair shop, the tech attempts to send you on your way, but you would like to see what he is doing and possibly learn how to make the system run better. You are fairly insistent, and finally work out that the tech will walk you through everything when you return.

PC Tech:

You set the system up on your test bench and boot into Windows 7. The system does take an inappropriate amount of time to boot and load all of the programs (you notice there are a large number of items in the system tray, but it is surprisingly devoid of an antivirus icon). You take a quick note of the version of Windows 7 and notice that no service packs are installed, so it's a good bet that Windows Update has not been running either.

You check Device Manager and Event Viewer to verify that there are no specific hardware issues; everything seems to check out there. You then run Disk Cleanup—which uncovers over 4 GB of temporary Internet files. It is a 500-GB hard drive that is almost filled to capacity. Finally, you double-check whether any antivirus/antiadware/antispyware programs are installed, and find nothing.

✔ **Cross-Reference**

Refer to Lab Exercise 18.03, "Cleaning and Protecting a Client's Computer," for more information on how to clean up a machine that appears to have no specific hardware problems causing issues, but merely an accumulation of junk files, adware, spyware, and viruses.

You contact the customer and recommend that she stop back by the shop to discuss your recommendations for the machine. You still do not know if the lost files are recoverable, but you know you'll have to work through the other problems before you get there.

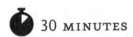 30 MINUTES

Lab Exercise 20.05: Scenario #4: No Documents, No E-Mail, and I Can't Print!

You arrive at work bright and early at 7:00 A.M. to find several voice mail messages blinking on your phone. You are one of the desktop support specialists at a large financial institution, and you usually make a point of arriving early to catch up on some of the studying you have been doing to pass your next IT certification exam. However, it looks like you will have to put this on the back burner for today. You check the messages, and it appears that the entire proposals department is in already, working on an investment proposal for a prominent client. The messages are frantic requests to fix the computer systems in the proposals department. Apparently, none of the computers are able to access the documents the team has been working with all week; they can not e-mail their concerns; and the network printer is down!

You have an idea of what might be happening, but you are going to drop by the proposals department and check some of the individual machines before you make a rash decision. You close your textbook and walk over to the proposals department.

Learning Objectives

Staying cool in high-stakes situations is the hallmark of a true tech, so look at this lab as an opportunity to improve your troubleshooting skills in the face of pressure. At the end of this lab, you'll be able to

- Verify that this is not an isolated problem with one or two machines

- Diagnose and troubleshoot from simple to complex, and record your findings

- Follow proper procedures to escalate the trouble ticket

Lab Materials and Setup

The materials you need for this lab are

- A partner or classmate to play the role of the client (optionally, if you do not have a partner, work through the scenario and complete the Lab Analysis Test at the end of the chapter)

- A notepad or computer-generated "trouble ticket" to simulate the practice followed in many computer support organizations

- Optional: A demo machine or Internet access to re-create the scenario and research options on vendor Web sites and tech forums

Getting Down to Business

To begin, have your partner read the Client section that follows. You will then read the PC Tech section and use the specifics to analyze the situation and recommend the best course of action. Now sit down and work through the scenario with your partner. If possible, use the Internet or demo machines to make the role-playing scenario more valid.

CLIENT:

You are the Chief Financial Officer (CFO) for this large financial institution. You have asked your entire team to come in today at 6:00 A.M. to finish up an investment proposal for a high-profile client. Everybody is on point, but as soon as things begin rolling, a number of your staff appear at your door: "The network is down!"

They inform you that they have left numerous messages with the IT department, but you do not expect anybody to be there until 8:30 A.M. or so. Just as you are preparing to call the Chief Information Officer (CIO) at home, one of the desktop support specialists arrives on the scene.

You ask the desktop support specialist if he is up to the challenge of determining the cause of the outage and, if so, whether he has the authority to complete the tasks involved to get the network up and running again. The specialist seems like a sincere individual, so you ask him to perform the initial investigation and report to you as soon as he has a handle on the situation.

PC Tech:

This issue is going to challenge you on a professionalism level more than it will challenge you as a technologist. You should run through some quick checks of the various computers in the proposals department. Check the physical connections and log on to a few of the machines to verify that the network connectivity is down.

As soon as you can verify that the entire department is down, make sure you communicate with the CFO to apprise him of the situation. This is a case of escalation—you need to get your network administrators online and have them troubleshoot the network. You have checked a few machines in other departments to verify that there is network connectivity in the building, and it is only the proposals department that is down.

You assure the CFO that you're on the issue and will inform him when the network admin is onsite. You then make a call to your friend, who just happens to be one of the network administrators; she is only a few minutes from the office, and tells you to hang tight and plan on joining her in the switch room. You're going to have an opportunity to work the issues through to the resolution. Don't forget to update the CFO!

Lab Analysis Test

1. Write a short essay summarizing the problem, discussion, and solution of the smashed laptop screen from Scenario #1.

2. Write a short essay summarizing the problem, discussion, and solution of the nonfunctioning monitor from Scenario #2. Be sure to include details on handling the analyst's stress level and frustration with the IT department.

3. Write a short essay summarizing the problem, discussion, and solution of the slow machine and Internet connection problems from Scenario #3. Be sure to include details on the steps and updates you would recommend that the client authorize.

4. Write a short essay summarizing the problem, discussion, and solution of the network outage in Scenario #4. Be sure to include details on the steps you would take to escalate the issue to the proper individual, the documentation paper path, and communication with the CFO.

5. Write a short essay describing the six steps included in the troubleshooting theory. List these steps in order and discuss the importance of each.

Key Term Quiz

Use the following terms to complete the following sentences. Not all terms will be used.

CFO

document

obsolescence

question

theory of probable cause

trouble ticket

troubleshooting theory

verify

1. There are six steps to the _____.

2. You should always _____ the repair after you verify full system functionality.

3. The limited lifetime of a PC is referred to as _____.

4. After you establish a(n) _____, you should always test.

5. A(n) _____ is a computer-generated report that usually includes contact information, the problem description, and the problem solution.

Index

Symbols

/ (forward slash), 195
\ (backslash), 195–199
* (asterisk character), 200
[ ] (brackets), 196

Numbers

5-V connections, 71
12-V connections, 71
16-bit color depth, 33
32-bit editions, of Windows, 19
64-bit editions
    Windows 7, 24, 109–112
    Windows Vista, 19
    Windows XP, 15
220-802 exam. *See* CompTIA A+
    certification
568A/568B standards, 254–257

A

The A-Team, 2
Accessibility Options applet, 47
ACPI (Advanced Configuration
    and Power Interface), 294
Active@ ISO File Manager, 61
ad hoc wireless networks, 274–276
Add New Hardware Wizard,
    180–182
Advanced Configuration and
    Power Interface (ACPI), 294
advanced utilities, 207–213
Aero, 29–34
AGP cards, 236–237
Android, 300–302
antivirus/malware software,
    331–333
APIPA (Automatic Private IP
    Addressing), 259–261

App Store, 304–305
Apple iOS
    Google Android vs., 300–302
    installing apps on, 302–306
    introduction to, 299–300
applets
    Accessibility Options, 47
    in Control Panel, 41
    Date and Time, 47–49
    Display, 44–45, 240–242, 247
    Ease of Access Center, 48
    Mouse, 46, 136
    Networking, 279
    Personalization, 44–45
    Power Options, 244, 294–295
    Sound, 45
    System, 44
Apply repairs automatically
    checkbox, 34
ASR (Automated System
    Recovery), 173–175
asterisk character (*), 200
ATA (AT Attachment). *See* PATA
    (Parallel ATA) interfaces; SATA
    (serial ATA) interfaces
ATX power supplies, 69
Automated System Recovery
    (ASR), 173–175
Automatic Private IP Addressing
    (APIPA), 259–261
automatic updates, 176–179
Avanquest, 76

B

backslash (\), 195–199
Backup and Restore Center, 173,
    175–176
backups, 173–176

batteries, 289–290, 293–295
bcdedit, 142–143
Best Buy, 331
BIOS
    CMOS and, 63
    CPU information and, 60
    introduction to, 58
BitLocker, 164–168
.bmp file extensions, 38
boot files
    in Windows Vista/7, 141–143
    in Windows XP, 137–140
boot order
    in CMOS setup program,
        78, 81
    in GParted, 84
booting faulty systems, 220–225
BOOT.INI tab, 229
Business Editions of Windows,
    19, 24

C

cabling, 254–258
career paths, 7–8
CAT 5/5e/CAT 6 UTP cabling,
    254–258
Category View, 42
cd (change directory) command,
    193, 198–199, 205
certifications. *See* CompTIA A+
    certification
chain of custody (CoC), 334–335
change directory (cd) command,
    193, 198–199, 205
Classic View, 42–43
clean installation, 121–124
cmd, 142